And he had trudged through Yorkshire dales,
Among the rocks and winding scars
Where deep and low the hamlets lie
Beneath their little patch of sky
And little lot of stars.

Wordsworth, "Peter Bell"

In Fox's Footsteps

a journey through three centuries

by David & Anthea Boulton

For Barbara, and in memory of Bernard

Dales Historical Monographs

Published by Dales Historical Monographs, Hobsons Farm, Dent, Cumbria
LA10 5RF, UK. Tel/Fax 015396 25321

ISBN 0 9511578 2 5

Typesetting by Dales Historical Monographs
Printed by Stramongate Press, Aynam Mills, Little Aynam, Kendal, Cumbria
LA9 7AH
This book is printed on recycled acid-free paper

Preface to third printing

George Fox walked from Pendle Hill to Swarthmoor in 1652 and we retraced his steps in 1994. *In Fox's Footsteps* was published in 1998, soon sold out, and was reprinted in 2000, only to sell out again. This is the third printing, production costs dictating that text and illustrations remain unchanged except for the addition of this preface.

But if our book is unchanged, the same cannot be said of the ground it covers. In the fourteen years since we did our Fox-trot, some of the B&Bs where we laid our weary heads and bathed our blistered feet have changed hands or gone out of business. Some of the Friends and assorted characters we met on the road have moved on, and some of the roads and trackways themselves have shifted: for instance, the "couple of miles of hell" we endured in traffic fumes on the A590 (see page 174) have now been replaced by a long-promised bypass. But of course the soft, sensuous landscape of the Yorkshire dales and south Lakeland remains defiantly unspoilt, and not only the hills, becks and byways but a number of relics of the seventeenth century building boom Fox would instantly recognise today if transported by time machine.

It has been our pleasure to hear from many Friends and sympathisers who have used the book as a guide to their own explorations of "1652 country". Our revisions of traditional, well-loved accounts of Fox's route and, more particularly, our reflections on both Fox's and modern Friends' theology, have sometimes been met with modified rapture: but that's what history does for you. Every generation sees the past in a new light, and we know that tomorrow's historians and pilgrims will subtly change the story again. But till then, *In Fox's Footsteps* has one more lease of life.

David & Anthea Boulton
davidboulton1@compuserve.com

THE MAPS

Our route from Pendle to Swarthmoor is indicated by a broken line, first in the general map opposite which shows the route in relation to the Yorkshire Dales, Lake District and North-West England, and then in the more detailed maps which follow.

The text makes clear where Fox's route is conjectural and where it is firmly established. The text also indicates where Fox's most likely route and ours slightly diverge (e.g. at Askrigg and Newby Bridge), and how our reconstruction of Fox's route differs from previous versions (e.g. at Dent and Garsdale).

Readers who feel stimulated to try the Foxtrot themselves, in whole or in part, will need to follow our maps in close consultation with the relevant text, and with the appropriate 1:25000 (two-and-a-half-inches to the mile) OS maps.

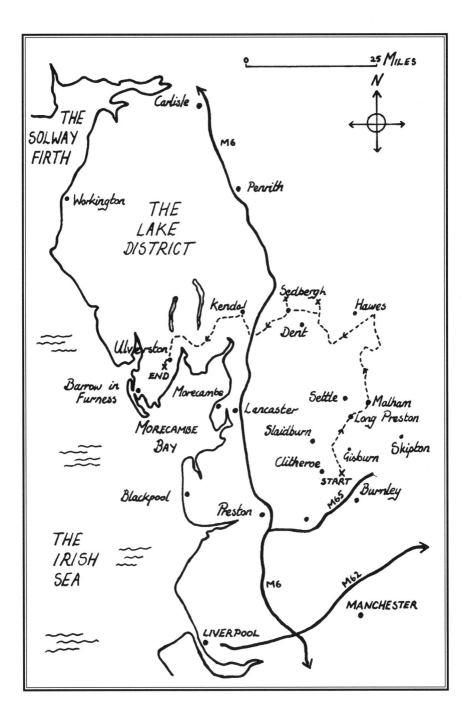

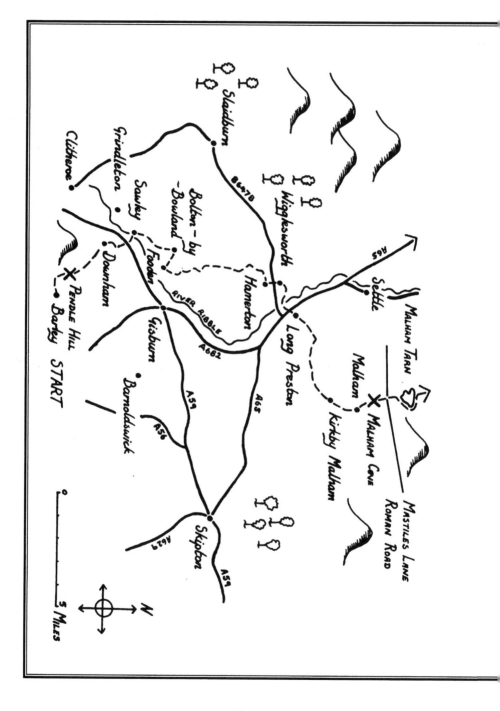

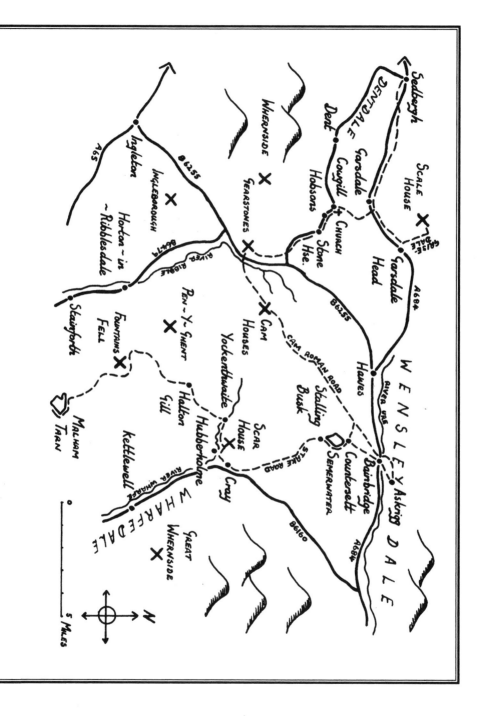

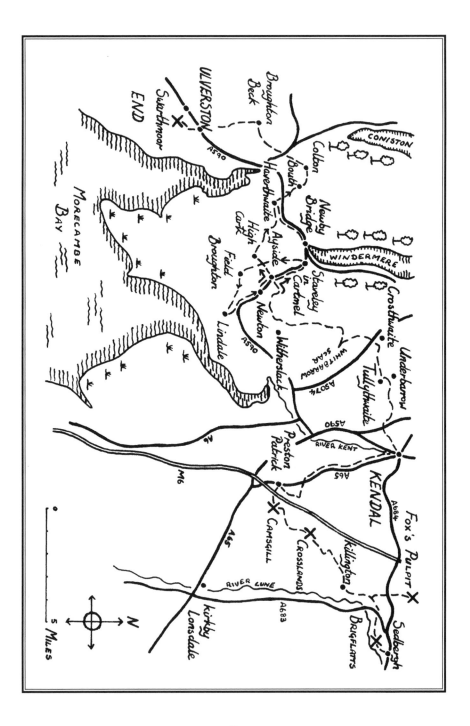

Contents

Introduction

This book is about two journeys from Pendle Hill, Lancashire, to Swarthmoor, Cumbria. The first, which is our real subject, was made by George Fox in May and June 1652. The second, which gives the book its framework, was made by Anthea and myself more than 350 years later, in May and June 1994.

Fox's journey had historic significance. It brought together different groups of religious and political radicals which fused into the Society of Friends. The new Society played a critical part in the English revolution and, when that failed, in the slow and painful process of turning a totalitarian kingdom into a diverse and pluralist community in which a culture of dissent could survive, if not always thrive. The story of Fox's eventful journey has been told many times, but its broader political, social and historical significance beyond the Society of Friends has not always been given due emphasis. One of our aims is to restore that balance.

Our reconstruction of Fox's route differs in some respects from that already familiar to Friends. We have made use of recent "revisionist" research into Quaker history, as well as our own work on the subject. Quaker readers who have derived pleasure and inspiration from a more traditional telling of the tale may not always welcome our reinterpretations and revised emphases. They should take comfort in the certainty that these too will be reworked and revised by others in the future. That is the nature of history-writing.

But our own walk in Fox's footsteps was not just an historical re-enactment. We were specially interested in marking the continuities and discontinuities of three and a half centuries. How has the landscape changed, and how has it stayed the same? What relationship is there between the trackways of the seventeenth century and the road network of the twentieth? What has happened to the houses Fox visited? Would Fox recognise those that still stand and still go by the same name? So this is not just a book about Fox and Friends. It is also a book about the Dales and South Lakeland, the jewels in Britain's landscape crown, and how they have both changed and remained the same, accommodated social transformations but retained their soft beauty and hard independence.

These themes of change and changelessness are explored in almost every chapter. But in the last chapter, the only one which falls out of the day-by-day framework of our walk, we ask the hard questions about what of significance remains in our day of Fox's message in his. Whatever continuities we may find in the physical topography of "1652 country", the thought-world we inhabit is almost immeasurably different from that of George Fox and his contemporaries. Can his message still ring true to a world which has outgrown and abandoned the supernatural framework which was still intact in the seventeenth century: to a world which has progressively abandoned divine reward and punishment, Truth as an absolute with a capital T, and God as an objective metaphysical entity?

Anthea and I planned this project together, and we walked every inch of it side by side. I made my notes, she made hers, and we married them at the end of each day. If my main concern was the history, hers was the natural history: the observations of flora and fauna which illuminate this otherwise prosaic manuscript almost always derive from her keen eye and ear. That is why this book is a joint work. At Anthea's insistence, I take responsibility for the final text. But Anthea is on the title-page by right. We did this together as a labour of love, in more senses than one.

This is not an academic treatise and we have avoided footnotes. Sources are mentioned in the text where this does not materially interrupt the flow of the narrative. Some important source-books are listed at the end of the book. We have not sought to be consistent in the style of quotations: where they have been modernised (as, for instance, in the Nickalls edition of the *Journal*) we have followed the modernisation, but where (for instance, in *First Publishers of Truth*) attempts have been made to preserve the contemporary spellings, punctuations and abbreviations, we have generally followed suit.

It remains for us to thank all those who helped us walk cheerfully, by making us comfortable *en route*, telling us things we didn't know, correcting our mistakes, and afterwards bullying us to get on with the hardest part: making a book of it (which has taken much longer than we planned, thanks to even more pressing commitments). Thanks too to those of our non-religious friends who have shown a keen interest despite the fact that they can't for the life of them understand our sympathy with Quakerism, and to Friends who have continued to welcome us into the heart of their fellowship despite our declarations of independence.

Thanks also, and not least, to two Friends who agreed to read through the first draft of the text and draw my attention to the howlers: David Blamires, editor of *Friends' Quarterly*, and Anne Ashworth, editor of *Universalist*. Remaining mistakes are likely to date from revisions undertaken after their careful scrutiny and, along with all interpretations, opinions and idiosyncracies, are mine alone. Thanks too to John Cooke (of The Studio, Dent, where his work can be enjoyed and purchased) for not letting the little matter of a painful arm fracture and its plaster straitjacket get in the way of providing some delightful line drawings.

Lastly, thanks to Martin Ellison for the maps. These are meant to help the reader keep track of us, and of Fox. They should be read and interpreted with the text.

David Boulton
Hobsons Farm, Dent

Round Big End and Buttock

DAY 1. Pendle-Sawley

On a late May day in 1994 Anthea and I stood on the summit of Pendle Hill, where the bleak fells of Lancashire meet the black moors of west Yorkshire, and looking west imagined we could see distant Morecambe Bay through the swirling white mists. A depression in what could have been a line of hills but may have been a line of cloud was perhaps the bay, perhaps not. We were vouchsafed occasional but more definite glimpses of Ingleborough and Pen-y-ghent, Pendle's big sisters to the north, looking less than inviting, but landmarks we would be passing on our journey, invited or not. This is the roof of England, and the spring comes slowly up this way.

George Fox was luckier. On a late May day in 1652 he stood where we were standing and looked down on green valleys and peaks reaching out to the sun. In that depression to the west a glint of gold marked "Lancashire sea" at Morecambe Bay, and as he looked down on the unenclosed pastoral landscape between Pendle and the far sands, his conviction grew that the Lord was showing him "in what places he had a great people to be gathered". William Penn, telling the tale in his more literary way, wrote that Fox "saw people as thick as motes in the sun, that should in time be brought home to the Lord".

So runs the story: a good story and a true story, if by no means the whole story. For this is the mythic tale of the origins of the Quaker movement. There were already a few score enthusiasts "in scorn called Quakers", but there was no organised Quaker movement when George Fox had his peak experience on Pendle. Barely one month later, when he reached the shining sea via the Yorkshire dales and the Lake District, a people had been gathered, and their religious, political and social radicalism would prove critical in transforming England from church and state totalitarianism to a more tolerant, democratic and pluralist society.

It started - if we accept the framework of the myth, and for the present we do, though we shall soon be looking at it more critically - at Pendle, and the foundation stones were in place 180 miles and four or five weeks later at Swarthmoor. So this is the story of George Fox's historic journey. It is also the story of a journey in Fox's footsteps three and a half centuries later. And if the story is about a journey from Pendle to Swarthmoor, it is also about a journey from the mid-seventeenth to the late twentieth century, a journey through a changing religious, intellectual, political and social landscape. Not least, it is also the story of a journey through one of Britain's most ravishing landscapes, one which has changed and yet remained the same in three hundred and fifty years.

George Fox was 28 when he "spied a great high hill called Pendle" and "was moved of the Lord to go atop of it". We know almost nothing of his life before this moment other than what he chooses to tell us later in the fragments of autobiography which, with bits suppressed and bits added, were published after his death as his famous *Journal*. Born in 1624 in the midland county of Leicestershire, the son of quite prosperous Puritan parents, he would have us know that as a small child he "had a gravity and stayedness of mind and spirit not usual in children", and that by the age of 11 he "knew pureness and righteousness". Modesty was never one of Fox's virtues. After being apprenticed to a shoemaker who also traded in wool and cattle, he left home at the age of 18 in September 1643 and began the wandering preaching life which he would continue for half a century. By the time he spied Pendle he had had a spell in Derby jail for blasphemy and had met up with small groups of fellow-radicals, mostly disunited Baptist groups in Yorkshire - "shattered Baptists" he called them. These groups were starting to call themselves "Children of the Light", and were mocked as "quakers" for their emotional zeal. Fox had already won a reputation as a firebrand for the "Good Old Cause" of Roundhead levellers and republicans who were looking to build the new Jerusalem in an England blood-stained by a decade of civil war.

The civil wars of the 1640s will provide the inescapable backcloth against which our drama is played. They mark the birth of modernity, and George Fox was one of the midwives of the modern world. By 1642, a year before young George bade goodbye to Leicestershire, the widening, deepening split between Royalists and Parliamentarians, between the bishops' Church and the people's churches, had erupted into armed warfare, first in Leicestershire's neighbour-county, Nottingham, and then throughout the land. By 1645 power lay with Parliament and the church reformers, but complex realignments over the next two years led to renewed civil war between the radical left, which controlled the New Model Army, and the royalist alliance. Only with the capture and execution of Charles 1 in 1649, and with the decisive defeat of his son's forces in 1651, could England try the experiment of living as a nation of citizens rather than subjects.

And where was young George in all this? The carefully edited *Journal* tells us little. We have to read between the lines, and there we meet a mixed-up young man, adrift from family and friends, wandering the country and freely tasting the heady variety of religious and political notions, programmes and heresies which abounded in the anarchy of war-torn England where censorship and thought control had collapsed. By 1647 his religious convictions, apparently developed by a mix of private contemplation, passionate public encounter with other enthusiasts and "phanaticks", and extensive reading of both Continental and English mystics and radicals, had moved far to the left of the orthodox Calvinist puritanism of his parents. But the new ideas he was embracing, and which he was quick to claim as his own, had political implications which were obvious to any shepherd-boy or apprentice, not to mention magistrate. A ferocious anti-clericalism, the emphatic rejection of all forms of church organisation and authority leading to refusal to pay the tithes and church taxes on which the clergy depended; the idea that personal conviction, an "inward light", could convey more of God's truth than any scripture and had more authority than any priest or judge; and a robust egalitarianism which led to the rejection of "hat honour" and class conventions in everyday speech: these were the inspirations of the man who was "moved to sound the day of the Lord" on Pendle Hill. These were also the inspirations of John Lilburne's Leveller party and Gerrard Winstanley's communist "True Levellers": the common inspirations of the Reformation republican left.

Fox's *Journal*, as I have said, is pretty silent on all this. Why so coy? Could the young George have been so wrapped up in himself, so absorbed by the condition of his own soul, that he simply failed to register any interest in the revolution through which he was living? Hardly, for his was not exactly a retiring, quietist piety. Rather was it a frenetic young man's religion of the streets, the markets, the ale-houses, a calling of the world to repentance, of judges to justice, of preachers to what they preached and of professors to what they professed. It was social religion - what the Leveller Richard Overton called "practical Christianity", concerned with the condition of the mass of humanity, of servants and the poor, castigating the gentry for fixing starvation wages for labourers and flaying the justices for hanging those who stole meat to feed their hungry dependents. If the later *Journal* editors, writing under restored royal censorship, downplayed young George's identification with the Good Old

Cause, that was because the Good Old Cause had by then become a seditious old cause, a seemingly defeated old cause which a second-generation of Quakers struggling for survival chose to keep in the closet.

One incident more plainly than any other demonstrates that the young troublemaker was clearly understood by his hearers and followers as a political radical, a republican, a zealot of the new social order. The *Journal* records that in 1651, a critical moment for the Good Old Cause, with the king dead but the royalists not yet decisively defeated, a New Model Army recruiting party called at the Derby House of Correction where George was completing a six-month sentence for refusing to stop causing trouble. Several prisoners joined up and demanded that Fox be made their captain, a post he was offered if he would "take up arms for the Commonwealth against the king". Fox chose to stay in his stinking jail rather than accept the commission, but it is clear that both his fellow prisoners and the New Model recruiting sergeants recognised on which side of the religious/political divide he stood. They knew what he had done, said, believed, preached. He might be an extremist, but he was their kind of extremist. He might be something of a "Ranter", possessed by that levelling spirit their high command had had to crush within their own ranks, but he was no neutral Clubman or - despite his defiantly long hair - a Cavalier. The army radicals recognised him as "one of us", one of God's own revolutionaries.

But let us not overdo our revisionist portrait. Our man on Pendle Hill is not a 1960s "make love not war" hippy, nor a torchbearer for the 1980s Militant Tendency, nor a twentieth century rationalist-humanist. George Fox believed he was in some special sense the son of God. There is no escaping it. He would concede that all true believers were in some measure sons or daughters of God, that there was "that of God" in everyone, but his deepest and most abiding conviction was that he, George Fox, was uniquely marked by the

Almighty as His mouthpiece. When, a few years later, other Quaker leaders claimed similar divine authority, George Fox crushed them. So we are following in the footsteps of a complex man, a man of the seventeenth century whose radicalism pointed forward to some of the key concerns of the twentieth, but a man possessed by the illusion that he alone, or he to a greater degree than any other, was God's chosen instrument for working out the divine purpose. He is not going to be an easy companion over the next few days!

*

So, on the morning of May 26 1994, Anthea and I cram our backpacks with the stuff real walkers cram their backpacks with: light-weight waterproofs, heavy sweaters, spare knickers, thick socks, sticking plaster and sandwich boxes, plus notebooks, maps, research notes and the addresses and phone numbers of our B&Bs. We are not used to this sort of thing. Strolls around our local lanes, the occasional sortie with friends up one (never more than one at a time) of Yorkshire's "three peaks", armchair sessions planning bold expeditions which somehow never materialise - this is the nearest we usually come to being long-distance walkers. We don't even know about the importance of lining our backpacks with plastic bags - though we soon find out. We have ancient boots, moulded to the nooks and crannies of four innocent feet which don't know what is about to hit them, and our antique waterproofs have seen service for ditching, pond-draining and coarse gardening - and waterproof they have long ceased to be. But we are looking forward to our Foxtrot. The weather has been kind, raising hopes of a merry May's end and a flaming June. We lock the door behind us - and it begins to rain.

Our home is in Dentdale, of which more later as George came this way, so it is slap in the centre of our route. We have the usual walkers' problem in an area where public transport exists only in history books, so our neighbour Jim Duffy offers to drive us to Pendle in his Fiat Uno. We are well aquainted with this vehicle. Once upon a time it had belonged to us, till in the evening of its life we passed it on to our daughter Katy. A newly-qualified driver, convinced that the rough tracks and pot-holed roads of the dales were expressly designed to test suspension bars, an otherwise gentle and pacific Katy had proceeded to batter the car to death, but Jim stepped in just before its last gasp and offered her a song for it. Katy accepted, and Jim drove off in a metal box which almost immediately separated from its chassis, the two entities parting company on the motorway. Jim (a survivor if ever there was one, and one who deserves a book to himself), lived not only to tell the tale but to rebuild his Uno and prove that, for automobiles at least, there is life after death. So, crammed close in this resurrected micro-car, shared with Jim, two of Jim's relations who wanted a day out, and two bulging rucksacks, we were driven through the rain to a great high hill called Pendle which we were moved to go atop of.

Jim stopped at Sawley, a village at Pendle's foot, and we fell out, followed by our baggage. Goodbyes were exchanged, along with remarks by Jim of the "rather you than me" variety and promises to come and fetch us when we got blisters or were tired of chasing after this Fox we kept going on about. A lighter Uno sped off, and we knocked on the door of the wardens' cottage at Sawley Quaker meetinghouse, where we had arranged to meet Martin and Alison Seddon.

Martin was a policeman for ten years, an unusual apprenticeship for a Quaker warden. He had hoped to be a police photographer, and his powerful, atmospheric photos of local Quaker sites suggest that the force's loss was Friends' gain. A few weeks earlier, when we met Martin for the first time while researching our trip, I had mentioned that we hoped to do a book which would be "a bit of this and a bit of that - you know, history, theology, topography" - if we could find anyone who might want to read it. "History! Theology! Topography!" enthused Martin, almost crossing himself in naming his trinity of special interests. "Put me down for the first copy!" And we did.

But first, Martin was to guide us over the hill that loomed over his front garden. Sawley is to the north of Pendle and Fox presumably approached it from the south, since two or three days earlier he had been chased out of a Derbyshire market town following a dispute with the local preacher in the parish church. After a night at an unnamed country house, where they were put up because there was no ale-house nearby, Fox and his companion, Richard Farnsworth, proceeded northwards. "And the next day," says the *Journal*,

"we passed on, warning people as we met them of the day of the Lord that was coming upon them. As we went I spied a great high hill called Pendle Hill, and I went on the top of it with much ado, it was so steep; but I was moved by the Lord to go atop of it; and when I came atop of it I saw Lancashire sea; and there atop of the hill I was moved to sound the day of the Lord; and the Lord let me see atop of the hill in what places he had a great people to be gathered. As I went down, on the hill side I found a spring of water and refreshed myself, for I had eaten little and drunk little for several days".

Five tops or atops in one sentence! George wasn't going to leave us in doubt that, however much ado it was to haul his stout body up the hillside, he had definitely reached the summit! But where did he start his climb (after parting company with Farnsworth, since George's "we" in the first sentence becomes an "I" in the second)? The tradition, Martin tells us - and tradition may not carry much authority, but it is all we have - is that he started at Barley, a tiny hamlet south-east of the summit, where a barley crop was said to have been grown in the 14th century. So we pile into Alison's car and she drives us the seven or eight miles of winding road below Pendle's Big End to a farm track above Barley. And here, with Martin as our guide, we step out - in Fox's footsteps.

The rain has stopped but a vicious wind is biting. The weathermen say it comes straight from Siberia - non-stop for Pendle, I swear. My hands are blue. Did Fox wear gloves? I note on the map the names of nearby farms and features: Pendle Side, Pendle House, Under Pendle, Nick of Pendle - and Buttock. In the distance Martin picks out for us a tiny rectangle at Red Syke farm, Twiston, which became a Quaker burial ground when there were Quakers to be buried, which persecution soon ensured there were. A pair of wheatears rise from the path, one fluttering and almost hovering over us in an effort to distract us, its "white arse" flashed to good effect. Perhaps it is nesting at Buttock. A lark sings in the distance, and meadow pippits are piping their accelerando calls.

I had imagined from all the fuss George made that the climb would take us half a day, perhaps, or at least a couple of huffing, puffing hours. But in half an hour we are at the summit: atop. True, we have been assisted by some conservation volunteers who have turned the steep but much-used and eroded path into an easily negotiated wooden staircase. George, mapless and without even a Wainwright to point him onwards and upwards, would have struggled through the lings and heathers that covered the hillside. But now, 557 metres or some 1830 feet above sea level, we stood where he had stood, on a mound known as the Beacon - perhaps a Bronze Age burial site, probably a mediaeval fire-beacon warning of hostile invaders - and imagined him, fevered by his recent fasting and intoxicated by his holy spirit, sounding the day of the Lord.

What does that mean? Did George, alone on a Pennine peak, open his mouth and bellow out a beacon-warning to the stones, the scrub and the odd lost sheep? Probably. High places brought out the visionary in him. Five years later, atop of Cader Idris in Wales (which he reckoned was "two or three miles high") he again "was moved to sound the day of the Lord". And as we have just seen, on his journey from Derbyshire to Pendle he and Richard Farnsworth were "warning people as we met them of the day of the Lord that was coming upon them".

Belief in an imminent second coming of Christ, preceding the Day of Judgement, was not confined to extremists. Millenial expectations were the common property of most puritans in the mid-seventeenth century, heightened by the "wars and rumours of wars" in the 1640s and the execution of King Charles, seen by many as a prelude to the crowning of King Jesus. Fox and the very early Quakers shared this popular conviction that they were living in the last days. They came to realise that they were mistaken, just as the first-generation followers of Jesus came to realise that their teacher was mistaken in preaching that the end of the world was at hand in the first century. Quakers adopted the view that the second coming was more a matter of mystery than history, that their own version of a purified primitive Christianity *was* the second coming. But that was a few years and much bitter experience ahead. George atop Pendle believed that the reign of King Jesus would begin in England in the 1650s, and that he was commissioned to proclaim it from the hilltops and in the valley bottoms in the language of the prophet Isaiah.

Looking into the valleys, north and west, he knew intuitively that down there was "a great people to be gathered", and he was indeed casting his eyes over what was to become the Galilee of the Quaker movement. There were good reasons for believing that in these deep and low hamlets there was fertile soil for his seed and open ears for his message, and we shall soon find ourselves musing to what extent George Fox was already aware that the dales housed communities of spiritual seekers thirsting for enlightenment and charismatic leadership. But after sounding the day of the Lord he began his north-westerly descent, and we shall head in the same direction, back to Sawley.

Martin tells us, as we leave the wide, flattened summit that Alison had been up here one day on a Quaker youth pilgrimage during which they sat on the grass for a short, silent meeting. Two or three fell runners panted past them, and Alison heard one of the runners say to his companion, "Hey, look, a whole load o' people doin' nowt!"

We follow a steep, indistinct path, perhaps just a sheep-trod, down the flank of Pendle's grit-stone cap, and come across an old stone trough and a bit of iron piping marking a long-abandoned attempt to control the course of a spring. This, traditionally, is Fox's Well, the spring where he refreshed himself, according to his *Journal*. Some maps mark it as Robin Hood's Well, but our George would seem to have the better-documented claim. This seems to be the one spot between Siberia and the Irish Sea where it is possible to get out of the wind, and we crouch uncomfortably in the wet grass to break our fast as Fox did, but drinking from cartons of orange juice rather than the sheep-coliformed spring waters, adding cheese and pickle sandwiches tasting none the worse for their cramped adventures at the bottom of a backpack. A kestrel hovers overhead, making us feel intruders.

We find a good path down to Hookcliffe plantation, then follow the quiet road to Downham, serenaded by three curlew, one singing in strange fifths - "like a cuckoo backwards and out of tune". says Anthea. We talk about Quakerism. It isn't what it was, says Martin - but of course it never was.

Fox's narrative picks up in the plural, so Richard Farnsworth presumably followed round below Big End and fixed up bed and breakfast for the two of them. They stayed at an alehouse, but they don't say where.

"And so at night we came to an alehouse and stayed all night and declared much to the man of the house, and writ a paper to the priests and the professors concerning the day of the Lord and how Christ was come to teach people himself by his power and spirit and to bring them off all the world's ways and teachers to his own free teaching, who had bought them and was the Saviour. And the man of the house [another version says the woman] did spread the paper up and down and was mightily affected with Truth."

One is tempted to guess that the alehouse with its co-operative man or woman of the house was the George and Dragon, now the Assheton Arms, in Downham. Then as now, Downham was the property of the Assheton family, and when Fox passed this way its lord was Ralph Assheton, Member of the Long Parliament and one of Cromwell's chief men of arms. In 1648 the New Model Army was quartered at Downham on its way to the Battle of Preston, and Ralph

Assheton was Major-General in command of 1500 foot and 1200 horsemen. These were the men who effectively cleared the whole north-west of Royalist garrisons, recovering Carlisle and Appleby for Parliament. But Fox wouldn't have heard much good said of the local lord, for the New Model men who did Parliament's dirty work had been short-changed in pay, and then disbanded to fend for themselves. The resultant disillusionment with grandee politicians was certainly a factor in the rapid growth of radicalism and the rise of Quakerism. Perhaps the landlord of the alehouse who was "mightily affected" by Fox's message, so much so that he or his wife undertook to make copies of Fox's paper and "spread it up and down", was one such disillusioned veteran, ready to embrace a new way of building Jerusalem.

Today's Downham is a regular contender for the "prettiest village in England" competition, and many who have never visited would know it instantly from its celebrity as the setting of numerous period film and television dramas. It would not have looked very different in 1652. The cottages would probably have carried thatch rather than flags on their roofs. Old Well Hall, the manor house, with low stone-mullioned windows and a two-storey porch, was already a century old, and its demotion into three cottages lay long in the future. The stocks near the church gate were no doubt more serviceable than they are today, and the 13th century church was largely rebuilt in 1800, preserving only the 15th century tower and ancient bells. The guidebooks proudly tell us that the late Queen Mary regarded the view as the most beautiful to be seen from any church porch in the land. But George Fox would have snorted "steeplehouse!" as he strode past.

Our first day's journey, however, will take us on to Sawley, where Martin and Alison have promised home comforts which no alehouse, ancient or modern, could match. Sawley is another contender for Fox's first night, as is Grindleton, a mile further. Today's motorised traveller reaches Sawley from Downham by heading westward to Chatburn before doubling back in a north-easterly direction, but Fox would have taken the direct route we choose, an old holloway or packhorse track leaving Twiston Lane and climbing to cross the ancient Roman road from Ribchester to Ilkely. The wind has died now, and our path runs by woods carpeted with ramsons or wild garlic, bluebells and a stand of purple spotted orchids. We cross the road which leads to Downham corn mill and pass under the railway line to reach a picture-book packhorse bridge over Swanside Beck. A pair of goosander fly over, and Martin's keen eye spots a handsome stonefly, motionless on the bank, with jazzy chestnut body and delicately veined, transparent wings. Following the holloway, now glorious with marsh marigolds, we cross first the new, then the old Clitheroe bypass, till the remains of Sawley abbey come into view.

Sawley was much knocked about by Henry VIII, and there wouldn't have been much more to see of it in 1652 than there is today. George Fox would certainly not have mourned its end, the more so if he had known that one of its monks was William de Rimmington who, as Chancellor of Oxford, became the scourge of John Wycliffe, intellectual leader and inspiration of the 14th century Lollards who anticipated some of the radical, subversive tenets of Quakerism by three centuries. The stones of the Cistercian abbey are now spread over a twenty-mile stretch from Gisburn to Clitheroe, embedded in farmhouses, barns and dry stone walls, and only a few masonry mounds, two fireplaces, a rebuilt archway and lines of footers mark the site its monks occupied for four hundred years. A pied wagtail is nesting in the remains of a wall which is mauve with patches of ivy-leaved toadflax. Behind the abbey is the Spread Eagle (another possible contender for Fox's alehouse), since where there are monks there is usually ale. And behind the pub, on the west side of the Ribble and down a lane off the Grindleton road, is Sawley meetinghouse and the adjoining wardens' cottage.

Sawley Quakers built their meetinghouse in 1777, by which time they had become part of a staid little sect, respectable and quaint. But the building, in the style of a local barn, elegantly simple and without trimmings, illustrates Friends' continuing horror of anything remotely churchy or ecclesiastical. The pitch-pine interior has a gallery built for women's meetings, in the days when women took on their own responsibilities in the meeting's business affairs. Attached to the meetinghouse, but built later, is the cottage where Martin and Alison now live with their two children, Rebecca and Ross. The garden is guarded by two giant beech trees, and the french windows frame a trim lawn behind flower beds, a sycamore and an ash which is still waiting for better weather before it will risk opening its buds, and an orchard beyond.

Alison feeds us handsomely, knowing from experience that Pendle weather produces Pennine-sized appetites. After dinner, Martin takes us to meet the Rector of Grindleton - but more of that anon. We are back in time for an early night, comfortably ensconced in a room full of soft toys and pop pin-up posters which Rebecca has vacated for us.

Drifting off to sleep, I can see George Fox and Richard Farnsworth at the ale house, their meal half eaten, their excitement intense as George describes the vision he had had on Pendle's beacon and the two men call for paper and quill to write their pamphlet for their landlord to circulate to "priests" - by which Fox meant all paid ministers - and "professors", meaning those professing to be religious. The *Journal* summarises their message in half a sentence: the day of the Lord was at hand; "Christ was come to teach people himself by his power and spirit and to bring them off all the world's ways and teachers", meaning that church teaching and bible teaching were superseded by direct one-to-one experience of Christ's spirit within; and this teaching was "free", not sold as the hireling priests sold it, not traded for tithes and church dues. And all this was not just true. To Fox, then and for ever, this was "Truth". And before I drift into sleep, I see the "man of the house" reading the paper over Fox's and Farnsworth's shoulders, "mightily affected", and promising that he (or his wife) would "spread it up and down" next morning.

And the evening and the morning were the first day.

On Quakers before Quakerism; and Witches

DAY 2. Sawley-Wigglesworth

An exceptionally full-throated thrush, the Pavarotti of the thrush world, awakens us next morning, Friday May 27. It isn't immediately clear what our winged alarm-clock is so thrilled about. The sky is a leaden sheet and there is still that wind from the northeast, though weaker than the one which thrust at us on Pendle. We are slow to join Martin and Alison for breakfast, and slower still to get our boots and backpacks on, but we finally wave our goodbyes half an hour before noon, by which time the wind has dropped and it has become one of those days when the world is becalmed, waiting for the weather gods to make up their minds whether maliciously to release a thunderclap or graciously part the clouds for a flash of sunlight.

Where next? George Fox gives us no help. First, we do not know whether he set off from Sawley, or Downham, or Grindleton, or somewhere else, because he doesn't tell us where he and Richard Farnsworth slept after Pendle. Nor do we know exactly where he went. His *Journal* says only that

"the next day we passed on among the fell countries and at night we got a little ferns or brackens and lay upon a common and the next morning went to a town where Richard Farnsworth parted with me and I was alone again. So I came up Wensleydale..."

All we know, then, is that Fox and his companion made their way from Pendle foot to Wensleydale, apparently in three days, via unspecified "fell countries", an equally anonymous common and an unnamed town. Even in Wensleydale we are not given the names of any towns, villages or hamlets through which he passed, so we cannot be sure whether he struck the long, winding valley at its lower eastern end, perhaps around Leyburn, or nearer the dale head towards Askrigg and Hawes. To add to our puzzlement, having come "up Wensleydale", Fox records that he came to "a man's house, one Tennant", since identified as James Tennant of Scarhouse, Langstrothdale. But Langstrothdale lies south of Wensleydale, in a direct line with Pendle, which means that Fox, having reached the northern dale, would have suddenly turned south again towards Pendle and then doubled back northwards before heading out towards the west. Such an erratic zig-zag is not impossible: Fox may have heard of Tennant in Wensleydale and decided this man was worth a visit, even if it took him off course - if, indeed, he had a course, other than the hidden one he believed was mapped out for him by God. But there may be another explanation for this puzzle: natural memory slip.

George Fox's *Journal* was not a day-by-day diary, nor was it written during the travels it describes. The various published versions are all edited compilations of several autobiographical and biographical fragments, of which the most important are an account written or dictated by Fox while he was in prison in Lancaster in 1664, known as the *Short Journal*, and a fuller account dictated in 1674 or 1675 and known as the *Spence MS*. So the earliest record of George's 1652 journeys was made twelve years after the events described, and the fullest record 22 or 23 years later. It would not be surprising if chronologies and itineraries were occasionally muddled: indeed, it would be miraculous if they were not.

So while I admire the scholarly attempts which have been made to reconcile the inconsistencies and fill the gaps, I am convinced that the best explanation of the *Journal*'s vagueness is simply that George remembered very well that he went from Pendle to Wensleydale but couldn't recall, and didn't think it particularly important to recall, exactly how he did it: which poses a problem for those trying to follow in his footsteps. We have chosen to resolve this problem by taking a direct route north from Pendle to Wensleydale, passing through "fell countries", commons and a town, and because this direct route passes Langstrothdale we shall visit James Tennant's house *en route* rather than doubling back. If any reader should grumble at our uncertainties, we can only answer that it is the best we can do with the record. We can also emphasise that these uncertainties diminish dramatically once we - and Fox - leave Wensleydale behind us and head west, when Fox's own record is much more detailed and can sometimes be supplemented from other contemporary sources.

So we take the path northwards on the left bank of the river Ribble, pausing on the elegant stone bridge to watch a goosander and her chicks paddling downstream, while swifts, swallows and martins swoop through the arches below us. Martin Seddon had seen an osprey fishing by the bridge a day or two earlier, blown off course, presumably, since this is not its natural habitat. The may blossom that is supposed to mark the arrival of the month is just beginning to show at its end, but a field by the river has been early-mown, and bunches of sugar-pink bistort lie fading in the severed grasses, the sight and scent of hay-timing offering a premonition of high summer. We put up several oyster-catchers as we follow the bank, first of the Ribble and then of its tributary Tosside Beck, and are so absorbed by their methodical care to keep themselves at a safe distance from unwelcome intruders on their territory that we miss the crossing to Bolton Hall and Bolton-by-Bowland and have to find our own way over the beck.

*

Behind us and a mile or so beyond Sawley lies Grindleton, and it has been suggested that George may have bed-and-breakfasted here, rather than at Downham, before striking out with Richard Farnsworth towards the fell countries. This tiny village was notorious in the seventeenth century as the hot-bed of a heresy known as Grindletonianism: "the only English sect", as Christopher Hill notes in *The World Turned Upside Down*, "which takes its name from a place rather than a person or a set of beliefs". Hill also notes, and he is not the first to do so, that the heresies attributed to the Grindletonians earlier in the seventeenth century bore a remarkable similarity to Fox's own teachings and the beliefs of first-generation Quakers.

In fact, despite Hill, it is not quite accurate to call Grindletonianism a sect, for Grindletonians never left the national church. This little village church first became notorious during the curacy of Roger Brierley or Brearley, from 1615 to 1622. In 1617 some fifty charges were brought by the church courts against Brierley and his congregation, starting with the heresy that "a motion rising from the spirit is more to be rested in than the Word itself". Other charges were that Grindletonians believed in the possibility of living without sin, and preached that "a man having the spirit may read, pray or preach without any other calling whatsoever" - that is, without ordination. Belief that "the spirit" within had more authority than the bible, that men and women were perfectible, and that ordination was wholly unnecessary to the business of preaching and teaching: all these, of course, were as important to early Quakers in the 1650s as they apparently were to the Grindletonians of 1617.

These Grindletonian ideas were themselves not original. They were strongly associated with a widespread but secretive network known as the Family of Love, or Familists, and it is likely that Brierley and his Grindleton congregation were part of the Family, which was also not a separatist sect (at least before the 1640s) but a tendency within the national church. The Family of Love was founded by a Dutch mystic, Hendrik Niclaes, in the 1540s and it spread to Germany and France as well as England. Modern research has shown that known Familists were sometimes tolerated in positions of power: they were particularly well represented at Queen Elizabeth's court, and the Queen herself may have had some sympathy with them. At times, however, as the politics of religion turned first this way then that, they were bitterly persecuted for their heretical beliefs. One student of Niclaes writes of him: "He aspired to be as sinless as Christ, and believed he could attain spiritual perfection in this life... He came very close to rejecting the literal validity of Scripture, and he probably conceived of heaven primarily as an illuminated state of mind. Finally, he scorned and threatened all who disagreed with him". How like our own George Fox!

The Grindletonian version of Familism seems to have spread into surrounding areas of Lancashire and Yorkshire during the seventeenth century. Brierley himself left Grindleton for Kildwick, some twenty miles away, in 1622, and another Grindletonian curate of Kildwick, John Webster, became a chaplain in the New Model Army, and was still active in the Pendle area in the 1650s. John Camm and Francis Howgill, whom we shall meet shortly, were described as Grindletonians (though they thought of themselves as Seekers) before they became Quakers, and another early Quaker, Thomas Bancroft, described his own conversion from Grindletonianism to Quakerism. Fox himself owned at least one book by Niclaes, whose works were extensively printed in English translations in the 1640s and '50s. William Penn, at the end of the century, acknowledged the Family of Love as an influence on early Quakerism, and in the 1680s a surviving group of Familists on the Isle of Ely described themselves as "a sort of refined Quakers".

The clear similarity and affinity between Fox's thought and that of Grindletonians and Familists was not something Fox himself was ever prepared to acknowledge. He never mentions Grindleton, and his only reference to Familists is when he lists them later as among the many "sects" with whom he had "disputes", when, he says, "the Lord's power gave us dominion over them all". George Fox believed, and wanted his followers to believe, that God was speaking uniquely through him and that the message was unmediated by book-learning or any other human influence. It is also important to bear in mind that by the time he was writing and dictating his *Journal*, groups like the Familists, Grindletonians, Ranters and Muggletonians were widely perceived as wild, fanatical remnants of the revolutionary period, the kinds of people respectable Quakers were all too anxious to distance themselves from, even if that involved a little creative rewriting of history. The Family of Love was even rumoured to have built its worship around ritual orgies - an accusation particularly sensitive to Restoration Quakers, who were constantly combating insinuations that their own refusal to marry in church made their men fornicators and their women whores.

But in the early 1650s it is by no means clear that Familism, Ranterism and Quakerism could be readily distinguished one from another. If George Fox was seeking out fellow spirits, men and women who had rejected orthodox institutional religion and were thrashing around in search of something better, it would be surprising if, with Grindleton lying at the foot of Pendle, and in the direction in which he was travelling, he didn't pay a visit to check out whether here indeed were a people to be gathered. With this in mind, I had asked Martin Seddon to run me into Grindleton the previous night after supper, since to walk there today would have taken us a little out of our way.

We met the rector, the Rev David Mewis, at the neat nineteenth century church. Yes, he knew of Grindleton's heretical past, but nothing more than he had read. There were no contemporary documents in the church chest waiting to cast new light on a seventeenth century congregation with views which even most twentieth century Christians would find too radical for their tastes. So faded my dream of blowing the dust off a yellowing manuscript and discovering the original of Fox's paper, written in the alehouse and distributed by the "man of the house" to local priests and professors; or a first-hand account by one of the churchwardens of how a Moses in leather trousers had come down from Pendle with a new message to proclaim, which had turned out to be little different from the one familiar to them ever since Roger Brierley had come to Grindleton forty years earlier.

However, David Mewis did tell us where Brierley's church stood: not on the site of its elegant replacement but at a place called Chapel Garth, down a mediaeval track called Higher Chapel Lane. It was nearly dark now, but Martin and I went to have a quick look. Maybe it was on that derelict patch covered in nettles, maybe where modern housing has encroached, but hereabouts the Grindletonian Familists, miles from any centre of learning and discipline, began questioning the literalism and authoritarianism of orthodox Calvinist protestantism, thereby laying one little foundation stone for modern pluralism. As Christopher Hill writes in *The World Turned Upside Down*, "Grindleton, lying at the foot of Pendle Hill, George Fox's Mount of Vision, should perhaps have a more prominent place on maps of seventeenth century England than is usually accorded it". And that is surely true whether or not George himself passed this way.

*

But back to our second day's walking. We stroll through the ordered parkland of Bolton Hall, a hidden chiffchaff marking our progress. The Hall itself is not to be seen, and we learn that it was demolished in the 1960s. This was the family seat of the Boltons - they *could* be my ancestors, since the Bolton/Boulton spellings were interchangeable - till 1322, when the estate went to the Pudsays. Ambrose Pudsay was just 14 when the civil wars broke out in 1642, but old enough to command a regiment of foot for the king. With the

Royalist defeat, the poor lad's lands were sequestrated for the Commonwealth, not to be returned to him till after the Restoration. Impoverishment forced him to mortgage them in 1667.

Massed rhododendrons, their flowers just beginning to show, give way to a a fine avenue of oak, sycamore and lime leading us to Bolton-by-Bowland. A cock pheasant parades in glorious spring plumage and a grey wagtail sees us through the great iron gates into the neat little village which boasts two village greens, one with ancient market cross and stocks, and a thirteenth century church with a fifteenth century tower said to have been part-designed by King Henry VI, who apparently anticipated a later royal by fancying himself as a bit of an architect. Henry was granted refuge here after losing the Battle of Hexham in 1464. Some eighteenth century cottages and some modern mock-Elizabethan complete the picture.

We rest briefly - though we haven't been going more than an hour - in a finely manicured garden of remembrance, huddling together to keep warm. "You won't get sunburnt today!" an old man tells us, stopping briefly to add that it may be the end of May but he hasn't dared bring anything out of his greenhouse yet. "Never knew a spring like it", he says, as he probably tells passers-by every year.

If George Fox did come this way he would have used any of a mass of criss-crossing tracks, some of which are today's roads and others the mere hint of paths. We are tempted to take the lane north to Fox Ghyll on the fancy that it commemorates our man, but no doubt the reference is to his four-footed namesakes, common in these parts. So, swifts screaming above us, we make a brief diversion eastwards instead to Fooden, only because a little guide-book we buy describes the tiny hamlet as "an absolute treasure", adding that "one can hardly believe that such a delightful nook could really exist". Truth to tell, we are a little disappointed when we get there. Fooden has a dilapidated, deserted air: there isn't a human soul in sight, but an extended family of ferocious guard dogs strain at their chains with the evident intention of sinking their fangs into our fleshy bits if they can only shake one link loose. Their demented barking, which never stops for a moment, makes this nook rather less delightful than the guide-book suggests. Perhaps its author passed by when the dogs were herding hapless sheep on the fells. But we note the once-fine seventeenth-century Fooden Hall, shockingly neglected and a sad reminder of better times, before sorting out a track across the fields to Raygill Moss, with roe deer breaking cover before us, and black-headed gulls and the occasional curlew maintaining a running commentary on our progress. Once we startle a pair of partridge as we cross a field stile, and once we meet a starling fooling us with a curlew's song. Wine-red wood-avens are opening up in the hedgerows.

Looking back, Pendle still seems almost on top of us, a lowering presence which threatens to follow us relentlessly all the way to Swarthmoor. We can understand its repution as a haunt of witches, hobgoblins and foul fiends. Fox's *Journal* makes no reference to the Pendle witches, which seems surprising till we remember that for him and his contemporaries witches were no more prevalent here than they were almost anywhere in rural England. There had been two much-publicised witch trials centred on Pendle in 1612 and 1633, and the souvenir-sellers of the future would make sure that they were not forgotten. But the truth is that mid-seventeenth century England seemed awash with witchcraft - or witchcraft accusations. The churches believed and taught that witches, mostly (but not always) women, were in league with the Devil in the service of evil. A more popular conception of witches saw them as practitioners of magic, sometimes good (the white witches and "wise men" or women), often bad (the black witches) with power to bring illness or death to people and livestock, to burn barns and houses, to spoil the beer or the butter or upset the apple-cart. "If any adversitie, greefe, sicknesse, losse of children, corne, cattell, or libertie happen unto them," wrote Reginald Scot at the end of the sixteenth century, "by and by they exclaime upon witches". *Malleus Maleficarum* ("The Hammer of Witches") was one of the earliest books produced by the newly invented printing press, and as a modern Quaker writer comments, it reads like "a combination of scholasticism and pornography: witches are described as having made a compact with the devil to indulge their sexual drives 'which in women are insatiable'" (Grace Jantzen, *Women, Witches and the Spirit* in *The Friend*, October 14 1994).

Single women, particularly the elderly, and especially the ragged, destitute and physically unattractive, were often singled out as witches and ducked, whipped, tortured or hanged. While George Fox was consorting with religious radicals and picking up ideas from them in the 1640s, perhaps the most famous of all witch hunters, Matthew Hopkins, was subjecting women to his own barbaric tests, pricking any bodily excrescences - warts, birth-marks, scars, which he supposed were extra paps for suckling imps - and pronouncing the woman a witch if she proved capable of withstanding the pain.

George Fox saw through many of the superstitions of his day, particularly those he could relate to pre-Reformation "popery" and paganism, but it didn't occur to him to challenge prevalent ideas on witchcraft, though others were beginning to do so. In the fields near Cockermouth in 1653 he met some "wicked women" and "saw that they were witches", so that he was moved to "declare unto them their condition". On another occasion, he tells us, "I cast my eye upon an unclean woman and told her she was a witch. And I was moved in the Lord's power to speak sharply to her... and people told me I had discovered a great thing, for all the country looked upon her to be a witch". Many times he was himself suspected of witchcraft and black magic, which might have alerted him to the misplaced suspicion and hysteria from which such accusations so often arose.

Quaker women, with their ecstatic preaching and rejection of normal gender roles of female subordination, were particularly open to accusations of witchcraft. Grace Jantzen instances a striking case as late as the end of the century: an engraving showing "The Quakeress and the Devil", in which "the Quaker woman, wearing a tall pointed hat, listens avidly to a horned devil whose clawed, bony hands point suggestively to her genitals. The inscription reads, in part...

'Presumptuous wretch, it were more fit that she
At home should keep, and mind her housewifery.
Their light within doth so prevail
It makes them hot about the tayle'."

A woman's place was in the home, and if a "light within" made them presumptuous enough to preach and teach, it was as likely to feed their overheated sensual appetites and turn them into sexual predators.

With witchcraft accusations so commonplace, then, it is no surprise that Fox makes no mention of the Pendle witches. If there were witches on the hill, there were also witches in the dale, and in the towns and cities. In many respects - not least his insistence on the equality of women - he was far ahead of his time. On witchcraft, however, he was quite simply a man of the seventeenth century, and rather slower than some to detect one of the great social evils of the day, even though he himself, and several of his own women followers, were sometimes numbered among its victims.

*

At Closes Hall, on the road to Monubent Head, we chat to a woman from the cottage at the Hall gates who is cutting flowers for the church. Where are we headed? she asks. We tell her we are treading in Fox's footsteps, in so far as we can track them. "I don't know which way *he* went, but the monks certainly came this way", she says. She is right. When the monks of Sawley Abbey were dispossessed at the dissolution of the monasteries in 1537, a deputation of tenants marched to Wigglesworth Hall to press-gang its owner, Sir Stephen Hamerton, to lead them against the king's men in an attempt to put the monks back in the abbey. Hamerton did so, claiming later that he acted under duress, which seems likely enough. He marched with the rebels as far as Monubent, where the rebellion collapsed, whereupon the reluctant hero was arrested, found guilty of treason and executed at Smithfield. The abbot of Sawley, William Trafford, likewise lost his head for his part in the revolt.

Past Monubent, we cross the flat fields, reclaimed from the flood plain between the Ribble and Tosside and heavily patterned by dyke and bank, to Lords farm and Hen Gill. Soon after four o'clock we notice our own pale shadows: the sun has half broken through - for perhaps thirty seconds. At Higher Agden a farmer finds us ankle-deep in his cow muck, having missed the path to Moss Side. Regaining the road with his help - "it's that way, like, you can't miss it, like" - we follow our noses to Pikeber. We could have avoided all this path-finding (and losing) by taking the modern road from Bolton to Wigglesworth, but by seeking out the field paths - which often show more distinctly on the map than they do on the ground - we feel we have a better sense of the untamed country through which George Fox walked before the roads were built.

At Pikeber we strike off-road again to Hamerton, which presumably gave its name to the unfortunate Sir Stephen's family, and thence into Wigglesworth village and on to our planned stop-over, Sir Stephen's own Wigglesworth Hall. No lying on the common in "a little ferns or brackens" for us! The ancient Hall is a fine farmhouse now, the centre of a 250-acre dairy and sheep farm. Odd sections of the house, an archway here, a section of wall there, seem to belong to Wigglesworth's mediaeval past, and a fine early sixteenth century tithe barn, built, unusually for the times, in stone rather than timber-frame and now rather cluttered by modern farm outbuildings, was described in 1694 as "the finest barn possibly in England". Wigglesworth gets its own mention in Domesday, and was no doubt much on the tongues of local gossips in 1307 when (according to some notes by George Wigglesworth which we were shown at the hall) the local lord, Reyner de Knoll, was caught in an act of adultery with one Alicia de Ribstan. Reyner appears to have got off scot-free, but the Registers of Archbishop Greenfield of York record poor Alicia's penance: "that on some Sunday, walking in front of a procession round the parish church of Preston in Craven, clad only in a smock, with bare shoulders, she shall undergo one whipping; and round the market place of Skipton in Craven on some market day, the next following, another whipping". A third whipping was to follow "on some Sunday or Holy Day", and a fourth in York market place. The fifth and final whipping was to take place on her own home ground, "humbly and devoutly, with the assistance of the people". Quakers would later take a stern view of sexual activity outside marriage (and sometimes within it), but their whippings were verbal and directed at both parties, challenging the prevailing view that most of the guilt lay with the temptress while the man could hardly be blamed for doing what came naturally to the stronger sex.

Our delightful, welcoming host at the hall was Mrs Booth, eager to hear news of our Foxtrot and to tell us of her own family connections with Quaker tradition. She brought out some old photographs of a gathering at Eldroth Hall, some miles to the north, near Settle, taken fifty or more years ago when the Society of Friends commemorated the setting aside of a small part of the farmyard as a Quaker burial ground in 1662. Mrs Booth's mother and aunt lived at Eldroth, and there they are in the pictures: two little girls, bewildered by this invasion of Quakers. Mrs Booth's mother never forgot that day, the first time she had ever seen so many people - perhaps fifty. "She didn't know there were so many people in the world". The family had moved on from the old place a few years later, driven out by the farming depression. The little girls' father - "a fairer man never walked" - died of heatstroke while out in the fields pulling turnips.

John Moore of Eldroth, who gave the burial plot, was an early convert to Quakerism and travelled to London and through the southern counties with George Fox in 1663. Fox visited Eldroth in 1669 during one of his journeys through Yorkshire, meeting up there with Margaret Fell's daughters Sarah and Susannah. "Not far off", he noted in his *Journal*, "lay Colonel Kirkby, sick of the gout, who had threatened that if I ever came near he would send me to prison again and had bid forty pounds to any man that could take me. And we had a very large meeting at this Eldroth". John Moore later married Mary Camm, daughter of Thomas Camm of Camsgill, who himself died at Eldroth in 1707.

After these reminiscences, we walk the mile or so back into Wigglesworth village for dinner at the Plough Inn, where they specialise in barbecued pork ribs, cooked American-style over scented wood chippings! A lark sings goodnight as we wander back in late, filtered sunshine, the shadows long and low. We both sleep the sleep of the well-fed and well-looked-after, content with the twenty miles we have put between ourselves and Pendle (though a crow could do it in little more than ten), but knowing that a hundred and sixty lie ahead.

The Horrid and the Picturesque

DAY 3. Wigglesworth-Malham

Our morning reading is printed on the apron Mrs Booth is wearing as she bustles around her kitchen:

"Let the wealthy and great
Roll in splendour and state,
I envy them not, I declare it.
I eat my own lamb,
My own chickens and ham,
I shear my own fleece and I wear it.
I have lawns, I have bowers,
I have fruits, I have flowers,
The lark is my morning alarmer.
So jolly boys now
Here's God speed to the plough,
Long life and success to the farmer!"

Rooks and jackdaws are *our* morning alarmers, and we wake to a cloudless blue sky and a wonderful whiff of bacon, egg, mushrooms and tomatoes. Mrs Booth's kitchen is hard to break away from, but we have to be off, briefly following the Ribble Way ramblers' footpath along Wigglesworth Beck. The beck is home to several mallard, some with chicks, and a goosander gathers up her eight fluffy bundles just in case we have designs on them.

George Fox tells us only that he "went to a town", where he and

Richard Farnsworth parted. There are two "towns" on our route, Long Preston and Malham. At Cow Bridge we join the road to Long Preston - no doubt the Preston-in-Craven where poor Alicia had her sins of the flesh whipped out of her. The village as it is today provides a busy through-route for traffic in the form of the Kendal-Skipton A65 trunk road, and we sit outside the post office for a short while, watching the cars go by.

Then we find the ancient green-road track, Scalehaw Lane, which takes us in a north-easterly direction across the rolling hill country to Malham. The "scale" name here is a reminder that this was Norse-settled country a thousand years ago, the *skali* marking their summer pastures. Over Scalehaw Hill the track divides, and we take the middle one towards Bookilber Barn, an ancient settlement astride Langber Lane, another old green road connecting Settle and Otterburn. East of Bookilber, we strike off towards Crake Moor, breaking for our sandwich lunch under a large, very ruinous stone bridge which once, perhaps in George's day, connected somewhere with somewhere else, but has long since been bypassed by new road systems. The early morning's promise of a fine day has not been fulfilled, and we munch silently in our wind-cheating greens.

The path, according to the map, runs straight ahead up a steep bank, but the bank has been ploughed out, probably for reseeding with new grass, and the path has gone the way of the tracks which once led to our ruined bridge. So we follow the field boundary till we strike the stile where the path re-emerges. Passing Crake Moor, a pretty house in a wooded hollow, accessible only by field paths, we reach Orms Gill, a limestone ravine which signals unmistakably that we are entering some of the most spectacular scenery in England. Here we become involuntary shepherds, driving a flock of sheep before us down the walled enclosure of Orms Gill Green Lane, till they eventually find a gap and make their escape.

Crossing Scosthrop Lane, another of the ageless trackways which criss-cross the moors, we climb to High Ings. Still uncomfortably close, to our south, is Pendle's Big End, but to the north we drop down by Deepdale plantation, out of Pendle's sight and over Kirkby beck into Kirkby Malham. Here we find the tea shops closed and the pub not yet open. So we head for the steeplehouse.

*

About two miles south of Kirkby Malham, just over the River Aire from Airton, stands Calton Hall. This, in Fox's day, was the home of John Lambert, Oliver Cromwell's henchman and for a time the second most powerful man in England. Lambert had distinguished himself early in the civil wars, at Nantwich in 1643 and again at Marston Moor, where he was second-in-command of the Yorkshire cavalry. When Fairfax relinquished leadership of the New Model Army, Lambert stepped into his shoes, and when Cromwell instituted full military dictatorship in 1655 he was widely tipped - not least by himself - as the next Lord Protector.

In 1652 John Lambert was seen as the champion of those who pressed for further reform and revolution - among whom, of course, was George Fox. Lambert recruited many Quakers to his regiments. The *Journal* has a tantalising reference to Fox meeting one described as "the greatest in the land", and it has been suggested that the reference is to Lambert, with the name censored out in view of the Major-General's subsequent disgrace. But that is speculation. In any case, Lambert spent most of his time on state affairs in London, and it is unlikely that George Fox would have found the great man in if he had knocked at the doors of Calton Hall.

The *Journal* does have two references to Lambert by name, a passing one to his defeat of a Royalist uprising in Cheshire in 1659, and another, rather more interesting, to his last-ditch stand against the restoration of the monarchy in 1660. Fox notes that "at Skegby in Nottinghamshire there came several that were going to be soldiers under Lambert and would have bought my horse; and because I would not sell him to them they were in a rage against me, using many threatening words; but I told them, and writ to them, that God would confound them and scatter them." A day or two later Lambert's dwindling forces were routed by General Monck, who was paving the way for the return of the king. If the later Fox saw the defeat of Lambert and the republic as God's work, a punishment perhaps for apostasy, this marked a radical change from the viewpoint of the younger Fox of 1652. In 1652 George's God was a republican. By 1660, swimming with the tide, even the Almighty seems to have turned royalist.

Lambert was lucky to escape with his head on his shoulders but spent the rest of his days in the Tower, though his son was permitted to return to Calton Hall, which he rebuilt after a disastrous fire. Well over three centuries later, in 1984, a memorial tablet was placed in the Lady Chapel of Kirkby Malham parish church, along with a modern painting based on a contemporary portrait, and a replica of the family banner. The Chapel of Our Lady became the Lambert Chapel - all somewhat incongruous, given the old soldier's implacable opposition to the established church and its crowned head.

The church also boasts a relic of a visit in 1653 by Cromwell himself, in the shape of the facsimile of his signature on a marriage certificate. The original has been stolen, whether by some outraged royalist or a more mercenary souvenir hunter is not known. Cromwell was presumably calling on Lambert at Calton, or Cowton as it was pronounced and sometimes spelt.

Fox, of course, would have been unimpressed by this steeplehouse dedicated to St Michael the Archangel. Built by the White Canons of the Premonstratensian Order and completed in the fifteenth century, its scale seems wholly out of proportion to the small, scattered population it served. Perhaps the White Canons were cocking a snook at their Cistercian neighbours, demonstrating that, although their order was smaller and not quite so wealthy, they could nevertheless build a dales church to rival Fountains or Bolton.

A little publication on the church bookstall notes that "after the national turmoil of the 17th century... there is little record of anything that disturbed the even tenor and tranquillity of life in the Dale". But it does mention that "some years ago on a fine Sunday morning, during prayer, a short-horn bull entered the church and proceeded down the middle aisle. The two churchwardens took their staffs and approached Mr Bull with some trepidation. Fortunately, the bull did an about turn and wandered out, to the thankful prayers of the parishioners. The vicar at the time had a habit of keeping his eyes closed during prayer and so was blisfully unaware that his flock had briefly included a four-footed visitor."

A visit by Oliver Cromwell and another by a short-horn bull: the two most exciting events to hit Kirkby Malham in four centuries.

*

But it is Malham proper, not Kirkby, which is our goal tonight, so we head north on the busy main road till, leaving the village behind, we strike off on a path to Scalegill. The mill here is said to be of eleventh century origin and was the village's main employer, working cotton, till the first world war. The infant stretches of the river beyond the mill are a delight and we are slow to move on, but we are soon in the confusion of Airehead Springs, which mingle the waters of Tanpits Beck, Malham Beck and Gordale Beck to form the River Aire, and Malham is below us.

The scene is familiar to hundreds of thousands of eager visitors to one of the most alluring tourist honey-pots in dales country. The nuclear village lies in a mile-wide basin, enclosed to the north by a wall of fells, scarred for their full length by exposed limestone. Directly ahead is Malham Cove, and to the east Gordale Scar. Since the invention of the Box Brownie, millions of snaps have attempted the impossible task of capturing this wild country on squares of coated paper no bigger than a man's hand. None can begin to do justice to the picturesque grandeur of the real thing.

Picturesque? Not a word that would have occurred to George Fox if this was indeed the "little town" where he rested. It is noticeable, in fact, that the *Journal* never offers us any description whatever of the landscape through which Fox passed, nor any mention of bird or wild flower. One reason, of course, is that George's mind was on other things: when a man is charged with proclaiming the day of the Lord, he doesn't stop to admire lapwings and woodavens. Another reason is that our hero was quite devoid of any aesthetic sense: he is never, ever, moved by music, poetry, the popular culture of his day - or by nature. But the third reason is that no-one in the seventeenth century, including those possessing all the aesthetic sensibilities so conspicuously lacking in George Fox, looked at the natural landscape and physical environment as we have learnt to do since the Romantic revolution a century after Fox's death.

To the seventeenth century these untamed regions were, above all, places to be avoided. If any adjective was appropriate to them, it was "horrid" or "terrible". Harsh landscapes were inhabited by rude men and women whose accents were as unintelligible as the barbarous names of the places they inhabited. The moors of Lancashire and the fells of the Pennines and Lakeland were England's dark corner, where jagged rocks and black superstitions haunted the imaginations of more cultured folk in cultivated country. In venturing north of Pendle, George Fox was carrying the Lord's message into the mouth of hell.

One hundred years later, the age of industry was beginning to blacken the cultivated gardens of polite landscape and provoke a reaction against urban artificiality. Burke published his *Inquiry into the Origin of Our Ideas of the Sublime and Beautiful* in 1756, and William Gilpin invented a third category for inquiry, what he called "Picturesque Beauty": the beautiful framed as a picture. Classical beauty was measured and orderly, like a meticulously planned country garden, whereas the picturesque was rough, irregular - and *natural*. (Gilpin himself said a Palladian mansion was beautiful, a broken ruin picturesque. Sidney Smith's caricature had it that the vicar's well-manicured horse was beautiful, the curate's hack picturesque). By the end of the century travellers were venturing into hitherto "horrid" territories to view them through picture-frames or Claude glasses and declare them indeed pretty as a picture. Soon the Lakeland poets and painters were reclaiming the old dark corners and hell-haunts for their new romantic paradise. So accustomed have we become to the romantic view of a Malhamdale, a Gordale, that we need reminding that a 1652 traveller saw something utterly different from what we see today, even if the object of his gaze was the same rocks and winding scars on which our own eyes are fixed.

Today, picturesque Malham is awash with visitors. It is the Spring Bank Holiday weekend, and the un-spring-like weather hasn't deterred them. The car parks are full and the cameras are clicking. There is even a troupe of morris dancers from Leeds, colourful and jingly, doing their stuff for the tourists. One has a fox head, another a horse head, another is the legendary Green Man, or perhaps a green goddess. Fox would not have approved. He tells us he was "sorely exercised... in testifying against their wakes or feasts, their May-games, sports, plays, and shows, which trained up people to vanity and looseness... I was also moved to cry against all sorts of music, and against the mountebanks playing tricks on their stages, for they burdened the pure life, and stirred up people's minds to vanity".

If the early Quakers vehemently rejected Puritan theology, they vociferously supported the Commonwealth's puritanical crackdown on popular arts and the pleasure principle. Fox almost certainly never went to the theatre, though contemporaries of Shakespeare were still alive; never listened to music, though masque was becoming opera. His friend Solomon Eccles gave up his profession as a music teacher when he became a Quaker, sold his violin, then bought it back again and destroyed it to ensure that no-one else would ever be seduced by its ungodly sweetness. As late as the nineteenth century the author Mary Howitt, daughter of Uttoxeter Quaker Samuel Botham, remembered her father hustling the young family indoors when a barrel-organ made its appearance on the street corner. For two and a half centuries Quaker life was crippled by the delusion that the arts derived from the devil. Today, of course, there are many Quaker actors and musicians, and Fox's crabbed and puritan views on the subject have been set aside. We shall even meet a Quaker morrisman later on our journey.

Fox's philistinism, as it seems to us today, is sometimes defended as a right-minded reaction against courtly vanities on one hand and the coarser vulgarities of popular culture on the other. His objection to theatre - "mountebanks on their stages" - was partly a protest against pretence. He was probably unaware that the Greek word *hypocrite* meant actor, but he would certainly have regarded the two terms as interchangeable. We must also remember that Fox lived at the end of a century of unprecedented iconoclasm. It has been estimated that no less than ninetyfive per cent of the paintings, murals, sculptures and stained glass of the pre-Reformation churches were systematically destroyed, not by Cromwell and his men but by the Anglican church, between 1540 and 1640. A glorious tradition of music and passion-drama was also suppressed, and the cultural gauleiters of the Reformation strove zealously to stamp out country dancing and festivities. A people's entire framework of both religious and secular imagery and symbolism was marginalised where it could not be wholly abolished. Fox was an inheritor, not an originator, of the view that the imagination was a barrier between humankind and God rather than a means of bringing the human and the divine together. This was an area in which he did not transcend his times.

English Reformation puritanism was itself only an extreme form of an ancient distrust of the arts, particularly music. Plato warned that music had a particularly insidious power to arouse undesirable passions, and in 1693 the Sorbonne itself decreed that musical drama in the new form of opera "is all the more dangerous since through music... the soul is much more susceptible to passion". So the puritans and Fox and his Quaker friends were by no means isolated. The idea that the arts had a moral function (as also Wordsworth's insistence that nature in the shape of a "vernal wood" may teach more of evil and good than all the sages can) came later. For Schiller, the theatre "punishes a thousand vices which civil justice tolerates with impunity, while a thousand virtues kept secret by the latter are acclaimed by the stage". Had Fox lived to hear the virtues of the arts lauded in this way he would have retorted that Schiller's theatre had assumed functions the godly assigned to God alone.

In his wholesale rejection of stage plays Fox may be said to have missed a trick in that he failed to appreciate the extent to which the folk theatre of his day could be a vehicle for popular protest, often against the very injustices Fox himself denounced. A protest play staged in the ruins of Kendal castle in 1621 so scandalised the authorities that it was prosecuted in the Court of Star Chamber. Written by a local schoolmaster, Jasper Garnett, and featuring as a leading actor a Grayrigg man named Henry Ward who, as we shall see, would become a Quaker thirty years later, it included a scene where two clowns persuade a young boy to peer down through a trap door in the stage and describe what he sees in hell. As well as the usual objects of popular contempt - self-righteous puritans, sheriffs, bailiffs - the boy sees a flock of croaking ravens feeding on sheeps' carcasses. The clowns interpret: the ravens are greedy landlords and the sheep "wee poore men, whose right these by their skill would take awaie, & make us tennantes at will, & when our ancient liberties are gone, theile puke & poole & peele us to the bare bone".

This was subversive stuff. No lesser lord than the king, James I, was leading northern landlords in an attempt to deprive their customary tenants of their ancient security of tenure and turn them into "tenants at will" - subject, that is, to the lord's will, no longer regulated by customary rights. It was no doubt because Jasper Garnett's play reviled not only the local gentry "to the greate abuse of the said Lordes", but also by implication the king himself, that the players were arraigned before the Star Chamber. Surprisingly (but perhaps because the king conveniently died while the court was considering the matter) Star Chamber effectively found for the tenants, and for preservation of their ancient customs. Subversive theatre, shunned by the godly for its reliance on "pretence", could be as effective as the radical preachers in securing social justice. Henry Ward worked for his New Jerusalem first as an actor and then as a Quaker. He probably achieved at least as much in the former as the latter role.

*

It is fortunate that we had the foresight to book our bed some weeks beforehand as the "no vacancies" signs are everywhere. But we find we have committed ourselves to one of the most expensive and least comfortable B&Bs of our trip in a guesthouse which, in charity, shall be nameless. We are some thirty miles from Pendle. Ahead of us lies wilder - or more picturesque - country than any we have yet trod.

The Other Pen

DAY 4. Malham-Yockenthwaite

After a breakfast which matches the meanness of the broom-cupboard we were given to sleep in, we make an early start. Today we must reach Langstrothdale where, at last, we can be certain we are on authentic Fox-trod ground. But Langstrothdale is twenty miles distant over rough highland country. Today will test our feet, and those odd little calf muscles which turn into quakers when you work them hard on a long downhill course.

First, however, we want to take a good look at Malham. Despite its recent adoption as a prime tourist centre, the village has probably undergone less change since Fox's day than any other village or town we shall be travelling through. Founded by English settlers (historians used to call them Angles) around the seventh century, when the newcomers conquered the native British (or Celts) in the Dales, it seems to have reached its present shape and size in the fourteenth century. The 1379 Poll Tax survey lists 31 married couples, 13 servants and an innkeeper, and the Lay Subsidy Roll adds a miller, all of which suggests between thirty and forty houses - roughly the size of the village in 1652, and in 1994.

Some of the houses we pass today would have been seen by any traveller in 1652. The cottage next to the Methodist chapel has a stone over the door carved with the date 1732, but Arthur Raistrick (in *Malham and Malham Moor*) argues that this is the date of a renovation, other structural details suggesting that the cottage itself was built a hundred or even a hundred and fifty years earlier. Another cottage at the south end of New Row, with attractive mullioned windows, is probably all that is left of Malham Hall, home of the steward of Fountains Abbey, which possessed the manor of Malham West from the thirteenth to the sixteenth century. The earliest hall, of timber and thatch, was built on the site of the present Reading Room and adjacent shop, and rebuilt in stone around 1600 with a wing extending northwards, of which the New Row cottage is all that is left. New Row itself was "new" in the seventeenth century, probably the 1660s or '70s. Up a narrow, winding lane is Hill Top, apparently dating from 1617, though the datestone is later. Finally, there is Beck Hall, which Raistrick has identified as the Old Hall given to Fountains in 1175 or earlier as the residence of their farm bailiff or other official, probably rebuilt in the seventeenth century and much altered since.

Most of the cottages and shops which make up today's village were there in 1652, but were timber framed and roofed with thatch. Raistrick quotes a 1600 deed giving a good description of a Malham house leased by Josias Lambert of Airton to Henry Hill of Malham:

"all that one mantion or dwelling house with the ground whereupon yt standethe and the fronte of the same house, one ladder or stee roome [an upstairs room] at ye sowthe end of ye house being threequarters of a yad onlie for ye theaking [thatching] of ye same house, one garth [yard] to ye middle of ye walls on both saides therunto adjoining commonlie called ye gill garth containing fifteen falls of ground, one croft adjoining to ye same garthe containinge thirtene falls and halfe a fall of ground as they are now agreed upon sett out and divided one third pte and parcel of ye turbary belonginge to that messuaige then late in thoccupacon of one Thomas Deane and John Hird. And all Brackans dailie in one close comonlie called and knowne by the name of Malham Cove Close on ye west side of Malham, and one hempe pitt for to rayt hempe in."

Such houses, with no chimney (the smoke from a central grate was allowed to escape through the thatch) and no upstairs other than a loft store-room reached by "stees" (ladders), were the typical homes of labourers and craftsmen in the mid-seventeenth century, and had changed little in hundreds of years. Once they had been typical for the whole of England, but by the late 1500s householders in the south and midlands were beginning to replace them with more solid homes, in which stone was used not just to fill the gaps between load-bearing timber frames but to construct walls of a sufficient thickness and strength to support a stone-flagged roof. Only wealthy gentry families in the north could afford to keep up with their southern Joneses in this way, and where smaller houses were concerned the new fashion hardly reached the north till the 1630s, and the upheavals and impoverishments of the civil wars and their aftermath effectively delayed wholesale rebuilding in stone till the 1660s and '70s. The great rebuilding spanned Fox's own lifetime, and had he returned to Malham shortly before his death in 1691 he would have seen the dilapidated timber and thatch cottages of 1652 transformed into the stone houses which are bed-and-breakfasting today's ramblers after three hundred years of domestic service.

Leaving Malham, we begin badly by taking the lane towards Gordale - Smearsbottoms Lane they call it at its easterly end - but soon realise our mistake, return to the village and turn northwards. Soon after Town Head we strike off to the right, on the Pennine Way footpath, making for Malham Cove. On our right now are the clearly-visible lynchets or plough terraces which are all that remain of seventh century English field systems, and on our left the less obvious boundaries of the tiny British fields laid out in the third century. Before us lies the Cove itself, towering above the ancient fields and daring us to enter its rock-strewn bowl.

The Cove is a vast, curved crag of limestone, its far wall rising nearly three hundred feet above the valley floor, its side walls some three hundred yards apart. Once, before the last ice age, a stream flowed over the top to create a mighty waterfall, but the waters eventually found an easier passage underground, leaving their old bed literally high and dry. In exceptionally wet weather, rainwater again finds its way over the lip of the gorge, encouraging vertical lines of mosses and lichens. Asked to explain these markings, a nineteenth century amateur geologist joked that the dark lines were probably made by a chimney sweep falling over the cliff and scattering soot as he slid down the rock face. The joker was Charles Kingsley, and the idea stuck in his mind, to be elaborated as *The Water Babies*: the tale of a boy-sweep whose early adventures take place around Malham. (I understand much the same tale is told of not-too-distant Arnclife).

The largest of the scatter of rocks which have fallen from the rim of the cove over the centuries has long been famous as marking a point where conversation is suddenly heard in multiple echo, bouncing backwards and forwards within the bowl of the Cove. As early as 1786 the local schoolmaster noted that from this stone "there is an Echo very distinctly repeated five times", producing "a most pleasing effect in a calm and clear evening from a French Horn or any other instrument from which the sound may be thrown forcibly against the Arches of the Cove". There are no French Horn players about today, but what might George Fox have made of the opportunity to sound the day of the Lord five times in one breath!

We follow the path through a thin hazel coppice, climbing to the top of the Cove on its western side. If the foot of the great bowl seems spectacular, the top is quite astonishing. Here is a bare lunar landscape, scraped dry of grass and surface vegetation by the ice ten thousand years ago. This limestone "pavement" is criss-crossed by natural joints which in time have widened into fissures called "grykes", a hiding place for alpine plants, some of which have virtually disappeared from surface habitats. The criss-cross effect does give the whole area the appearance of a giant crazy-paving, and the strangeness and insecurity of the landscape is accentuated by the slipperiness of the surface, and by the occasional rocking movement of the huge blocks of stone under one's feet. The Cove's limestone pavement is by no means unique: there are hundreds scattered across the dales. There used to be more, till the garden-centre industry discovered them and started ripping them out to sell as picturesque adornments to suburban rock gardens.

We cannot linger, for we have a long day ahead of us. Grass again grows under our feet on Ewe Moor, one of four large pastures reclaimed from the waste in mediaeval times, two - including this one - for sheep and two for cattle. We cross Watlowes, the dry valley which once carried the ice and water which quarried out the Cove, to find an ancient track called Trougate, running between more Celtic settlements, visible as heaps of stones and marked on the map in romantic gothic type as *homestead, hut circle, settlements,* or *cairn.* Unmarked, and visible only to the trained eye, is a large dew pond, a man-made shallow depression expertly designed perhaps a thousand years ago to hold moisture abstracted from the dew-laden air and keep the stock well watered.

Perhaps a mile from the Cove we start descending again and catch our first glimpse of Malham Tarn, less than a mile ahead. Crossing us at right angles is Mastiles Lane, probably the most famous of the long-distance tracks used by the monks of Fountains to travel between their far-flung colonies, though it must be Roman in origin: a rectangular camp platform, clearly Roman, stands astride it, a mile to the east. Mastiles has been badly damaged by the thoughtlessness of off-the-road drivers who have gouged their ruts into its surface before departing in search of other beauty-spots to ruin. Where the two tracks cross each other there is a stone base with a groove cut into it, one of three on this section of Mastiles. Embedded in the grooves were once the bases of wooden crosses, destroyed by earlier generations of vandals, or perhaps by the greatest vandal of them all: time.

Malham Tarn is a natural lake formed by the run-off from Fountains Fell, the water being contained at the southern end by a wall of clay and gravel deposited by a passing glacier. It was granted to

Fountains Abbey in the twelfth century and kept the monks in good fat trout for four hundred years. As we approach the eastern side we are welcomed by the smiling faces of a thousand little yellow mountain pansies. Anthea's eyes are on the waters, searching for the crested grebes we have seen on earlier excursions. They are not at home today.

On the north shore is Tarn House, built in the nineteenth century and now a popular field studies centre. We promise each other that they are sure to do coffee there. But they don't: not for passing strangers. Peering through the windows, however, we see a group of students evidently taking a break and helping themselves to coffee from a machine. Leaving our backpacks outside, we try to look like mature students and join them, dispensing coffee to ourselves and nodding knowledgably as their friendly conversation touches on matters unfathomably geological.

Leaving behind us the domesticated woodland of Tarn House we head for Fountains Fell, still following the Pennine Way. It is a slow trudge onwards and upwards towards the 2000ft contour, through heather and peat-land pitted with shake holes indicating underground watercourses. The lower slopes, divided into Little Fell, Middle Fell, Far Fell and Stangill Fell, are now National Trust property. They were once part of the Fountains sheep run, and a 1539 valuation tells us that "Fontaunce Fell" with "all the sole [soil], waste and ground... and also the Fedings and pastor" was worth forty shillings a year. Our track takes us over the shoulder rather than the summit, skirting Fountains Fell Tarn where generations of monastic mutton quenched its thirst. Over the brow, we are surprised to find ourselves among mounds and shafts indicating a disused colliery, probably opened in the eighteenth century and closed perhaps a hundred years later. The track on which we have ascended is the route, cut in 1807, by which the colliers brought down their black gold in the panniers of their ponies. Here, with a stunning view down into Pen-y-ghent gill and up again to Pen-y-ghent hill, we pause for a late sandwich lunch, the energising effect of our stolen coffee already dissipated by our climb.

Then steeply down to join the narrow lane through the delightful gorge which drops to Littondale. Taking the old line of the road, a little south of the modern lane, we stop to look at a heap of huge slab-stones, some set on edge, appropriately called Giant's Grave. They do indeed indicate a much disturbed burial mound thought to date back to Neolithic - New Stone Age - times. On the far side of the gill below us, on the well-drained limestone ledges, are more ancient settlements. The steep sides of the gorge are lightly wooded with ash, at the flowering stage but with no leaves yet in evidence, and with hawthorn showing off their light green newborn leaves, but with no hint as yet of the May blossom, postponed this year till June. A pair of young ring-ouzels take cover in a young ash.

*

Since crossing Fountains we have been skirting the huge mass of Pen-y-ghent. While preparing for our trip, we had been visited by Susan Bell, a Friend from Southampton, who had put to us the startling suggestion that Pen-y-ghent rather than Pendle Hill was George Fox's "hill of vision". Just over a year later, in July 1995, Sue published her theory in the *Friends' Quarterly*, where it created quite a stir. Had Friends got their basic history wrong? Had hundreds of young Quaker pilgrims been climbing the wrong Pen all these years? Would America's famous Quaker college, Pendle Hill, have to change its name? Would we have to do our walk all over again on different terrain?

Susan Bell's argument may be summarised as follows. 1, Fox started his journey not in Derbyshire, as he writes in the *Journal*, but at Bradford, and the direct Bradford-Wensleydale route runs nowhere near Pendle Hill but does include Pen-y-ghent. 2, Fox's climbing "with much ado" better fits the steeper Pen-y-ghent than the gentler Pendle. 3, the sea, which Fox saw from the top, is "very far from obvious" at Pendle, but "much closer" at Pen-y-ghent. 4, the topography Fox refers to better fits the fell country around Pen-y-ghent than the "Lancashire plains" around Pendle. 5, William Penn says Fox's hill of vision was in Yorkshire, as Pen-y-ghent is, while Pendle is in Lancashire. 6, Fox's vision of the places where "a great people" were to be "gathered", where two rivers meet, should be understood literally, and only from Pen-y-ghent is it possible to see the precise place Fox was refering to, the confluence of the Rawthey and the Lune near Sedbergh. 7, evidence in the *Journal* conflicting with the Pen-y-ghent hypothesis is "either...an uncharacteristic blunder" of Fox's editor, or "a deliberate red herring" to produce "a cover-up".

We have of course acknowledged at the outset that Fox's *Journal*, in its various forms, is bound to puzzle the historian who tries to disentangle from its text a precise itinerary and chronology. Our George had a keen sense of his own historical importance, but his primary purpose in writing and dictating the various versions of his mis-named *Journal* was not academic documentation but evangelism. Putting together two versions many years after the events would be bound to result in some topographical and chronological inaccuracies, even if topographical and chronological accuracy rather than evangelism had been his primary purpose. Add to these uncertainties the confusions, accidental or censorial, of later editors, and the more complex the problem becomes. We are dealing with a middle-aged man's memory, possibly defective and certainly selective, and with texts from different periods written in different hands and collated by different editors. So Susan Bell is right to insist that it is all a matter of interpretation. The question is whether her new interpretation is more convincing than the old. I believe it is not, because the arguments she advances seem to me flawed.

First, the question of where Fox started from. He mentions in the *Journal* that he was in the Wakefield/Liversedge/Bradford area with James Nayler and Richard Farnsworth, from which location he "Passed through the country...and came into a market town in

Derbyshire". Susan Bell says bluntly that a venture into Derbyshire at this point is "clearly an impossibility...an elementary geographical error". But it is hard to see why. Bradford is some twenty miles, Liversedge about fifteen and Glossop around twenty-two from the Derbyshire border. It is admittedly hard to identify any Derbyshire "market town" within an easy day's walk, but there is nothing in the *Journal* to suggest that the foray over the county boundary was accomplished in a single day. On the contrary, it is clear that the return journey from the Derbyshire market town to the hill of vision took two days and nights. The descent into Derbyshire *is* problematic, but it is far from being an "impossibility" or an "obvious geographical error".

Susan Bell buttresses her case for a direct Bradford-Pen-y-gent route by pointing out that this would have taken Fox through Skipton, which would in turn account for that town being an early Quaker stronghold. But there is no evidence of Skipton being the key Quaker centre she supposes before 1658, and the reference she gives to a Quaker burial ground said to have been marked with a datestone of 1637 (which can no longer be found) derives from a nineteenth century antiquarian, Harry Speight, who frequently got his dates wrong.

Next there is the argument that Pendle Hill, "from the angle Fox had been travelling", "doesn't stand out from other hills", "is not a particularly difficult hill to climb", and offers no clear view of the sea. Certainly if Fox *was* on the Bradford-Skipton line he would have caught only distant and not particularly impressive glimpses of Pendle. But on a line from Derbyshire, Pendle would have reared up before him out of flat land with an air of mystery and menace which still stirs the imagination. True, the climb to the summit seems easy enough to the modern traveller who leaves his car at Barley and then completes his mountaineering by using the newly-cut steps, but Fox, whether or not he took the Barley route, presumably started from the floor of the Calder valley and would have had to carry his stoutish frame up 1800 feet of unpaved moorland on a hot June day. And if the "Lancashire Sea" - the great Morecambe estuary inlet - is often obscured (as it was for us, and presumably for Susan Bell), countless Quaker pilgrims will testify that it can be seen shining in the distance on a clear day.

Nor do I see much in the argument that the topography of Pendle country is less fitted to Fox's "fell countries" than that of Pen-y-ghent. His journey northwards from the inn at Pendle foot would have taken him little more than fifteen miles across flattish Lancashire plain before he hit proper "fell countries". And what of Penn's reference to Fox's hill being in Yorkshire? What he actually wrote (in the Preface to Fox's *Journal*) is that the unnamed hill was "in some of the hither parts of Yorkshire, as I take it". It seems more likely that Penn was a little unsure as to which side of the county boundary the hill lay on than that he was offering posterity a coded reference to Pen-y-ghent.

Susan Bell's most pressing argument, however, is that by naming Pendle Hill in the published *Journal* either Fox or his editors were guilty of a "cover-up". The suggestion is that between Bradford and Skipton Fox may have associated with republican elements whose names political expediency required should be excised in the counter-revolutionary climate of the Restoration. So great was the danger of mentioning such subversives (Lambert is the obvious candidate) that it was thought necessary not only to censor them but also to throw in red herrings to suggest Fox had taken a quite different (but allegedly impossible) route.

But this conspiracy theory, I am afraid, is full of holes. First, there is no actual *evidence* that "Derbyshire" and "Pendle Hill" were inserted by Fox's first editor, Ellwood, or any subsequent one for that matter. The modern scholarly Nickalls edition distinguishes between the *Short Journal*, the *Cambridge Journal* and Ellwood's additions. It does not mark "Derbyshire" and "Pendle Hill" as Ellwood's interpolations. They appear to be Fox's own work. Was *he*, then, the author and instigator of the cover-up? The suggestion might be credible if Fox had been conspicuously wary of mentioning earlier politically incorrect connections, but he made no secret - indeed, he made much of - his familiarity with the "great usurper" Cromwell himself. If he didn't trouble to hide that in the dangerously vengeful climate of the Restoration, why so deviously hide possible encounters with lesser rebels? The *Journal* is full of sympathetic references to radical republicans who had taken arms against the king: Major Bousfield, Colonel Benson, Lambert's own quartermaster James Nayler, and many more. So why introduce elaborate red herrings, false trails, editorial censorship and a cover-up to hide a purely conjectural meeting with a possible anonymous Skipton revolutionary? The theory is stimulating, but unconvincing.

There is one more reason why Fox would not have said Pendle Hill if he meant Pen-y-ghent. As we shall see, Fox's later travels were to take him through the Pen-y-ghent region more than once, including a stay nearby in 1669, the year he put together the so-called Cambridge version of the *Journal*, the one in which Pendle is mentioned by name. By then, when the whole territory had become thoroughly familiar to him, he must certainly have known the one hill from the other.

So, while applauding Susan Bell's insistance that Friends bring questioning minds to their origin-myths and received histories, I believe she failed to make her case. Fox climbed Pendle Hill. But his subsequent journey northwards led him around Pen-y-ghent, as we have seen. He probably sounded the day of the Lord here too, at its foot if not its peak.

*

Passing a shake-hole - a natural depression formed by a partial roof-collapse over an underground watercourse - melodramatically marked "Flamethrower Hole" on the map, we reach the magical little settlement of Halton Gill. Hiding away in the valley bottom, the modern road dropping from Malham cuts ruthlessly through yet another ancient field system, more noticeable from the opposite slopes. Halton Gill is remote today: how much more so before these modern roads. Its neat little houses are datestoned - 1623, 1641 - and some of them retain unaltered seventeenth century fenestration. But we are frustrated to find no tea-shop open. The tourist season, with the summer, is a late visitor to these parts.

From the south, the track we are to take on the far side of the dale is clearly discernible - and apparently vertical. How our sore feet can be persuaded to open a new offensive against gravity we cannot imagine. But once reached, it turns out to be not as steep as it looked. We haul ourselves up to Horse Head Gate where we are rewarded by the seductive sight of Langstrothdale far below us, and there, straight ahead, the tight little cluster of three or four houses which form Yockenthwaite: our night halt.

As we drop down towards Yockenthwaite bridge we find ourselves hailed by a stocky farmer. Is he berating us for trespassing on his pastures? It seems not, for his face is a mass of broad smiles. A little nearer and we recognise him as an old friend: Richard Charnley, who used to be a neighbour of ours in Dentdale till he decamped with his wife Barbara to run a National Trust farm here. Richard marches us off to renew acquaintance with Barbara, the jolliest and most hospitable of daleswives. Soon we are deep in tales of Dent.

Such as the occasion when Richard was organising a farmers' demo against Margaret Thatcher's agricultural policies, and asked me if I could lean on my television contacts to get the loan of some Spitting Image face masks of the said lady. Maggie-masks being unobtainable - demand was far outstripping supply - I acquired instead some very realistic rubberised monkey faces, ready to wear. The Charnleys were out when I delivered them that night to their farm at Borranhead, so I left them in the porch in a large box, the lid secured by a heavy stone against the curiosity of the farm dogs which were showing a noisy and somewhat menacing interest in my exotic deliveries.

Next morning I phoned Richard to check that he had found them and that they would suit his purpose. "We found them all right!" he said. "We were driving up the farm track at midnight and my headlights picked out this black hairy face with big red eyes staring up at us from the ground. Then we saw another, and another. The closer we got to the house, the more there were. The yard was full of them! It looked like a bloody massacre!" The dogs, it seemed, had worried the stone off the lid and scattered their enemies. With peals of laughter, Richard and Barbara recalled how they had collected their grisly trophies, put in a few running repairs, and made them the centrepiece of the Kendal National Farmers Union float on their demo, under the slogan: "Don't let Maggie make monkeys out of us!"

Reluctantly we said goodbye and crossed the bridge to the middle of three houses at Yockenthwaite: an elegant Georgian structure surrounded by white pales. The Hird family welcomed us, but they were off to a farmers' thanksgiving service for lambing time at Kettlewell church, so two helpful young bed-and-breakfasters, Tim and Justine from New Zealand, offered to drive us the mile or so to the George at Hubberholme, where I consumed an enormous ham, egg and chips and Anthea virtuously tucked into something more healthy. The Hirds, as they told us later that night, had lived at Yockenthwaite for five generations - some 150 years. Much grander than most dales farmhouses, it boasts high ceilings, fine multi-paned windows and a gracious staircase leading to a wide, arched landing. They thought it had originated as a hunting lodge for a "big family".

Yockenthwaite, or Yoghannesthweit in its earliest recorded form in the thirteenth century, derives from *Eogan's thwaite*, thwaite being a common Norse word or suffix for clearing. The Eogan bit is particularly interesting, being an Old Norse adaptation of an Old Irish name which today would probably be rendered O'Gan - a reminder than many of the Norse settlers in these parts came not direct from Scandinavia but via Ireland and the Isle of Man.

Deliciously picturesque in its typical Norse dale-head setting, it has had nearly as much attention from rambling photographers as Malham. Like most properties here, it is now owned by the National Trust. "It's a beautiful place, all right", agrees Mr Hird, "but it's a devil to work". He points to the old, narrow stone bridge over the Wharfe which is its only access. "Everything has to come over there, you see, and it was built for packhorses, not modern waggons".

One sees his problem, and hopes it may long continue. And if that seems selfish, it is perhaps a little less so in that the Hirds who steward this beautiful spot so lovingly would no doubt be the last to allow anyone to change it.

An Avenging Angel; and a Naked Quaker

DAY 5. Yockenthwaite-Semerwater

The last day of May was one of those glorious sunny mornings of which we dream through long wintry nights. After a banquet of a farmhouse breakfast we are reluctant to leave Yockenthwaite, so we sit in the garden, soaking up the sunshine and making the notes which will one day make this book. Anthea draws my attention first to the song of willow warblers, then the twittering of swallows, then to the squeaking and squawking of a family of young jackdaws in the chimneys above, then to the music of goldfinches glimpsed in the nearby sycamore. Paradise has some competition on its hands if it is to beat this.

But with only half an hour of the morning left, we finally tear ourselves away. There is a spring in our step, brought on not only by the refreshment of a night's rest and the ministry of sunshine and birdsong, but also by the knowledge that today we really are on Fox's trail. Till now we have followed his *most likely* route: the most direct line, given sevententh century trackway systems, from Pendle towards Wensleydale. But - conspiracies, cover-ups and cock-ups apart - we cannot be sure that he came precisely the way we have come. It has mostly been guesswork so far: informed and intelligent guesswork, we hope, but guesswork nonetheless. Today we reach surer ground.

Fox tells us in the *Journal* that he "came through the dales to a man's house, one Tennant". Another early (1704) account says significantly that Fox was "*directed* to ye house of James Tennant, called Scarhouse, in Langstroth Dale" - about a mile east of Yockenthwaite. Here Fox was "moved to speak to the family". As he turned away to continue his journey, something stopped him. He turned back "to declare God's everlasting Truth to [Tennant] and he was convinced, and his family, and lived and died in the Truth". The Tennant family became firm friends of Fox, and Scarhouse an important Quaker centre in the dales.

As noted earlier, however, there is a puzzle in the placing of this story in the *Journal*. Fox puts this, his first of what were to be several visits to Scarhouse, *after* rather than before his arrival in Wensleydale. Three possible interpretations of this apparent anomaly may be offered. First, Fox passed close by on his Pendle-Wensleydale route without calling at Scarhouse, then heard of Tennant when he was in Wensleydale and retraced his steps to call on him and "convince" him before proceeding westwards towards Sedbergh and Westmorland. Second, Fox's Pendle-Wensleydale route lay (as Susan Bell suggests) further to the east than the more direct line we have followed, so that in visiting Scarhouse he would only have had to take a short detour southwards rather than actually retrace his steps. Third, Fox did call at Scarhouse *en route* to Wensleydale, but when he came to write it up many years later he placed it out of sequence. Take your pick. If we choose the third alternative, that is because it makes most sense for our purposes. We are not going to pass Scarhouse with eyes averted, only to have to make our way back there after Wensleydale. Nor are we going to embrace a much more conjectural easterly route just to accommodate Fox's puzzling and probably mistaken chronology.

By whatever route, however, and from whatever direction, and at whatever precise point in his itinerary, George Fox came to Scarhouse, and that is where we are headed now. First we climb steeply, our faces set directly northward, up on to the ridge, the "scar", above Yockenthwaite, then turn sharply eastwards following an ancient track which once accommodated the travellers whose descendants now move more swiftly and surely along the tarmac road which hugs the south bank of the Wharfe.

The limestone along this ridge is worn into fantastic shapes. The steep slopes are still well wooded, remnants of the old Langstrothdale forest which made a happy hunting ground for the mediaeval gentry. We read in a local guide that the remains of five buildings may be detected among the trees, all that is left of the lodges used by twelfth century deer-hunters. Forgetting George Fox for a while, we make it our business to search them out and find two, one a mere pile of stones but the other with immense foundation platforms and strong gable walls still intact. They were probably ruins when Fox came this way. But the accompanying laughter of green woodpeckers was surely as merry in his day, and for twelfth century huntsmen, as it is today for us.

Suddenly we reach Scarhouse, its back to what seems at first sight a man-made quarry but what is in fact a natural scar or clint, its front elevation commanding a view down a long, rough track into the lower valley. This is not quite the house Fox visited. James Tennant had leased the property, with six and a half perches of land, from the absentee landholders, the Earls of Cork and Cumberland, for one penny a year in 1650. The original house is said to have had three storeys. It was altered in 1698, perhaps to accommodate the large Quaker meetings which were regularly held there, and the inscription I.A.T. 1698 over the door (no distinction being made between I and J at that time) indicates that the work was done by James and Ann Tennant, James being the grandson of Fox's convert.

James senior, according to the records of Settle Monthly Meeting, written in 1704 and printed in *The First Publishers of Truth* in 1907, "became a Serviceable Man to friends and truth in his Day, wch was not long, after the time of his convincemt, being taken Prisoner for his Testimony against Tythes, fro which he did not decline, but Patiently Endured Close Jmprisonment untill Death".

He died in 1674 and was buried in Scarhouse burial ground under a slab roughly carved I.T 1674. The stone was later unearthed and used as a butter-slab in the dairy.

Three years later, in 1677, a frailer George Fox came this way again with a party of friends on horseback. They made their way to Scarhouse over the high, bleak Stake Road (which we shall soon encounter), "the way many times deep and bad with snow," as he wrote home, "and our horses sometimes were down, and we were not able to ride". At Scarhouse he preached for "severall houres" to Friends who came to hear him from "Wensydaile, & Littendaile, & Bishopsdaile, & Skipton, & Coverdaile, & from Kellet in Lancashire, & from Sedbergh etc". It is good to think of these scattered bands of dissidents making their way across this rugged country to gather in one of the very first meetinghouses of Commonwealth republican Quakerism, to hear the man who turned back to talk James Tennant into the new movement.

The Tennants remained faithful to Scarhouse, and Scarhouse to the Tennants, for many more generations. Nine Tennants are named in the incomplete records of Friends buried there between 1674 and 1792. Seven are listed as attending what became the parent meeting at Settle between 1702 and 1784. In 1785 Scarhouse meeting came under Richmond Monthly Meeting, new roads making distant Richmond marginally more accessible, and thence to Brighouse in 1908. The house was refronted by its owner, Sir J W Ramsden, in 1876, when it lost most of what remained of its original appearance. Since 1989 it has been owned by the National Trust, which has not always found it easy to place tenants willing and able to negotiate the steep and stony access track down to Hubberholme. It was empty and a little desolate when we called, but has since found new occupants. Its re-opening was celebrated with a gathering to which former tenants as well as local Friends were invited. Our friend Elizabeth Middleton of Dent, who had family connections there, told us "It was a grand do. It was far too good a house to leave empty". And one of her relatives remembers visiting as a child. "And, you know, I'll swear we could hear singing at night, coming from where they had them meetings." Early Quakers may not have done much singing, but their ghosts evidently made up for it. Or perhaps it was the silence that was singing.

Careful scrutiny of our map reveals that there is a pub at Cray, where our high track meets the Buckden road a mile further east. If we get a move on, we can reach it before closing time. So we get a move on, pausing only briefly to glimpse the little toy-town of Hubberholme through the trees and down in the valley. Huburgheha to the perhaps aurally-challenged commissioner who wrote its entry in Domesday Book, Hulberham in 1220, Huberam in 1241, Hobram in 1545 and Hubbram (the present pronunciation) in 1657, the name means Hunberg's homestead. The twelfth-century church of St Michael and All Angels, around which Hubberholme's houses huddle protectively, was originally a forest chapel, and so remote was it from ecclesiastical authority at the Reformation that it audaciously preserved its forbidden rood screen and loft, embellishing them further in the last year of Mary's reign. They are its glory (though Fox would have considered them shameful relics of popery), along with the choir stalls, pews and chairs carved by Robert Thompson of Kilburn in 1934. Thompson's trademark was a mouse, and many of his pews and chairs are so decorated. Visitors' children can be observed playing hunt-the-mouse: a useful way to keep them occupied and interested while their parents wander from rood loft to Elizabethan bell, reading bits of the guide leaflet to each other.

"Hubbram" was J B Priestley's favourite church (though he was a non-believer), and his ashes are buried in the churchyard. His widow, the archeologist, philosopher and peace campaigner Jacquetta Hawkes, told me one day on the road from Aldermaston to Trafalgar Square that Jack had threatened never to speak to her again if she buried him anywhere but here! She showed me a photo of the hamlet, which I assumed to be some exotic Scandinavian hide-out, Yorkshire being an unknown land to me in those days.

Quite irrevelant to our story, but of some personal interest, we discovered many years later that Hubberholme church owned half of our own Hobsons farm at Dent for a time in the 19th century, when dales churches used their Queen Anne's Bounty to invest in whatever pieces of land, near or distant, they could snap up at bargain prices during the agricultural recession. Hubberholme must have bought the land from the last of the Quaker Thistlethwaite family at Hobsons, who must have been impoverished indeed to sell out to a steeplehouse.

*

We reach the White Lion at Cray just in time for a quick lager and crisps. Heading north on the tarmac road, we cross the moss at Buckden Causeway, then strike off to the left along the southern end of the old Stake Road track, marked Gilbert Lane on the map. There are ancient enclosures and settlements on either side of us, but our inexpert eyes fail to pick them out. Beyond Stake Moss, where we cross the ancient boundary dividing the West from the North Riding or "thirding" of Yorkshire, the line of the old track has been diverted to skirt the presumably 18th or 19th century enclosures, but we adopt the purist (and shorter) original line. The road becomes spectacular where it runs across the steep slopes of Cragdale. Here, more than anywhere, we can imagine "the way deep and bad with snow", and Fox and his party having to dismount and urge their horses through the drifts. But we have only a cooling wind to contend with, and soon below us we get our first sight of Semerwater, to which we descend via Bob Lane, through Stalling Busk, past the romantic ruins of an ancient chapel, and so to the edge

Top: *atop of Pendle*
Bottom: *Pendle Hill from Sawley Abbey*

Top: Pen-y-ghent
Bottom: Scar House, Langstrothdale

Right: Looking down on Hubberholme from the Scar.

Bottom left: Preston Patrick Hall courtroom.

Bottom right: Brigflatts meeting schoolroom.

Lea Yeat, Dentdale, from Hobsons Farm

of Semerwater itself, lying like a brooch of lapis lazuli pinned into folds of green velvet. A hare starts away through purple orchids and a tree pippit serenades us with a dazzling aria, soaring from its chosen tree top and gliding back again with accelerating notes. There are a few holiday-makers on the beach, and one or two brightly-coloured wind-surfers are dipping in and out of the water.

Semerwater is a glacial lake, filled by the waters of Marsett and Crooks becks flowing through Raydale, and emptied by what is said to be the shortest river in England, the Bain, which runs into the Wensleydale Ure a couple of miles northward. Three dales meet here: "Cragd'le", "Rayd'le" and "Bard'le". "Say that quickly", writes Norman Duerden in *Portrait of the Dales*, "and you have the sound of boots on the stony track that leads by Cragdale over the Stake to Buckden". But Semerwater is famous not only for the startling beauty of its setting but for no less than three legends, one concerning a siren mermaid, another a giant's stone, and the third a drowned city.

Once upon a time, the last and best of the three stories goes, the druids of the Celtic town which stood on what is now the bed of the lake were celebrating the winter solstice. On a "weatherly night", as the dalesfolk have it, a mighty storm blew up, and a lone traveller interrupted the ceremonies asking for shelter. The druids refused, which was unfortunate for them as the traveller turned out to be an angel disguised as a poor man, come to deliver Christian good news. His words were rejected as blasphemy against the heathen gods and he was sent packing. On the outskirts of the town, however, he came to a shepherd's hut where he was given food and shelter, and where the shepherd and his wife were duly converted to the faith of the angel's master.

The following morning, the angel ascended the fellside overlooking the town which had rejected him and cursed it as "the habitation of hard, unfeeling and uncharitable men", concluding with the rhyme:

"Semerwater rise, Semerwater sink,
And swallow all the town, save this lile house
Where they gave me meat and drink".

Whereupon there was a mighty rushing of waters which soon filled the hollow, burying for ever the inhospitable town, all except the shepherd's hut. And even today, it is said, boatmen (and perhaps windsurfers) may catch glimpses of towers and roofs in the depths below (though, truth to tell, the depths are pretty shallow), and on a still night the faint tolling of bells may be heard from the drowned steeples of the unhappy town. Quite why the Christian angel, presumably with God's blessing, should treat the town's innocent fidelity to its own religion with such ruthless lack of Christian charity, and why church bells may be heard tolling from heathen temples, the legend does not explain, legends being properly impatient of such quibbles.

Similar tales of submerged cities are of course told elsewhere. But in 1937 evidence was found suggesting that the Semerwater story may have a factual origin. Silting had raised the bed and therefore the water level over the centuries, so work was begun to lower the level and recover some land around the margins. In the recovered area a timber structure was found, which archeologists identified as the remains of a small platform set on piles. Bones of red deer, rings and fragments of iron tools proved it to be an Iron Age habitation, and a bronze spear-head and flint arrow-heads indicated that Bronze Age folk had lived nearby too. Arthur Raistrick and others have surmised that the remains are those of an Iron Age lake dwelling, of a type uncovered in other lakes, built over the water for additional protection. As the water level rose, either slowly through natural silting or suddenly as the result of a catastrophic flood, the dwellings were submerged - and the legend was born.

We follow the grassy path round the eastern shore-line to the road at High Blean, turning left to pass the Giant's Stone (painted by Turner), crossing the little stone bridge over the Bain (built by 18th century Quakers) before trudging wearily up the steep road to Countersett - and Countersett Hall.

George Fox certainly visited Countersett Hall - but not in 1652, though his friendship with the Hall's occupant, Richard Robinson, began that year, and Fox records being entertained there on future journeys, including the one in 1677 when he was snowbound on the Stake Road. Richard Robinson was 23 years old in 1652, from a long line of Wensleydale Robinsons, "brought up a Scholr (but not in the Univrsities"), newly-wed and newly-established at the Hall. The seeking urge so common among puritans of the age led him to try several varieties of religion, but "haveing Inspected them all, & was at astand where to find a people to Joyn himselfe to...he could find no true satisfaction amongst any of them". His sense of being different, of standing apart, is vividly captured in a contemporary description of him as "a specled Bird in the wilderness, or as an owle in the Desert". It was written of him by his friends that before he ever met George Fox he heard of his preaching and "joyned wh it in his mind". By 1652 it seems that Robinson was involved with the loose groupings of Seekers forming in the dales and further west in Westmorland, led by a dissenting minister named Thomas Taylor. This was the group Fox would meet up with at Sedbergh. It is surprising that he missed contact with them on his way through Wensleydale and within a couple of miles of Countersett Hall. But he evidently did, or he would surely have told us about them.

It was no doubt this Seeker network which brought Richard Robinson news of Fox's eventual encounter with them in Sedbergh a few days later, and Robinson lost no time in going off to find out for himself what was happening. He talked with Seeker leaders Francis Howgill, John Audland, John Snowdon and Thomas Taylor himself, and like them became a convinced "Child of the Light", as future Friends had begun to call themselves. Returning to Countersett Hall, he made it the centre of his own lifetime's Quaker work, "freely given up for the Entertainment of friends & also for a meeting house". Together with another former Seeker, Richard Hubberthorne - "dear innocent Richard" George Fox called him - they began to preach their subversive new gospel to a suspicious and unconvinced Wensleydale populace. They were abused at Carperby and attacked at Robinson's home market town of Askrigg, where "Many of the People were Exceeding Rude". Nevertheless a regular Friends' meeting was established at Countersett before the end of 1652, and in the next few years, writes his biographer David Hall (*Richard Robinson of Countersett*), "there was hardly a town or village between York and Newcastle which did not hear him 'proclaiming the Truth' in the church, the market place or the court house".

He made two visits to London,

"in which service he suffered many beatings, buffitings, scoffings, scornings & revileings, Especially from the Ruder Sort... He Traveled much on foot, being a lusty, strong man of body, & likewise finding it to be more agreeable to his service in those publick places, the roughness of the people in those times considered, for he was forced to lay sometimes out of doors in the fields, & to Travel in the night as well as the day, & in winter seasons as well as Sumbr, without shrinking from the violence of wether. And after this manner the Lord led him on his way throug many rough and untrodden paths, but the Lords power was with him and supported him through them all, and notwithstanding the many blows and stroaks he gott by staves and Clubs, several of which were broaken upon him with such violence that peices thereof flew up into the aire".

Richard Robinson was prosecuted many times for refusing to pay his tithes, and in 1661 he was jailed at York Castle. The castle was so full of prisoners - the Fifth Monarchy Rising, which Friends were falsely accused of aiding and abetting, had only just been suppressed - that Robinson was "forced to Lay in a great Oven which stood in the Castle yard wall". He was twice committed to Richmond jail, where he spent three years for refusing to pay church rates of 10d. He narrowly escaped a worse fate when in 1663 he was suspected of complicity in the "Yorkshire Plot" to restore a republic by armed force. Under examination in London, he accepted that he knew John Atkinson, who was deeply involved in the plot as a kinsman of

Robert Atkinson, its leader, and agreed that they may have "discussed the government" while they "lay together in York Castle". But Robinson was eventually freed. Robert Atkinson was hanged, drawn and quartered.

The account of Richard Robinson's life from which I have drawn, apparently written shortly after his death in 1693 (and printed in *The First Publishers of Truth*), makes a short, coy reference to one startling habit of this sturdy Quaker pioneer: that of walking "almost Naked" through the streets. He went to Askrigg church, "Sometimes in his shift", and to Middleham "once in his Shift on a market day". In Richmond "he was sore bett, and had urine thrown upon him being in his shift". "Going naked as a sign" was seen as a prophetic act, a sermon-in-action, by several early Friends, women as well as men. Fox, though never called to "perform the service" himself, defended it in the days of "Oliver and his Parliament...and Priests" as a signal that "God would Strip them of their Power, and that they should be Naked... and stript of their Benefices".

William Simpson "was made before many times to go through Markets, to preists-houses, and to great Mens-houses, and Magistrates-houses, and to Cambridge, stark naked". In London "he did receive many stripes upon his naked body with Thorn Bushes, so that when his service was done, Freinds were forst to pluck the Thorns out of his flesh". James Nayler in 1654 refers to Friends who "go naked along your streets, as in Kendal and Kirkby-Stephen", adding significantly that they did so "contrary to their own wils". Solomon Eccles begged the Lord to relieve him of such service, but felt compelled to continue it in obedience. Thomas Holme of Kendal wrote to Margaret Fell from Chester in 1655 that "the word of the lord came vnto mee, & said I shuld goe A signe in this Cittie; and as I was comanded soe I did. I went to the hy way nacked, & great dread fell vpon many harts. I sufered sum percution, stripes, stones, & durt cast vpon mee, but by the mighty power of the lord I was keep from harme".

In 1659, according to the new vicar William Brownsword, more Kendal Friends, including William Strickland, Thomas Cortley, Elizabeth Levens and Miles Newby "went up the streets naked except that Strickland had a shirt on". Later, "the wife of Edmund Albighton went naked through the streets with other members of the society, male and female, and did the same, calling themselves Adam and Eve". Pepys refers to naked Quakers, and William Lowther wrote in 1661 from Swillington, Yorkshire, to a Government official in London, "In all the great towns, Quakers go naked on market-days through the town, crying 'Woe to Yorkshire', and declare strange doctrine against the Government, some officers being amongst them". Richard Robinson was more sedate than some: like William Strickland, he kept his shirt on. But such actions clearly played into the hands of those who wanted to discredit Quakerism and its radical challenge to current political, social and religious values, and while it was never formally disowned, "going naked as a sign", along with other extravagant expressions of enthusiasm, was gradually and sensibly abandoned after the Restoration.

But we have knocked on the door of Countersett Hall, a house of pure delight. It is not significantly changed from Richard Robinson's day. He moved in with his new wife Margaret in 1650 as a tenant of the City of London, which had purchased the manor from the Crown in 1628. His 180 acres of enclosed land with extensive grazing rights on the unenclosed Crag, Bardale and Bainbridge pastures, made up the largest holding of any tenant in Bainbridge or Raydale, and despite his activities as Quaker preacher, traveller and jailbird after 1652 he found time to organise his fellow tenants in the collective purchase of manorial rights in 1663. As fully franchised freeholders, the Robinsons and their neighbours had the incentive to improve the properties they now owned outright. The house Richard and Margaret had moved into was of the simple dales two-bay pattern, a firehouse or hall as kitchen/living-room and a service room attached. There was a chamber above, reached either by a curved stair by the main hearth in the hall or by a "stee" which preceded it. The surviving line of a steep-pitched roof in the central wall suggests the house was ling-thatched. Richard now added a parlour to the east, with a new chamber above it, and the magnificent two-storey porch, on which he set his and Margaret's initials, RRM (the middle initial being the surname), and the date of their marriage and first occupancy, 1650.

The small stone mullioned windows so characteristic of 17th century buildings, but since replaced by larger sashes in most houses of the period, are here for the most part retained in all their glory. Pat and Robin West, the present owners, have succeeded in preserving the Hall's timeless atmosphere without being afraid to stamp their own creative personalities on its ancient features. Our large, low-beamed bedroom is inscribed with fragments of poetry. Skelton:

"With lullay lullay, like a childe,
Thou slepist to long, thou art begilde".

And Christina Rossetti:

"Young love lies dreaming:
But who shall tell the dream?"

No more Quakerly, but no less delightful, is the painting of the unclothed girl in the bathroom, bathing in the limpid waters of Semer, perhaps, redhaired above and below the waist, looking surprised but not alarmed at being observed. It could be a Chagall, but it is signed Moishe Abraham. George Fox would not have liked it at all.

But before bed and bath time we dine sumptuously with Pat and Robin and their two other guests, Brian and Sue from Birmingham. Yes, Brian has heard of Quakers. Didn't they come from America, and were they not rather good businessmen - like the Jews? Brian talks a lot about money. He began life in a council house and he and Sue started a printing business in their back bedroom. They worked hard, the business grew, they prospered. "You don't have to be clever to be rich," he advises us, "you just have to want it". He says he is vaguely thinking of buying Lord Peel's vast estate in

Swaledale, now that the new Lady Peel has persuaded her husband to abandon the grouse moors for London... Printers have always made more money than mere writers.

Before the light dies, we go to take a quick look at the simple meetinghouse, adjoining the Hall, built by Richard's son Michael around 1710. It has had several renovations and virtual rebuildings, and by the early 19th century it had been largely superseded by the more conveniently placed meetinghouses in Hawes and Bainbridge. But when William Howitt came this way one Sunday in 1836 with his wife Mary he found that

"the people were flocking from all sides, down the fells, along the Dales, to the Meeting, not only the Friends themselves, but other Dalespeople; and we found Mr John Pease, brother of the MP, and his lady, from Darlington, addressing a crowded audience. The old times of Fox seemed indeed returned. The preacher's discourse was one of an earnest and affectionate eloquence, and the audience was of a most simple and unworldly character. Almost every person, man or woman, had a nosegay in hand; nosegays in truth, for they very liberally and repeatedly applied them to the organ whence they are named. The herbs, for they consisted rather of herbs than flowers, were as singular as the appearance of such a host of nosegays itself. Not one of them was without a piece of southernwood, in some instances almost amounting to a bush, and evidently there entitled to its ancient name, lads'-love and lasses'-delight. With this was grasped in many a hardy hand, thyme, and alcost, and in many, mint! No doubt the pungent qualities of these herbs are found very useful stimulants in close and crowded places of worship, and especially under a drowsy preacher, by those whose occupations for the other six days lie chiefly out-of-doors, in the keen air of hills and moors. That such is the object of them was sufficiently indicated by a poor woman who offered us a little bunch of these herbs as we entered the Meeting-house, saying with a smile, 'They are so reviving!'"

Maybe the nosegays also helped dispel a smell of decay as, despite this special occasion, the meetinghouse was already beginning to crumble. When it was again repaired in the 1850s it was the Primitive Methodists who footed the bill. Methodists continued to use it till 1977, when another massive overhaul took place, to enable Friends to reclaim it for meetings on the first Sunday each summer month.

"Now sleeps the crimson petal, now the white",

Tennyson tells us from another beam over our bed. It does not take us long to join the petals.

John Cooke

A Tithe Strike

DAY 6. *Semerwater-Dent*

"So I came up Wensleydale," writes Fox,

"and at the market town in that dale there was a lecture on the market day. I went into the steeplehouse, and after the priest had done I declared the day of the Lord to the priest and people, and bid them repent and take heed of deceitful merchandise; and turned them from the darkness to the light and from the power of Satan unto God, that they might come to God and Christ's teaching freely. I declared freely and largely the word of life to the people and had not much persecution."

We do not know where Fox entered Wensleydale, but it is recorded in *The First Publishers of Truth* that he did not "stay overnight in that dale that is remembered", (which adds one more piece of evidence against the suggestion that he entered at the foot of the dale via Skipton and then traversed its full length). It was once thought that the market town where he preached in the "steeplehouse" was Wensley, but the town which gave its name to the dale had long lost its market and declined to village status. Hawes was then suggested, but "t'haws" did not achieve market-town status till 1699. The chief market town of the upper dale in 1652 was Askrigg, just across the river Ure or Yore from the Semerwater hamlets and Bainbridge, and there is little doubt that this is where George Fox preached the day of the Lord and warned against deceitful merchandise, typically combining a religious and a social message.

The *First Publishers* account adds that "as he passed thorrow Wenslaydale, [he] advised the people, as he met or passed by them, To fear God, which, togather with his grave Look or Countenance, did much Alarum the people, it being a time that many people were filled with Zeall". The vicar of St Oswald's church, Askrigg, in 1652 was one Henry Hodges, who had presumably appointed the "lecture" or sermon-day, perhaps to take advantage of the crowded market at his church gate. Fox waited till he or his guest lecturer "had done", which courtesy he by no means always observed, then said his own piece. By urging his listeners to come to Christ's teaching "freely" he was attacking the status of "hireling" priests and ministers, who "sold" their gospel for stipends, tithes, church dues and other monetary reward. Priests, and churches run by priests, were an abomination to him.

There is little in the church today which would have caught his eye, since the Victorians comprehensively did it over: perhaps the mediaeval font, which would have had a lockable lid in Commonwealth times to prevent the holy water from being stolen for use either in secret papist ceremonies or for black magic. A seventeenth century holy water stoup - later hollowed out and used as a chimney pot before being recaptured for ecclesiastical service - probably dates from the restoration of prayer-book services in 1662.

It was our intention to make direct for Askrigg from Countersett via Semerdale Hall, another Robinson family property, crossing the river by Yorebridge (and passing the site at Fors where the Cistercians founded a monastery in 1145 which they moved eleven years later to Jervaulx). But before we left Countersett Hall we had news which caused us to change our plans. A close family friend, Bernard Crossley, had died after a long fight against cancer. We wanted to be with his wife, Barbara, and to attend his funeral in the Lake District. So we set Askrigg aside for a future visit and decided to walk the twenty miles home.

As it happened, this involved only a minor departure from Fox's most likely itinerary. He tells us that, immediately after preaching in the Wensleydale market town, he "afterwards passed up the dales...and went into Dent". Dent is our destination, and the most direct line from Countersett is also the likeliest route from Askrigg.

First, however, it must be admitted that the three dots I have inserted between his "passing up the dales" and arriving in Dent cover a number of intriguing events and chronological puzzles. Let us take the passage in full:

"and afterwards passed up the dales warning people to fear God and declaring his Truth to them through all the towns as I went. And people took me for a mad man and distracted, and some followed me and questioned with me and were astonished, and at last I came to a great house where there was a schoolmaster, and they got me into the house; and I declared the Truth to them, asking them questions about their religion and worship, and they had me into a parlor and locked me in and said I was a young man that was mad and was got away from my relations and they would keep me till they could send to my relations. But they being astonished at my answers and the Truth I spoke to them I convinced them of that, and they let me forth and would have had me to have stayed all night, but I was not to stay but admonished them and turned them to the light of Christ by which they might come to see their salvation, and so passed away and wandered in the night.

"And at last I came to a little alehouse upon a common where there were some fellows drinking. And I walked up and down in the house and after a time they began to drink to me. I would not drink with them and I spoke to them the Truth, warning them of the mighty day of the Lord that was coming and bid them take heed of that which showed them sin and evil in their hearts, upon which one rose against me with a club. And they held one another and then they were quiet. I was walking out as to have lien all night out of doors, and he that would have struck me followed me, with a batch of knives by his side, under pretence that he would have whispered with me. But I kept him off and warned him to repent. So the Lord preserved me by his power from him, and he went into the house again. And I was moved to go into the house again, and so staid there all night. The next morning I passed away and came through other dales and warned and exhorted people to repent and turn to the Lord, and several were convinced. I came to one house, to a kinsman of John Blaykling and he would have given me money but I was moved to shake my hand at it and would not receive it."

At this point Fox inserts his call on James Tennant at Scarhouse, which I have suggested probably took place on his way to rather than from Wensleydale. Then he concludes: "And after this I went into Dent where many were convinced also".

Let us look at the problems and puzzles this passage throws up. First, we need not trouble ourselves too much about the reference to passing through "dales" in the plural: he probably meant "dales country", but even if he is understood literally he could be referring to the Sleddale and Snaizeholme valleys, just off the Cam road, and Widdale, which meets the head of Ribblesdale between Cam and Dent head. Declaring Truth "through all the towns" is more problematic, as there are no towns at all in this thinly-populated upland area, unless the huddle of perhaps a dozen houses at Cam could be called a town. It seems more likely that once again Fox's memory and chronology are hazy here. It would greatly help if we could identify the "great house" where the perplexed schoolmaster supposed him to be a runaway madman, but so far we cannot. Nor have we yet identified the location of the house occupied by "a kinsman of John Blaykling", though this should not be impossible from a systematic study of contemporary wills and deeds. The "little alehouse upon a common" is easier: there was certainly an alehouse at Cam Houses and another at Gearstones.

Today's motor route from Wensleydale to Dentdale is through Hawes and up Widdale by the turnpike road towards Ingleton, turning off by the Dent road at Newby Head. But this was not available to George Fox. The turnpike dates from 1802 and cut through virgin pasture. Before this, the traveller might make use of a track on the west side of Widdale beck, or possibly the high West Cam track above Snaizeholme; but by far the best-used route was the old Roman road over Cam from Bainbridge to Ribchester, turnpiked in the eighteenth century and not abandoned till the road through Hawes was constructed in the nineteenth. This Cam Road is almost certainly the way George Fox used, and it is the one we choose now as the shortest route home.

From Askrigg, Fox would have picked it up at Bainbridge, where the artificially flattened square of the Roman fort was and is still prominent. From Countersett, we meet it on Bainbridge High Pasture and climb steadily to the 2000ft summit of Wether Fell, with a biting westerly in our faces. We are both rather glum, for the road is straight, steep, hard under foot, and we have clearly lost the balmy weather of yesterday. Our rucksacks press into our backs, as if some mountain imp has stealthily filled them with a selection of the limestone slabs all about us. Shortly after losing sight of the now grey and less enticing waters of Semerdale behind us, we are enveloped in swirling mist. We are on the rooftop of England, and that's what it feels like.

We are also shocked and miserable at Bernard's death. It was Bernard and Barbara who had originally stirred our interest in the Lakes and Dales, introducing us to Dentdale in the 1970s and encouraging us to take the plunge, mortgage ourselves to the hilt, and buy our beloved delapidated farmhouse there. Researching its history, we discovered its Quaker connections, which stimulated our interest in Fox country. Raised a Friend, Bernard's generation had faced the agonising dilemma of how to respond to Hitler in 1939. Bernard's deeply-held pacifism warred with his conviction that the almost unimaginable evils of Nazism had to be confronted, and after a terrible struggle he joined the forces, resigning from the Society rather than compromise its peace testimony. After the war he built up a sucessful business in Bolton and became chairman of the Labour-controlled Bolton Council, but politics was not greatly to his liking, and his distate grew when, as it seemed to him, trades union restrictive practices hampered the development of his own company. In the 1979 general election he shocked his friends - and subsequently himself - by supporting Margaret Thatcher, on the ground that a complacent, backward-looking country needed the shake-up she promised - or threatened. Bernard soon came to regret his momentary lack of judgement. It was partly our own interest in Quakerism which rekindled his own, and he began to attend Bolton meeting again, and subsequently, after his retirement to the Lake District, the little meeting at Colthouse. He was thinking about reapplying for full membership when the cancer struck. He was a most special man, with a great gift for friendship, inexhaustible warmth and generosity, and the intellectual integrity to follow where his reason led him, even when that meant admitting he had been wrong in the past. In this latter respect at least, George Fox could have learnt much from him.

*

On its descent from Wether Fell, the Roman track merges with a minor tarmac road which carries adventurous summer motorists from Hawes over the desolate heights of Green Side (where a nineteenth century Dent Quaker traveller, resting for the night, was to freeze to death) and down to Oughtershaw and Langstrothdale. After half a mile we strike off to the right, continuing on the line of the Romans' Cam High Road after noting with astonishment the daffodils in the verges, in full bloom in June! Rounding Dodd Fell, we catch fleeting sight through the mists of the "three peaks": Whernside, Ingleborough and - by looking back - Pen-y-ghent. Passing some ancient coal pits and sparing a thought for the eighteenth century colliers who worked these thin, barely accessible seams, we drop down the steep side-track to Cam House, the one surviving farm of an ancient settlement and, as we suppose, the site of George Fox's "little alehouse upon a common". We get a more cordial greeting than Fox got from the drinking party he encountered. The Pennine Way and Dales Way long-distance footpaths meet here, and there are a score of water- and wind-proofed hardy types munching sandwiches the size of their knapsacks, biting into Kendal mint-cake and downing great mugs of tea and coffee. We join them in the lee of the stone wall and order our tray of goodies. "Doing the Pennine or the Dales?" they ask us, as they all ask each other. "Fox", we reply. "Don't know that one", they say, and we explain.

Cam House looks and feels as ancient as the records confirm it to be. It is surrounded by the remnants of the other buildings which once made up a settlement living on exploitation of the high sheep pastures. Improbable as it seems today, it flourished briefly as a coach stop when the Roman road was turnpiked, and before the nineteenth century road system left it high and wet for sheep and ramblers. We follow the Dales Way footpath across Cam Pasture to rejoin the Roman road, which brings us down the steep incline of Cam End and over a wooden footbridge alongside the ford across Gayle Beck, the infant Ribble, and up to Gearstones. Once, many years ago, we had taken our two young children a Christmas walk from Gearstones to Cam End, meeting a blinding snow-storm on the way. We kept their spirits up by telling them stories of Roman legions marching this very road two thousand years ago - "and if you listen very carefully, you can just hear the echo of their marching songs and see the ghostly glitter of their shields and helmets as they pass". At that moment the whine of the wind did seem to assume a musical shape, and then, unmistakably, the wind had words. Out of the swirling snow ahead of us appeared a band of ramblers, bellowing their own marching song into the teeth of the gale. Our little girls' faces were white as the snow of which the whole world seemed made.

Gearstones was once a famous droving inn, certainly by the eighteenth century and probably in Fox's day. In 1792 Lord Torrington travelled the Cam road, and wrote:

"I was much fatigued by the tediousness of the road where we met two farming men, with whom we conversed about the grouse, and their abundance. Crossing a ford, Mr Blakey led me to a public house called Grierstones, the seat of misery, in a desert; and tho' filled with company, yet the Scotch fair held upon the heath added to the horror of the curious scenery: the ground in front crowded by Scotch cattle and the drovers; and the house cramm'd by the buyers and sellers most of whom were in plaids, fillibegs, etc. The stable did not aford hay. The only custom of this hotel or rather hovel, is derived from the grouse shooters, or from two Scotch Fairs; when at the conclusion of the days squabble the two Nations agree in mutual drunkenness, the Scotch are always wrapped up in their plaids - as a defence against heat, cold or wet; but they are preventions of speed or activity: so whenever any cattle stray'd, they instantly threw down the plaid, that they might overtake them. All the Yorkshire around, tho' black and frightful, seems of small account in the comparison of Ingleborough - at whose base we now travel."

The "squabble" between the two nations had been a major component of the civil wars immediately prior to Fox's journey. But the droving trade had probably recommenced by 1652, so perhaps it was drunken drovers and cattle-buyers he encountered at Gearstones or Cam, and maybe it was a Scots dirk with which he was threatened. Gearstones retained its reputation as a somewhat rough and ready halt well into the nineteenth century, when a navvy engaged in building the nearby Ribblehead viaduct to carry the Settle-Carlisle railway tested the strength of his gelignite by tossing a stick into the fire. He and his mates somehow survived the explosion. "Gearstones" has nothing to do with machinery but probably derives from a compound of Old English *gar*, a spear, and by extension a triangular plot of land, and *stan* or *ston*, a stone or post. A H Smith points out in *The Place-Names of the West Riding* that it "may well refer to stone posts marking the course of the Roman road; between this and Gayle Beck there is a narrow triangle of land". Gearstones and Cam were both Norse farms later incorporated in the great Cistercian estates. Wild and remote they seem today, but they have been active centres of trade and travel for many a century.

The old road climbs from Gearstones to High Gayle and runs northwards as Black Rake Road to the west of the modern Hawes-Ingleton highway. It is often little more than an indistinct path through the rough grasses, and we are grateful for the occasional Dales Way signs indicating that we are still on course. I have a blister now. The "driving road", as these droveways were known, picks its way through difficult country, climbing steeply up Wold Fell to Arten Gill Moss, where it veers round the flank of Great Knoutberry to become Galloway Gate, the road of the drovers' Galloway ponies and cattle, heading for Garsdale Head, Mallerstang and the Scottish border. We leave it before it climbs Wold Fell and take the early nineteenth century tarmac road down into the valley bottom of Dentdale, where the browns of the fells are replaced by lush greens and flushes of bluebells. Some commissioners preparing an agricultural report in the eighteenth century made a similar descent and declared Dentdale a "terrestrial paradise". It is not hard to see why. The infant river Dee splashes through a deep, wooded gorge, cutting through pastures divided by irregular stone walls enfolding a cottage, a barn, a ruin. A couple of miles on, and some twenty from the day's point of departure at Countersett Hall, over the hills and far away, we reach Stone House. Fox stopped here, but we trudge on the final mile to our own Hobsons farm, and soups, sticking-plasters and scalding-hot baths.

*

Stone House, however, was George Fox's destination, and it plays an important part in our story since here, for the first time, we have a detailed account from someone other than Fox himself of one of his meetings on this historic journey. Today it is almost a hamlet, with the old Stone House farm on Arten Gill track, East Stonehouse a stone's throw away towards Dent Head, and a scatter of homes between. Stonehouses it was then, just two farms above the narrow stone bridge over the Dee, and at the foot of what was then the main road out of the dale head: the steep, ankle-breaking track running up Arten Gill to join our "driving road" and the old Cross Gate over Cross Wold to Widdale. The name Stonehouses dates at least from the sixteenth century and suggests that, when the norm was still cruck-framed, ling-thatched dwellings, someone bucked tradition by building a house with load-bearing stone walls and a stone-flagged roof. The original is probably part of the structure of the present Stone House farm, which looks to have been substantially rebuilt in the eighteenth century.

Unlikely as it must seem, this tiny, out-of-the way half-hamlet would win itself a footnote in the history of the industrial revolution.

Around the turn of the nineteenth century a Dent Quaker, Richard Alderson, built or converted an existing mill here to cut and polish the local hard limestone known as "Dent marble". Alderson's handsome house is still there, as are the remains of his remarkable enterprise. In 1835 a young lawyer's clerk named George Armstrong, holidaying in the dale with his new bride, came across Alderson's enormous iron water-wheel, sixty feet in diameter, turned by the dammed waters of Arten Gill beck, and geared to power the saws which, lubricated by sharp sand and water, cut the raw limestone blocks into chimney-pieces and stair treads. Already fascinated by and experimenting with water power, Armstrong traced the beck to its source high on Great Knoutberry, estimated the volume of water and the power generated by its fall, and came to the conclusion that the giant wheel was using efficiently only about a twentieth of the power available. Stone House marble mill may not have benefited from his calculations, but on returning to his Tyneside home he was stimulated to abandon the law and take up the full-time study of hydraulics. Three years later he submitted his first scientific paper and was commissioned to build his first rotary hydraulic machine. From this grew the mighty Armstrong works which became Armstrong-Vickers, bringing George Armstrong immense wealth and a barony. What the Quaker Richard Alderson would have thought had he known that contemplation of his inadequate wheel would lead to the creation of a mighty armaments empire we can only imagine.

The building of the Settle-Carlisle railway in the 1870s put one vast viaduct over Arten Gill beck above the mill and another through the heart of the marble quarry at Dent Head. Adding injury to insult, the railway also brought in cheap Italian marble (on which import duties had been removed), which eventually closed Stone House mill. So this bustling little hive of industry became once again the quiet backwater it must have seemed when George Fox arrived to rally the local radicals.

George's own account is laconic in the extreme: "I went into Dent where many were convinced". But we have a rather fuller narrative, written half a century later by a local grocer, Richard Harrison, who was 12 years old when Fox came to Dent, was instantly "convinced", and spent much of the rest of the seventeenth century in and out of jail for his robust Quaker trouble-making. "In the year 1652", he wrote,

"did George Fox Come unto Dent, & had a Meeting at Stonehouses in Dent wth & amongst several that were in a great pfession of Religion, as Independants or the like, but they, being rich and full of knowledg in their own Conseit, were not sensible of want of Information or need of a phisician, so they mostly opposed & Rejected his offerrs, & Testimony Conserning the Light, & Manifestation of Christ, in the hearts and Consciences of peopl, to be Come in power to Restore into pfect health, happyness, & peace with God againe. Nay, they did believe any such Condition was not attainable in this life, Altho some of them said they had sought after such an estate of owning & Confessing to be a miserable sinner, and could not otherwise be while in this life, and who psessed more was deceiued & deluded, etc."

Deconstructing this tangled language gives us some interesting insights into Fox's target audiences and his religious message. First, we must presume that by some means Fox had sent ahead word of his coming and his wish to hold a meeting. We recall that, after his Pendle vision of a "people to be gathered", he had organised the innkeeper and his wife in writing and sending out papers. In the days before the Royal Mail, such letters and papers were routinely carried by travellers for a small consideration. This would explain why Fox is often clearly expected, and a meeting set up for him. As we shall see later, one of the Stonehouses dwellings was the home of an active dissenter, James Burton, who was leading a local campaign against the payment of tithes. So we may make a reasonable guess that Fox had consciously decided to come this way and had sent ahead to call together those who might be sympathetic to his radical message.

What was his message? At Stonehouses, according to Richard Harrison (who does not seem to have been present, so must have been relying on the accounts of others who were), the main point of contention was one we would find particularly abstruse. Prevailing orthodoxy was that we are all "miserable sinners", in the language of the prayer book, and can be no other. Fox and the early Quakers challenged this doctrine of original sin and preached instead something akin to original blessing. By turning to the inward light of Christ in our conscience, they insisted, we can overcome sin and be "restored into perfect health, happyness and peace with God again", as Adam and Eve were before the Fall. It wasn't good enough to "sit down short" and settle for a sinful state. Just such complacency, said the Quakers, was holding back the godly reformation of England, and the realisation of its vision of social justice. The orthodox answered that this was a counsel of perfection: "Nay, they did believe any such condition was not attainable in this life", and anyone who thought otherwise was "deceived and deluded". We may sympathise with that view: bitter experience has made us deeply suspicious of anyone claiming even the possibility of perfection. But we must remember that Fox made his challenge in a day and at a time when profession of godliness was everywhere and the practice of it nowhere: when the high ideals of the Commonwealth were being betrayed by greed and corruption. Fox and early Friends stood out by insisting that it was necessary to practise what one preached, and by their conspicuous (though never wholly successful) efforts to live with integrity.

So despite George Fox's own over-optimistic recollection that by his visit to Dent "many were convinced", it is clear from the local record that these convincements were not exactly instant. One account written or collected by Harrison says flatly "it was but a ffew yt then was Convinced", and of these few there were "none of the greatest accounted". Only after several years missionary work in the dale could it be said honestly (if ungrammatically) that "since they Cast theire bread upon ye waters has found it after many days, many since Convinced in ye Towne & Dale of Dent". But Harrison does name some of the few ("who were not so high in pfession") who did respond immediately to the visiting preacher-reformer. They included Thomas and George Mason of Cowgill, who were joined within days by Alexander Hebblethwaite and his wife Agnes, Thomas Greenwood and his wife Isabell, and the young Richard Harrison himself: four men, two women and a boy. As meetings were soon being held in William Mason's barn at Stonehouses, James Capstacke's "parrock" at Gawthrop and Robert Lund's house in Deepdale, the little band of pioneers evidently grew, eventually justifying Fox's claim that "many" were convinced in Dent, if not all of them by his own preaching.

By searching out information about these converts, buried in parish and Quaker registers, deeds, wills and other contemporary documents, we can begin to build a profile of the kinds of people George Fox and his colleagues were recruiting to their new movement.

Thomas and George Mason of Cowgill (then just two farms by Cowgill beck, which later gave its name to the whole of upper Dentdale), were both small farmers of the "middling sort". A dales farmer held his estate by customary tenants' right, which meant that, although not the freeholder, he had security of tenure and could sell or bequeath at will. Until the 1980s an old house behind West Cowgill farm remained substantially as it must have been in the Masons' day. It has since been rebuilt as an outhouse. Thomas was 34 in 1652, his brother George 31. Thomas had goods valued at £79 when he died in 1673, including "one old mare" and some "wool and stockings", which suggests that he and his family supplemented their income by knitting. He marked his will with a cross, indicating that he was illiterate, or at least unable to write. Brother George's wife had given birth to a daughter, Mellery, three months before Fox's visit, and the fact that she was christened suggests that the Masons were "Independents or the like" (who were still using the parish churches) rather than members of the Seeker network, which did not believe in "sprinkling".

Twelve-year-old Richard Harrison was the son of John Harrison of West Banks (possibly the oldest surviving house in the dale, though now a cow-house), who probably ran the grocery or general shop in the Laning, Dent, to which Richard succeeded. Despite continual distraints and imprisonments, Richard was worth a healthy £368 1s 8d when he died in his 90th year in 1720. The accounts of "the coming of Truth to Dent" from which I have quoted, written around 1702, testify to his literacy. He was probably educated at Dent Grammar School, founded in 1604. Unhappily, after a lifetime of heroic service to the Quaker movement, which included supervising the building of two meetinghouses, one in Dent Town (where the Methodist chapel now stands) and one at Lea Yeat, near Cowgill (now a cottage), he was sadly "disowned" for persistent drunkenness in his old age and disappears from the records shortly before his death. So much for perfection.

If the Masons and Harrison belonged to the "middling sort", Alexander Hebblethwaite was a notch higher in local society. 46 years old in 1652, he lived at the lower end of the dale at Gate, then a modest home (it seems to have had only one hearth for tax purposes), but since rebuilt in mock-Jacobean style as an imposing gentleman's residence. Alexander's grandfather James had been granted a coat of arms by Henry VI, which carried with it the rank of gentleman. One of James's daughters, Anne, married into the powerful Otway family of Ingmire Hall, Sedbergh, and the civil wars found the Sedbergh Otways and the Dent Hebblethwaites on opposite sides, the Otways backing the king while Alexander Hebblethwaite served as a captain in the New Model Army or the local Parliamentary militia. Hebblethwaite suffered intense persecution as Cromwell's grip weakened, being despatched to the Fleet prison in London in 1657 for refusing to pay tithes and refusing the oath of allegiance. He was not released until the collapse of the republic for which he had taken up arms and the restoration of a monarchy he detested. He was frequently in and out of jail for the rest of his long life, since he too lived to his 90th year, dying in 1696 with goods valued at £235 18s 8d. These included £10 worth of oats, £7 5s worth of "bigg" (barley), hay and straw worth £11 10s, "black cattell" worth £45, horses worth £6 and sheep worth £21 10s, all suggestive of a fairly prosperous mixed arable and stock farm. The £85 listed as "creditts" indicates that, like many men of his standing before the days of banks, he lent money to his neighbours and invested in their businesses. His inventory also includes £6 12s "in gold". His wife Agnes shared his privations, but his son Joshua reverted to the established church and the local squierachy.

Alexander's sister Isabell was the wife of Thomas Greenwood of Gailegarth, across the river from Gate via Rash bridge. Thomas was one of Dent's relatively comfortably-off yeomen-farmers, being the possessor of a freehold. About 40 in 1652, he was able to leave £190 to be shared by his three daughters when he died in 1671, and his inventory lists a full cooking range (when most dales kitchens were confined to a bakestone and a pot over the fire), and some "fine vessells" alongside the everyday wood and pewter. Like Alexander Hebblethwaite and Richard Harrison, he was literate. His daughter Sara was christened on April 6 1652, only a couple of months before Fox's arrival, emphasising again that the Dent converts, although political and religious radicals, were not Seekers.

Clearly Dent's first Friends were not exactly the men "of lower note" suggested by Richard Harrison, who perhaps shared a Quaker tendency to exaggerate modesty on the subject of social origins. Expanding our analysis to include every known Friend in Dent from 1652 to 1681, it is clear that most lived in the remoter extremities of the dale rather than in Dent's Town itself; that 16 out of 29 men called themselves or were called by their neighbours "yeomen", with one grocer, one joiner, one "body maker" (the bodies being those of carts), two servants and eight with trades unknown. A statistical analysis of the inventories of Dent Quakers compared with non-Quakers indicates that Friends were clearly drawn from the better-off (55% of Dent Quakers were worth £50 or more at death compared with only 16% non-Quakers). About half the men were literate - much the same as for those of the non-Quaker population who left wills, though probably most of those who didn't were illiterate. While there were young singles and older converts, the largest group was young marrieds in their 20s and 30s, most with young children. Early Quakerism was a youthful rebellion.

The women are less visible in contemporary records, but of 14 named in a 1681 list, five are married and some of the others are probably servants. One, Dorothy Winster, was the sister of Phillip Winster, a petty constable and paid informer against Quakers, while another probable kinsman, Thomas Winster, was an accomplished coin-clipper and forger of fake half-crowns! Two, Ann Salkeld and Agnes Wilkinson, died while their men-folk were in jail for their Quaker activities.

With all this in mind, let us return to the question of why George Fox chose to come to Dent. Was he simply on his way to Sedbergh to meet the Seekers, of whom perhaps John Blaykling's unknown kinsman had told him? Or had he heard something of the Stonehouses Independents which drew him specifically to them? It seems certain that, as he travelled through the dales, rather less haphazardly than appears to be the case from a reading of his *Journal*, he was gathering intelligence of potential like minds and sending letters ahead to those who were recommended to him as potential sympathisers. If so, there was good reason why he might be directed to Dent.

At Easter 1652, five weeks before Fox appeared on the scene, there were dramatic developments in the dale's relationship with church and state authorities. A substantial number of customary tenants here and in neighbouring Garsdale and Grisedale began a tithe strike. As it spread to include most of the dale's inhabitants, news of this civil disobedience campaign must have travelled. It is hardly conceivable that George Fox, whose vehement opposition to tithes was a principal plank in his radical programme, did not get wind of the rebellion in Dent during his treks over the Yorkshire hills.

Moreover, one of the eleven men subsequently indicted as ringleaders of the strike was John Burton of Stonehouses, where Fox had his meeting. Others were Edmund Dawson of Ewegales, whose daughter Em joined Friends, William Thistlethwaite of Harbergill, whose grandson would become the leading Quaker in the dale, and Reighnold Wynn of Grisedale, whose family would also become Quakers. Another, Thomas Mason of Bowmanhill, was probably a kinsman of the Mason brothers up-dale at Cowgill. Five of the ringleaders lived in the upper dale, just below Stonehouses. It was among just such activists that Fox would hope to find a following.

Tithes were one of the hottest issues on the political and religious agenda. It was compulsory tithes which financed the priesthood of the national church, so those who favoured a national church allied to the state were passionately attached to the system, the Independents who wanted a reformed, congregational church were for reforming it, and the radical sects were for its total abolition. Left-wing political movements such as the Levellers also proposed abolition on the grounds that tithes were an intolerable burden on the poor. The matter was further complicated by the fact that, over the course of the years, tithes once paid to the monasteries had been "impropriated" - we would say expropriated - by rich laymen, who used them to swell their own revenues. So tithes raised issues of class as well as clerical exploitation. General Monck called them "that issue of blood", at the heart of the quarrel which had driven the nation to civil war. Repeated attempts in Parliament to reform or abolish tithes were thwarted by Members who themselves benefited directly from the wretchedly corrupt system, in which church and gentry had a deeply vested interest. Cromwell, though favouring reform, was himself a tithe-owner. When the Nominated Parliament of 1653 mustered a two-vote majority for abolition, Cromwell dissolved it before the Act could be passed.

Dent's tithe strike was to last eight long years. Not till the Rump Parliament of 1659 passed an Act enabling tithe-owners to recover their losses, which was endorsed by the newly restored monarchy the following year, were the strike leaders defeated and ordered by the courts to resume payments. Even then, the sums confirmed were those agreed in a schedule of 1505, with no allowance for inflation over the intervening century-and-a-half, which meant that Dent farmers paid an average of little more than 10d each per year. The court records show that the rebels' case for withholding tithes was technical rather than principled: they argued that the 1505 agreement related only to the parish of Sedbergh, of which, they claimed, Dent and Garsdale were no longer a part, having achieved the status of an independent parish. This was but the latest shot in an age-long conflict between Dent and Sedbergh which had seen earlier tithe strikes in the fifteenth century (when the entire dale was threatened with excommunication) and endless financial disputes thereafter. But it is doubtful whether the legal arguments employed in 1660 adequately reflected the complex motives of the Dent strikers in 1652. Seeing in the confusion of the times an opportunity to rid themselves of a hated burden, they made use of the best pretext available, with no more care than George Fox had for the livelihood of hireling priests.

In the circumstances, Fox must have been surprised and disappointed not to have won more followers at Stonehouses. But he did collect the name of an influential parliamentary soldier, Major Miles Bousfield of Garsdale, and when he had done preaching perfection in Dent it was to seek out the major that he set his face to the more northerly dale.

The Corpse Road to Fea Fow and Flust

DAY 7. Dent-Garsdale-Grisedale

The attractive pictorial map of "George Fox's Journey to the Westmorland Seekers" drawn by Geoffrey Makins in 1952 for the Friends' North-West 1652 Committee has Fox walking the length of Dentdale to Sedbergh. This is almost certainly a mistake. The mistake arises from confusion over what Fox meant when he wrote that he "went into Dent". Today, Dent commonly means the village at the centre of the dale, and if Fox went there he would certainly have followed the road down-dale from Stone House. But until recent times Dent meant (and still properly means) the entire dale, which, with the lateral valley of Deepdale, made up the ancient township of Dent. Today's Dent village was Dent's Town. So the fact that Fox "went into Dent" simply means that he entered the *dale*, not that he went through the *town*. The *Journal* tells us that from Stone House he "came to Major Bousfield's in Garsdale where he and several more received me, and some were convinced and stand to this day. And I passed through Grisedale and several other of those dales, where some were convinced".

Garsdale and Grisedale lie directly north of Dentdale, with the long low whaleback of Rise Hill intervening. There are and were at least three more or less direct routes from Stone House to Garsdale - and none of them run through Dent's Town. One is the steep track up Arten Gill, already noted, which joins the Galloway Gate "driving" or drove road to cross Cowgill head and drop down to Garsdale head at Hawes Junction. Another is the "coal road" from Lea Yeat, which led to Kirthwaite and Garsdale pits, joining up with Galloway Gate. A third is possibly the oldest route of all, and certainly the only one to take the traveller to the heart rather than the extremities of the dale: a track zig-zagging up the hill from behind West Cowgill farm to flank Cowgill beck and meet the Garsdale road at Dandra Garth. We choose this last.

So, after taking a day out for Bernard's funeral, where we express our gratitude for his life and friendship, we hoist our packs on our backs and make for the clouds which are waiting to envelop us on Black Moss at the east end of Rise Hill. We pass through a community rich in Quaker associations. Between Stone House and Lea Yeat is Harbergill, home of William Thistlethwaite the anti-tithe agitator and William his Quaker grandson. Harbergill was a registered meetinghouse before one was built at Lea Yeat, and the Quaker William who had his initials and 1700 carved over the porch was described as "a handsome man of middle stature, of friendly genteel manners, his disposition somewhat reserved, and his words few": a typical dalesman! Lea Yeat itself is a cluster of homes, all with early Quaker associations. One, now River View, is the converted meetinghouse built by Richard Harrison in 1701. More than two hundred Friends lie buried under its gravel and concrete drive. On the north-facing slopes are Holme Hill or Hollow Mill, Fletchers (in ruins) and Hobsons, all former Quaker houses. A Quaker schoolmaster, John Bleamire, ran a school from Hobsons in the 1750s. On the south-facing "sunny side" are Rayside and East and West Cowgill, all Mason family homes. Every one of these houses was rebuilt in the late seventeenth or early eighteenth century, but the farms and closes would still be recognisable to their seventeenth century occupants, and to George Fox.

More Quaker houses dot the valley below Cowgill: Hud's House, where James Mason "was so compassionate to travellers that he set apart for the reception of the poorer class of them a sort of hay loft, where he provided beds for their repose"; Spice Gill, where a descendant of the Thistlethwaite family still lives and farms; Broadmire, once owned by local Friends and rented out to earn funds for poor relief; and Blands, the home of Thomas and Ann Salkeld who were prosecuted by the vicar of Sedbergh in 1676 for refusing to pay a church tax of 2d. Thomas remained in York Castle jail till the vicar died and his widow pleaded for his release. He returned home to find his wife and two young children had starved to death. Small wonder that Friends feel a special affinity for the dale: there is martyrs' blood below the green grass.

We leave the riverside road at Cowgill Church, built in the 19th century just before the Gothic revivalists took full posession of ecclesiastical architecture. The plain, country church, made for a plain, country people, is the second on this site where Cowgill beck tumbles into "Big Beck", the Dee, by a narrow bridge which carries the roughly-cut inscription, "Repered at the charg of th West Riding 1702". A chapel was first put up here around 1750 by Inghamites, a sect led by an early associate of John Wesley named Benjamin Ingham. Quakers seem to have seen off this challenge to their local nonconformist monopoly, however, since within ten years the chapel was reported to be largely deserted. For many years it was used irregularly by Sandemanians and Congregationalists, but in the 1830s it was pulled down and replaced by the present Anglican church. Adam Sedgwick, the Dent-born pioneer geologist, whose father and brother were both incumbents at Dent, laid the foundation stone on June 30 1837, and named it Cowgill Chapel.

Unhappily, a later curate decided that Cowgill, with its suggestion of bovine associations, was altogether too vulgar a designation. Learning that the ancient name for upper Dentdale was Kirkthwaite, which had more of an ecclesiastical ring to it, he registered the chapel accordingly. But he failed to reckon with old Adam, who penned a furious *Memorial* to the church authorities demanding the restoration of the honest-to-goodness Cowgill name. The curate won the first round when the bishop of Ripon proved reluctant to undo a perfectly legal registration, but Adam Sedgwick was not to be thwarted. He got Queen Victoria on his side, and she told Gladstone to pass an act of parliament restoring the name of Cowgill. Gladstone did as he was told - he had bigger battles to fight - and in 1869 the mighty Parliament of Great Britain solemnly turned Kirkthwaite back to Cowgill. The following year, Cowgill actually became a parish in its own right (but as the dales population declined it was reunited with Dent parish in 1974). Poor Mr Sumner, the thwarted curate, had one consolation: he had his church school inscribed over the porch with the name "Kirkthwaite School", and even Adam Sedgwick wasn't going to pay for a new stone. So "Kirkthwaite School" it still proclaims itself to passers-by - though it has been a private home (at present occupied by a Quaker) since the school closed in the 1970s.

The track to Garsdale runs along the east wall of the churchyard, with the Mason brothers' Cowgill farmhouses on the right, till it crosses Cowgill beck by Dockra bridge and commences a steep zig-zagged climb to some old quarries on High Ellershaw Edge. I have said this is possibly the oldest of the tracks linking Dentdale and Garsdale. Before the Reformation, Garsdale chapel had no burial rights and the dead were carried to Dent over what Garsdalesmen complained, with pardonable exaggeration, were "great daungrous mountaynes". I suspect that our track is the "corpse road" they used. The only alternatives would have involved either long journeys via the two dales heads on the "driving road" or via the two dales foots through Frostrow - or by a route now lost over the summit of Rise Hill, which seems most unlikely. In 1548 Garsdale chapel is mentioned as a dependency of Dent, "being in the mounteynez, so that in wynter many tymez ther can nothinge passe betwixt the same and the paroch church". The church authorities at last got the message and from about 1560 Garsdale was licensed to bury its own dead. But the corpse road continued to provide the shortest distance between the two dales, whose churches and townships remained closely linked. The stone quarries no doubt extended its life, and the track was walled on the Dent side during the nineteenth century enclosures.

We are grateful for those walls, as visibility is soon all but blotted out when the menacing clouds spring their ambush and pelt us with hailstones as large as humbugs and heavy as Dent marble. We trudge on to Will's Hill or Peggy's Hill - did Will and Peggy dispute ownership, one perhaps from the Dent side, the other from Garsdale? Here on the watershed the walls run out and we are deposited in a featureless morass appropriately known as Black Moss. Eyes down, we soon discern the faint depression of the track as it drops down to Dandra Garth farm. We drop with it, leaving the hail to reimpose the ice age on the tops behind us.

The elderly farmer at Dandra Garth - a house which, at the end of the twentieth century, still relies on candles and oil lamps rather than new-fangled electricity - tells us the Quaker burial ground we are looking for is "up yonder", and has "one auld 'eadst'n". We find it, and read that the headstone marks the resting place of "Thomas Moore, died at Badger Dub Cottage, Garsdale, 13th of third month 1901 Aged 77 years". Dandra Garth belonged to one William Thistlethwaite (who may or may not have been the very same man as the Dent WT) and he sold the 400-square-yards burial plot to Friends for £4 in 1699. (We are told that Friends are now thinking of selling it, no doubt for a modest profit). Four years later Quakers bought a farmhouse called Birkrigg half a mile up the valley for use as a meetinghouse for both Garsdale and Grisedale Friends. But as David Butler's authoritative study *Quaker Meeting Houses of the Lake Counties* tells us that the land on which it stood has reverted to meadow we do not search it out.

I would like to have found the home of Major Miles Bousfield, the puritan army officer to whom Fox was recommended and who was duly convinced, but his Garsdale residence is not recorded. The one record I find of him in the Sedbergh parish registers is that of the death of Elizabeth, wife of "Mr Milles Bowsfield of the towne", in 1651. Major Bousfield is credited by William C Braithwaite (in *The Beginnings of Quakerism*) with having introduced Fox to the Seekers, but his own attachment to Friends seems to have been short-lived. A year or two later he was in Ireland, presumably on Cromwell's military business there, where he met William Edmondson, another Cromwellian soldier from the dales who would become the founder of Irish Quakerism. They seem to have been temperamental opposites. Edmondson carried the burdens of Quaker evangelism on his shoulders, and his spirits were often troubled. Miles Bousfield told him to cheer up and be merry. This seems to have convinced Edmondson that the major was all talk of religion without "the power". Thereafter Major Bousfield disappears from the Quaker story. Maybe Bousfield was a little less merry when George Fox called on him in Garsdale. Fox distrusted laughter and merriment. Perhaps the most chilling story he tells in his *Journal* is one about an unnamed army captain he met in Weymouth in 1655.

"And this captain was the fattest, merriest, cheerfulest man and the most given to laughter that ever I met with; so that I several times was moved of the Lord to speak to him in the dreadful power of the Lord. And yet still he would presently after laugh at anything that he saw; and I still admonished him to sobriety and the fear of the Lord and sincerity. And we lay at an inn that night. And the next morning I was moved to speak to him again, and then he parted from us the next morning. But he confessed next time I saw him that the power of the Lord had so amazed him that before he got home he was serious enough and left his laughing. And the man came to be convinced, and became a serious and good man..."

But what price convincement if laughter is banished?

We push up-dale towards Grisedale, at first following the modern road up Garsdale which replaced a much more winding track when motor traffic intruded into these parts. But, anxious for authenticity in following as closely as possible in Fox's footsteps, we take the old line of the road at Cross Thwaite, only to retrace our steps hastily when we find our way blocked by some belligerent geese whose hisses and honks speak plainly "They shall not pass". Crossing the River Clough at Mill Bridge we again pick up the old road, this bit under tarmac, which takes us up Cock Brow, past Garth Gill House, Grouse Hall and Knudmaning farm to the secret entrance to Grisedale, the valley of the young pigs.

Grisedale was popularised by a television documentary *The Dale that Died*, made in the 1970s by an old friend and colleague of ours, Barry Cockcroft (whose affectionate portrayals of dales life for Yorkshire Television, including the immensely popular Hannah Hauxwell series, won him the honorary title of Lord Cockcroft of the Dales). In the book accompanying the film, Barry wrote of Grisedale:

"A million eager tourists pass close by its entrance every summer, hugging road maps that do not even acknowledge the existence of Grisedale, as though the gods which protect its privacy blinded the cartographer when they came to draw the area. Yet Grisedale is perhaps the most romantic dale in all Yorkshire, the dream dale which those million people seek, complete in its unspoilt beauty, serenity and vivid history... There is only one way into it, for the dale is an enclosed place sealed off at its northern extremity by the impassable heights of Wild Boar fell. And even this narrow road joins the conspiracy to keep Grisedale a secret. It loops surreptitiously off the main Hawes to Sedbergh highway and will lead the unwary straight back to the main road again. But half way along it is joined by a thin strip of tarmacadam which is unmarked save for a 'No Through Road' sign. It could be a well-metalled farm track; it is, in fact, the entrance to Grisedale."

By this little road and over the protective riggs, we descend to Double Hole Bridge and Mouse Syke farm. The dale is as enchanting as the poetry of its farm and field names, golden with marsh marigolds and pink with proud melancholy thistles. Below the bridge the stream exposes limestone pavement embellished with innumerable crinoid and more complex fossils of creatures which lived and breathed and died some 250 million years ago. Anthea searches the beck for sandpipers. She found two pairs here last summer, but surveys show them to be withdrawing from the tributary becks in recent years. None are to be seen today, but blackcocks - also diminishing in numbers - are said to hold their leck near a small plantation, and the oyster-catchers are out too.

We have arranged to meet a photographer from the *Westmorland Gazette*, which has decided there is a story in our Foxtrot. He arrives by car and pulls off the road near the bridge. Within seconds, the farmer from Mouse Syke is into his farm buggy and bearing down on us. The photographer can't park there! Where can he park? Nowhere: the road itself is too narrow, and the grass on either side is private property. We explain that he is only going to take one or two quick pictures, but far from appeasing our farmer, that makes him more determined to see us off. He looks after this dale. He doesn't want any photos. They only bring in more visitors, and visitors spoil it. I try gently pointing out that there is a public right of way through the dale, and the photographer from the *Gazette* has his rights too. There is a tense stand-off. Then the farmer explains. Visitors are a menace. They leave gates open. Only the other day one of his stallions in heat had taken advantage of a gate carelesly left open and attacked a rival in the adjoining field, half killing it. I have some sympathy: walkers who leave gates open are the bane of a countryman's life. We begin swapping stories of careless ramblers. He relents.

Photo-call over, we head up-dale, taking a footpath which follows the line of the old road which was swept away by floods in 1889. The dale was held by Jervaulx Abbey before the Dissolution. Necolas Wyn was one of their tenants in 1530, the first of many Wyns, Winnes and Whynnes recorded here. The wealthy Wharton family acquired it in the sixteenth century and leased it to Jervaulx's former tenants for one thousand years. George Winne leased Rowantree in 1584, and in 1596 John Winne's will mentions "a litel howse in aldershawe", along with fields and farms with names like Westaldersgarth, Holkstarkstead, Overcakt and Calfe Flawe. Aldershaw is still there, rebuilt in 1775 and again more recently, and now not so "litel". When Fox came there were perhaps fifteen or twenty farms here: Flust and High Flust, Fea Fow, Howshaw Head, Reacher and many more as melodious.

Richard Harrison's manuscript tells us that Fox met and convinced "Thomas Winn & his wife & familly". Among the extensive family was probably Reighnold or Reynold Wynn, one of the indicted leaders of the Dent/Garsdale/Grisdale tithe strike, and a man of modest wealth as indicated by his will of 1677, by which he left £167 to friends, neighbours, family and servants. Thomas or Reighnold or both are thought to have lived at Scales, at the head of the dale, and that is our destination.

Scales is now two houses, both in an advanced state of ruin since being abandoned after the first world war, but evidently once large and prosperous. Between them, over a tiny packhorse bridge, is the former Friends' burial ground, designated for the purpose by the family but never transferred to Friends' ownership. There isn't a single "'eadst'n" in sight, but at least a hundred burials are recorded here. The grass is close-cropped by the resident sheep, and swallows are darting between the big sycamores. In the early years, Grisedale Friends met for worship here, but in 1706 they built a meetinghouse on a piece of ground called Stubstacks, near Grisedale beck: too near, as damp and even flooding were constant problems. By the 1880s they were renting it out to the Wesleyans at 5s per annum, but when they too rebelled against the damp and decided to build a place of their own on drier land, Friends had to decide what to do with their old building. "To patch the place up seems out of the question, to rebuild seems rather like a waste of money, and to sell seems objectionable", as the worried clerk wrote in the monthly meeting minute. The dilemma was resolved by Act of God when the beck in full flood reduced the meetinghouse to a pile of stones, which the Methodists were allowed to cart away to build their chapel. David Butler notes that nothing now remains "but a slight irregularity in the ground"; but as the ground hereabouts is nothing but irregularities, it helps to know where to look to locate the remains of the platform where Quakers once sat stolidly even when "the floor was all swimming".

There were some Grisedale Quakers who were not named Winn, but not many. John Banks, in his book *The Silent Stream*, traces 19 Winn wills between 1530 and 1818, and some of the most interesting are those of Winn women. In 1648 Dorothy Winn left her bible to Ann Bland and her "best red petticoate" to her sister Elizabeth. Her "best hatt", "best ruffed band", a "white happin [quilt]", "yarne and stockings", "a petticote with a lethern bodice", her "best white coate", a "double happin" and a "browne carsey [kersey, or Kendal worsted] coate" were bequeathed to the wives and daughters of other friends and neighbours. Some only got the second-best: Dorothy Hobson got her "greatest pan but one". Grace Winn in 1632 left "a red petticote, a Gowne, a Couerlitt, one pare of Furred gloves [and] one Hatt". One wonders what became of the red petticoats, gowns and luxurious "furred gloves" when the Winn women were restricted to drab Quaker greys. I suspect they kept them hidden in their cupboards, and perhaps brought them out and guiltily tried them on from time to time when no-one was about to see and judge them. Margaret Fell (who, as a gentlelady, never abandoned her silks and satins) let it be known at the end of her life that she considered insistence on dull greys and blacks "a silly poor gospel". But by then the gospel of drabness had become a Quaker shibboleth, and shibboleths are not easily shaken off.

Having inspected High Scales, admiring the characteristic round bump concealing a circular stone staircase on the back of the house, and imagining George Fox passing through the walled-in doorways to sup with the Winn family and change their lives for ever, we begin to move back down dale. On our way we call on our friends Linda and William Garnett at East House, one of only three homes in the dale which can boast continuous occupation since the thousand year leases were granted in 1584. As we approach, we find the hills are alive with the sound of music. An amateur singing group is bravely tackling a piece George Fox would not have approved of: Byrd's four-part Mass. We stand in the porch for a minute or two, savouring the sound, before knocking. Linda is a professional musician and William writes children's stories, which he markets in a most original way. He places his books in boxes fixed to trees along the track by the house, and invites passers-by to pick one and leave a contribution. He is the only author we know whose work almost literally grows on trees. Sadly, William has died since our memorable visit, and Garsdale church was packed with family, friends, neighbours and dalesfolk celebrating the life of one who, in Penn's words about Fox, was "an original, and no man's copy".

After joining the warblers in a few stop-and-start attempts at the Kyrie we take our leave. As we head down the dale, the wind is up and the rain is driving into our faces. Soon our boots, our weatherproofs and our backpacks are awash. We have arranged to call our neighbour Jim from the callbox in Garsdale so that he can pick us up and bring us back to Hobsons, but when we cram our sodden, ice-cold bodies into the box we get no reply. Un-Quakerly thoughts flit through our heads. Without a lift, we have five miles to walk, over a 1700-ft pass which is lost in vicious black vapours - and isn't even on-course. So we wait ten minutes and try again. Jim answers: he has just got in after driving around looking for us, convinced that the storm will be the death of us. Twenty minutes later we are huddled in the back of his Uno, too cold and tired to thank him properly. I try to keep my mind fixed on the glory that is Grisedale, but it is overwhelmed with visions of hot buttered toast.

Finding Seekers

DAY 8. Garsdale-Sedbergh-Brigflatts

Our bedtime prayers last night were that it would stop raining. Throwing back the curtains this morning, we see our prayers have been answered - but the answer is No. Jim has offered to drive us back to Dandra Garth where we can resume Fox's route on foot, and as he drops us the rain stops and we are welcomed by a hint of sunshine.

The *Journal* is clear that Fox came from Grisedale and Garsdale to Sedbergh, and there seems no doubt that he would do this by following the track along the Clough, through Garsdale Street, to the dale foot and into town, rather than looping back over Rise Hill to Dent. He is certainly not wandering aimlessly. He must by now have heard, perhaps from that unnamed kinsman of John Blaykling, or the Dent Independents, or from Major Bousfield, about the concentration of Seekers in and around Sedbergh. No doubt he has also heard that the town will be filling up for the big Whitsun Fair. He is going to be in the right place at the right time.

Garsdale, the valley settled by a Norseman named Garz or Gards, spelled Garstall in the fourteenth century and pronounced Garsd'l today, is another gem. Since the winding little road, criss-crossing the river, was turnpiked and numbered A684, its privacy has been less well guarded than that of Dentdale and Grisedale. It is also narrower than Dent, as its river, the Clough (which means ravine), does indeed run through a ravine, which severely rations available meadow land. But Garsdale is said to have clung to its old ways - haytiming by sledge, milking by backcan - when even Dent had bowed to modern technology. The litany of farm and field names produces a "found poem":

Badger Dub and Bellow End,
Blades, Blirtses, Bullstones and Butterbeck,
Coat Weggs and Cock Lakes,
Dandra Garth and Dingle,
Fold House and Fox Hole,
Hard Ing and Hining Brea,
Liquor Gill and Lousegill Wold,
Mostard and Mudbeck,
Pogs House and Paradise,
Rackenthwaite, Rattenrow, Roger Pot and Rowantree,
Swarthgill, Smorthwaite, Smout Gill and Stephen Wives,
Thrush Gill, Toad Crag, Tod Hole,
and Witcherhouse.

One of the finest of the old houses is Swarthgill, hard on the roadside and overlooking the river. It was the birthplace in 1740 of Dr John Haygarth, the medical pioneer who first recognised the importance of isolating patients with infectious diseases. The initials I.H.A. are over the porch, representing John's parents, together with the date when they presumably moved in and substantially rebuilt the house, or perhaps built the porch: 1712. Seeing us admiring the place, the current owners, Ray and Avril Whittle, invite us inside to show us two spice cupboards also inscribed 1712 and the initial H. They tell us they are about to open an arts and crafts bookshop here.

Just beyond Badger Dub, we escape the main road to follow the old track above the north bank of the river and on the lower slopes of Baugh Fell. Some of the fields here are so white with the frothy heads of cow-parsley that we wonder whether it is being grown as a crop. A tea-break is due, and we call on Penny Constantine at Bellow End, whose kettle is soon whistling. Penny has recently added a new kitchen. Most of these houses were here in George Fox's time, but almost every one has been extended, refenestrated, knocked about a bit and generally adapted to the changing needs of each new generation. Penny has only done what all her predecessors at Bellow End, and all their neighbours, have been doing for centuries.

But if the houses have changed with changing times, so too has the farmland around them. The dales through which we are walking show not a trace of arable, every farm having its own meadow lands at the bottom, pasture on the lower slopes and rough grazing on the tops. These same dales looked very different to George Fox. Four fifths of the bottom land and lower slopes were ploughed for crops: mostly oats, barley and peas, a little wheat and perhaps some flax for linen or cannabis for hemp. The other fifth was kept as meadow for a hay crop and the tops were used for pasturing. Arable crops continued to play a part in the dales economy, though a gradually diminishing one, till the nineteenth century. Winter snows in the hollows, or evening sunshine casting tell-tale shadows, expose these abandoned plough-marks, confirming the clear evidence of Elizabethan manorial records and Victorian tithe awards. Where we see nothing but grass and meadow herbs, and suppose this to be the "natural" state, as it was in the beginning, is now and ever shall be, George Fox saw waving corn.

Below Danny Bridge, a mile down-dale, it is sometimes possible to hear the earth move. The Clough is crossed here by the line of the Dent Fault, a mighty fracture in the earth's crust which runs across both dales and meets the Craven Fault at Ingleton. Some 290 million years ago, in late Carboniferous times, a seismic event lifted the ancient Silurian rocks of the Lake District far above the younger limestones of the dales, crumpling the new against the old in startling striations exposed by later ice ages in the bed of the Clough.

It is possible to stand astride the two ages, one foot planted on 300-million-year-old Carboniferous and the other on 440-million-year-old Silurian rocks. The fault still quakes from time to time, rattling the tea-cups in dales kitchens. An unusually violent rumble split Dent church tower from footings to toppings in the 1770s, and the steeplehouse lost its steeple.

The path along the south side of the river has been designated the Sedgwick Trail, as it was the Dent geologist Adam Sedgwick who first began to make sense of what he saw here. The theories he developed in the early nineteenth century still form the basis of modern geology. But Sedgwick was an Anglican clergyman before he became (by accident) a geologist, and the poor man was increasingly torn between what the bible seemed to tell him of a creation one busy week in 4004 BC and the evidence in the Clough of a world several hundred million years old. Such anguish was common in his day. Another evangelical scientist, Philip Gosse, suggested an explanation for the apparent discrepancies between biblical authority and empirical evidence: God had planted fossils in the rocks, making them *appear* to be of immense age, in order to test the faithful. Adam was too intelligent to accept such a notion, but unable to devise a better. One of his pupils at Cambridge was Charles Darwin, whose demonstration of evolution by natural selection brought the crisis between religion and science to a head. But it was a crisis which troubled Friends less than it did the mainstream churches. From George Fox on, Friends had rejected biblical literalism, and if the bible didn't have to be upheld as literally true, an infallible guide to all things including science, natural selection posed no insoluble problem.

But none of this was in the mind of our predecessor as he walked over this quaking landscape, oblivious of the way in which the rocks beneath his feet would shake the intellectual foundations of generations to come. George Fox may even have missed this enchanting stretch of the river altogether, as the old road from

Danny Bridge climbed up the north bank to Dovecote Gill and Dowbiggin Foot, to cross the River Rawthey at Burnt Mill bridge before entering Sedbergh at the foot of Winder and the Howgills, then as now one of the wildest and least-spoilt uplands in England.

The old spelling of the little town, Sebber in the fifteenth century, accurately reproduces its pronunciation by natives over the years. It is just permissible to sound the middle d, but to articulate the final g is to declare yourself a foreigner. Mid-seventeenth-century Sedbergh was a market town of small, thatched houses, workshops and barns along the line of what is now called Main Street, with long, narrow strips of land behind each house, some perhaps already being built on and turned into yards. At the east end, covering the junction of a Roman road up the Rawthey valley and the Garsdale road to Wensleydale and the east, there was once a Norman motte and bailey castle on the hill still called Castle Haw. At the west end, at the junction of Finkle Street with the Kendal road and Howgill Lane (which joins another Roman road running up the Lune) is the parish church, fronted by a tiny square which is all that remains of the old market place.

Today's town is dominated by Sedbergh School and a spread of Victorian housing. The school was there in Fox's day, though much smaller, and happened to be embroiled in bitter controversy. The headmaster, Richard Jackson, who was also minister of the church in Garsdale, was a radical Parliamentarian who was soon in conflict with the more conservative Fellows of St John's College, Cambridge, who effectively governed the school. Jackson was pronounced "unconformable to reason" in 1651, and subsequently denounced as "a constant haunter of alehouses, frequently intoxicated with immoderate drinking". An attempt was made to oust him altogether, when several witnesses deposed on oath that they had seen him drunk, and an assistant master he had sacked accused him of failing to put in an appearance at the school for three months. Jackson retaliated by producing parishioners from Garsdale and Grisedale who swore that he was a godly minister and that the tales of his frequent inebriation were malicious fabrications. Jackson himself claimed he had only been drunk once, when a royalist "crew of villains" had forced liquor on him. He had sacked the assistant master, he said, "because he turned apostate proselyte" and had "introduced the observation of the holy days with their eves, which I had abolished and brought to the Parliament order".

That the dispute directly reflected the political-religious divide of the day is made explicit by Jackson's appeal to Cromwell's "triers", who were commissioned to test ministers' loyalty to the regime. He warned them that to pay heed to his enemies would be to "abandon all sound principles upon which honest and godly patriots ingaged in judgment and conscience against the late King", and would expose to reproach and prejudice "such as sincerely close with the Government, in favour of the few and wilde fellows who adhere to those old principles and that cursed interest which they cannot renounce". Jackson's headmastership was confirmed in 1654, but he was finally ousted in 1656 when Cromwell's revolution was in full retreat and the "few wilde fellows" of the old "cursed interest" were recovering their power and influence. His name is still execrated in the school. Its twentieth century historians conclude their account of this "sordid story": "Farewell, Richard Jackson, with your gospel preaching and your hypocrisies, your love of ale-houses and unlettered companions, not even the wish to bury your name in oblivion shall cause the School to forget your well-merited fate". A better-balanced judgment would take account of the political and religious prejudices of Jackson's enemies.

The schoolmaster was by no means the first Sedbergh townsman to fall foul of religious party politics. Half a century earlier, in 1585, the vicar, Giles Wigginton, was thrown out of his living in a national purge of puritan ministers, accused of working to "overthrow the state ecclesiastical", and locked up in the notorious White Lion prison, London. He was released in 1586 and returned to Sedbergh where he set up an independent church with some 140 members. Jailed again the following year, he was eventually reinstated as vicar in 1592 when the purge of radical puritans petered out. The struggle between puritan and anti-puritan parties, which became an armed struggle between Parliamentarians and Royalists, had deep roots in Sedbergh.

Gervase Benson, who will soon be properly introduced into our story, complained in 1653 that Sedbergh had fourteen alehouses and the priest was a frequenter of all of them. He was probably referring to the curate, Leonard Burton, who became vicar a year or two later. Burton belonged to the puritan party but was no friend of the Quakers, perhaps because they stole so many of his flock. Fox says that, on a later visit, Burton physically attacked him. Benson complained that he made no attempt to enforce the Commonwealth's reforms, continuing, for instance, to register births in church rather than by civil registrar as decreed by parliament. The impression is reinforced of a bitterly divided community, unenthusiastic about radical religious and political change and probably thoroughly disillusioned by the violent upheavals of the preceding decade. In this, Sedbergh was no doubt little different from the vast majority of rural towns in England in the critical early years of the experimental Commonwealth.

Fox probably walked right through the town. We stop to chat with a group of travellers who are feeding and watering their horses at the roadside, *en route* to the annual horse fair at Appleby. Then we make for the White Rose fish shop and a generous plate of fish, chips and mushy peas. The inner man and woman thus refreshed, we proceed down Main Street, paved with granite setts which give the town an old-fashioned air - falsely so, as it happens, since the setts have only just replaced modern tarmacadam at the behest of the Yorkshire Dales National Park with an eye to attracting tourists here from the Lakes. Since the burghers of Sedbergh were not consulted, they are threatening a new civil war. (Over the next few months the National

Park is forced to retreat, and the setts which replaced tarmac are themselves replaced - by tarmac.)

But are we, then, in Yorkshire still? Yes and No. Sedbergh, Garsdale and Dent were all part of the West Riding of Yorkshire and within the Yorkshire Dales National Park till 1974, when the West Riding, Westmorland and Cumberland were all abolished as administrative entities and the three western dales were lumped together with former Westmorland, former Cumberland and bits of northern Lancashire as the new county of Cumbria. But the three dales remained within the Yorkshire Dales National Park. So they now belong to both Cumbria and Yorkshire - or, as some of the locals would prefer, to neither.

But these geo-political confusions are nothing new. In the fourteenth and fifteenth centuries the region was known as "Frendeles" because it was perceived by both Yorkshire-proper to the east and Westmorland-proper to the west as a friendless and unfriendly area which neither much wanted to claim. If geography had been the determinant, the territory must have been awarded to Westmorland as it lies on the western side of the Pennine watershed, and when Friends began to organise themselves into an orderly structure in the later 1650s they anticipated the 1974 commissioners by more than three hundred years in placing Sedbergh, Garsdale and Dent under Westmorland rather than Yorkshire. On the other hand, if neither geography nor geo-politics but geology had decided the matter, we would have crossed the boundary as we stepped over the Dent Fault.

George Fox knew exactly where he was heading, and for the moment it wasn't Sedbergh town. He had been given the name Richard Robinson - a different Richard Robinson, of course, from the one at Countersett. So he tells us: "As I was passing along the way I asked a man, which was Richard Robinson's; he asked me from whence I came and I told him, 'From the Lord'". If the local man thought the stranger's answer evasive or enigmatic, he nevertheless gave directions, and soon George Fox was knocking on Robinson's door at Brigflatts.

Brigflatts lies a mile or so west of Sedbergh where the Roman road once forded the Rawthey just above its confluence with the Lune. The ford must have been replaced by a bridge, but frequent flooding of the meadow flats has obliterated the line of the road and the location of the bridge which gave the hamlet its name. Surrounded by the heights of Holme Fell, Whernside and the Howgills, Brigflatts is often said to have been a sizeable community in those days. David Butler actually describes it as "a much larger place than we now know, where several hundred people who were employed in the manufacture of flax lived in cottages around the green". I am dubious. The Sedbergh parish registers only name three families in Brigflatts over the entire period of the first half of the seventeenth century: we would surely expect more if there were "several hundred" people in the hamlet, or even several dozen. The population of Sedbergh town itself was probably no more than "several hundred": perhaps approaching a thousand at most. The tradition of a large flax-making community is part of the Quaker mythology, but the available documentary evidence suggests that in 1652 Brigflatts was little, if at all, bigger than the three-house hamlet of 1994. Indeed, with the conversion of outbuildings into homes in 1995, the hamlet is probably larger today than ever.

Richard Robinson's house lay and lies at the foot of the lane which winds down to Brigflatts from the Sedbergh to Kirkby Lonsdale road. It was renovated and enlarged after Robinson's death in 1673, and has since been cement-rendered against "weatherly days", but the small windows to the left of the porch indicate the old house, and visitors are sometimes shown the room where George Fox is said to have slept. Fox says tersely that "when I came to Richard Robinson's I declared the everlasting Truth to him and he was convinced". But the convincement may not have been instantaneous, as the *Journal* adds: "And yet a dark jealousy riz up in him, after I was gone to bed, that I might be somebody that was come to rob his house, and he locked all his doors fast". It was more usual, no doubt, to lock a burglar out, but once he had gained entrance the next best thing was to lock him in to prevent him making off with the family pewter.

Perhaps reassured by finding his suspicious guest still declaring everlasting Truth the following morning, Richard Robinson told Fox of a "Separate meeting" - a meeting of separatists - called for that very day, Whit Sunday, at Borret farm nearby, on the Kirkby Lonsdale road. This was to be Fox's introduction to the Westmorland Seekers. Again, the *Journal* is almost comically laconic: "the people were generally convinced", it says. But by the end of the meeting George Fox knew he had found the following he was seeking, and some at least of the Seekers knew they had met the prophet who could turn them into finders. "This was the place", Fox realised, "that I had seen a people coming forth in white raiment": the place of his Pendle vision.

It is time for us, too, to meet the Seekers. The word is very hard to pin down, and it is a mistake to try. The Seekers, despite their capital initial, were not a single organised sect. The label was often applied loosely to all who turned away from state religion and embraced freer forms of worship in "gathered churches" of like-minded men and women. There was no clear demarcation between those dubbed Ranters, Familists, Anabaptists, Antinomians, Grindletonians, Separatists: all might be called Seekers, and even the derisive term "Quaker" is said to have been used of some enthusiasts in the late 1640s, before Fox or his associates were on the scene. Cromwell himself declared that the best state for a believer was that of a seeker, but that didn't make the Protector a member of any sect. Indeed, one characteristic of seeking was moving from one group to another in search of true religion - and in search of leadership. Seekers increasingly came to believe, by 1650, that some mighty act of God was imminent: perhaps the Second Coming itself, perhaps a new prophet who would gather the diaspora of true believers and give them direction and authority.

Seekers had no one form of worship or organisation, and although Westmorland and Yorkshire Seekers had established links with each other by the 1650s it is by no means clear that these links extended to others called, or calling themselves, Seekers elsewhere. There were certainly groups of Seekers in the religiously radicalised New Model Army, and they no doubt took their faith with them into their home communities on demobilisation. Some met in private homes or taverns, their worship consisting of little more than religious debate and discussion. In 1647 Anne Newby returned from London to Kendal where she "joined herself to a company of sincere seekers who often met together for Divine worship, sometimes sitting in silence, at others holding religious conference, and frequently were engaged in fervent prayer". The similarity to later Quaker meetings is striking - but we cannot be sure whether this is because Seeker meetings *were* like Quaker meetings and perhaps provided a model for them, or whether the later Quaker friends of Anne Newby who wrote this appreciation of her unconsciously read back Quaker features into the Seeker meetings.

There were Seeker groups in Preston Patrick, Kendal, Underbarrow, Grayrigg, Hutton and Sedbergh in Westmorland and the West Riding, and in Swaledale in the North Riding. Their leader was an ordained minister, a Yorkshireman named Thomas Taylor, "a comely man of person, fair and ruddy", eight years older than George Fox. Taylor was an admirer of the German mystic philosopher/theologian Jakob Boehme (1575-1624) who had been influenced by the twelfth century heretic Joachim of Fiore. Joachim preached "the Everlasting Gospel" - a phrase which became the coded badge of underground radical religious dissent for hundreds of years before it was appropriated by Fox and early Friends and other antinomian groups such as the Muggletonians. It carried a sense of an authority over and above that of the institutionalised church, a belief in inward light rather than outward rules. This powerful idea, with its huge potential for subverting all external authority, links anti-clerical heresy in the middle ages to Familism, the Seekers and Fox.

In 1650 Taylor disputed infant baptism with three other ministers in Kendal parish church. When he got the better of his orthodox opponents, writes William C Braithwaite, "his hearers ran up Kendal street crying, 'Mr Taylor hath got the day! Mr Taylor hath got the day!' with an enthusiasm now reserved for a game of football". By this time he had accepted a position as minister at Preston Patrick, refusing tithes but taking a stipend of £50 a year from voluntary contributions. Preston Patrick church, presumably vacated by the national church since the legal abolition of Anglicanism during the civil war, became the centre of Westmorland Seeker activity and the venue for their general meetings which attracted "the most zealous and religious Roundheads and Puritans" within a twenty mile radius.

In 1651 the Swaledale Seekers asked for a share of Taylor's services, but he had come under the influence of Richard Baxter, an Independent minister who was trying to halt the tendency of puritanism to split into competing sects. Baxter's dream was to re-unite Independents, Presbyterians, Baptists and other separatists, and that meant some agreement had to be reached on basic doctrine. In the interests of unity, Thomas Taylor agreed to resume infant baptism, but failed to carry his Westmorland Seekers with him. The Swaledale Seekers, however, proved persuadable, and Taylor moved to Richmond as a "lecturer" - an approved preacher supported by voluntary contributions. By June 1652, when George Fox walked into their fellowship, pastoral leadership of the Westmorland Seekers had been taken over by two lay ministers, Francis Howgill and John Audland, supported by Gervase Benson.

If Taylor, Howgill and Audland were the spiritual leaders, the highest-ranking and most powerful member of the group was Colonel Gervase Benson, at whose home at Borret farm, near Brigflatts, Fox attended his first Seeker meeting that Whit Sunday.

A thumb-nail sketch of Benson's "pilgrim's progress" tells us a great deal about the turbulent religious atmosphere of the times. A native of Kendal and a lawyer, he had held prior to the civil wars the powerful post of Commissary to the Archdeaconry of Richmond, which made him the archdeacon's head of legal affairs. But the commencement of hostilities in 1642 found him a convinced Presbyterian, and when episcopacy was abolished by parliament he became a member of the Westmorland Presbyterian "classis", the church's administrative body. In 1643 he was elected Mayor of Kendal, and was by now leaning towards Independency. In 1645 he took a commission in the New Model Army or its local militia, was captured in a skirmish with Royalist troops, and released in an exchange of prisoners.

In 1648 much of the Presbyterian party switched sides to join the King and the Scots against the Independents, fearing that Independency and its radical allies would make good their promise to introduce liberty of religious and political opinion: anarchy, as the gentry saw it. But Benson was by now a fully politicised republican and he became one of Cromwell's chief men in Westmorland: a Justice of the Peace, and a member of the powerful Westmorland Militia Commission which was charged with raising funds by the sequestration and sale of royalists' estates. It may be that it was through this latter office that he was able to purchase, perhaps at advantageous terms, the two farms which belonged to him in Sedbergh: Borret, near Brigflatts, and High Haygarth at Cautley (now the Cross Keys temperance inn). He was one of the "new men" who rose to positions of influence and power previously monopolised by the gentry, and one displaced gentleman sourly declared it a disgrace that such power should now reside in the hands of one who "hath but a house and land", and no pedigree to go with them.

Some time before 1652 the pilgrim had progressed one stage further, from the Independents to the Westmorland Seekers. He retained his commissions as a Justice and in the military (until 1653), but the next few years show him as an increasingly vociferous critic of Cromwell's inability to see the revolution through. Even his attachment to Friends, which began the day he met George Fox at Borret, did not mark the end of his spiritual and political journey. After many years of working, writing, preaching and suffering for the Quaker cause, and often acting as Friends' legal adviser, he briefly joined a group of dissidents who broke with Fox's leadership in the 1670s, protesting at the movement's drift, as he saw it, from the radical libertarianism of the early days to the more disciplined and institutionalised Society Fox was bent on creating. But he was reconciled to Fox and rejoined the mainstream before his death in 1679. It was noted then that despite all his "Titells of the World...He generally stiled himself Husbandman" - the lowest class in the social pecking order. His first wife Dorothy was imprisoned at York "for speaking to [or heckling] a priest", and there gave birth to their son, Immanuel, in 1653. (When she died, a year or two later, she was buried in the garden at High Haygarth, below the awesome heights of Cautley Spout, where Cautley beck plunges from the tops of the Howgills in an almost unbroken fall to the valley bottom).This, then, was the mettle of George Fox's hosts at Borret farm, as the future Society of Friends began to take shape over the next few action-packed days.

Leaving Sedbergh town behind us, we take the Kirkby Lonsdale road at Tollbar corner and soon pass Borret, now a modern house on the right with outbuildings and a camp site on the left. (Our daily pints of milk come from here). Minutes later we are walking down the little lane to Brigflatts. The skies open again as we reach the meetinghouse and take up residency in the tiny guest room which was once the gallery over the women's meeting-room. Melvyn Roberts, a former Nottingham miner, whose broad-brimmed Quaker hat suggests a whiff of puritanism which is instantly dispelled by his laugh (GF would have put a stop to that) plus a miner's thirst (and some Friends would put a stop to *that*), pops in to welcome us.

Melvyn is the warden and lives with Sandra and their family at Rosebank, just above the meetinghouse. "It's not the Ritz", he says, and we agree it is not: no Ritz was ever built in so perfect a setting. If Quakerism ever had a holy of holies, we had entered it at the end of our eighth day hard on Fox's heels.

Sermon on the Fell

DAY 9. Brigflatts-Firbank

That great northern nationalist poet Basil Bunting called his master-work *Briggflatts* (using an antiquated spelling). He had spent childhood holidays in the hamlet, and the song of the river and the roar of the bull and the annual explosion of may are vividly present in his famous opening lines:

"Brag, sweet tenor bull,
descant on Rawthey's madrigal,
each pebble its part
for the fell's late spring.
Dance tiptoe, bull,
black against may.
Ridiculous and lovely
chase hurtling shadows
morning into noon.
May on the bull's hide
and through the dale
furrows fill with may,
paving the slowworm's way."

"Call it God, call it the universe", wrote Bunting in the prefatory note to the poem, "all we know of it, extended far beyond our telescopes or even inferences, detailed more minutely than our physicists can grope... The day's incidents hide our ignorance from us; yet we know it, beneath our routine. In silence, having swept dust and litter from our minds, we can detect the pulse of God's blood in our veins, more persuasive than words, more demonstrative than a diagram. That is what a Quaker meeting tries to be, and that is why my poem is called *Briggflatts.*"

His plain little gravestone, identical to all the rest but a bit whiter, stands in the burial ground by the meetinghouse, simply inscribed with his name and dates, 1900-1980. But though he returned to meeting here as often as he could manage till the end of his life, Basil Bunting was no conventional Quaker. The sensuality of *Briggflatts*, expressed in a few lines now framed and displayed in the meetinghouse, was much disapproved of by the elders of his day:

"My love is young but wise. Oak, applewood,
her fire is banked with ashes till day.
The fell's reek of her hearth's scent,
her girdle is greased with lard;
hunger is stayed on her settle, lust on her bed.
Light as spider floss her hair on my cheek which a puff scatters,
light as a moth her fingers on my thigh.
We have eaten and loved and the sun is up,
We have only to sing before parting:
Goodbye, dear love."

And his theology was hardly less perplexing to the orthodox. As he wrote to the American poet Louis Zukovsky, "Adjectives, numbers, symbols like the word God, eat away all sense of reality and land us in every kind of social and economic mess, when people begin to think they correspond to anything genuine".

"Words!
Pens are too light.
Take a chisel to write..."

Brigflatts was not immediately the epicentre of local Quakerism. Richard Robinson's was only one of a dozen or more farmhouses in and around Sedbergh where meetings began to be held after Fox's dramatic first visit. But when one Rebecca Laughton (some records say Langle) died in 1656, Richard Robinson allowed her to be be buried in one of his fields instead of the steeplehouse garth. Five more Friends were buried there over the next four years, and in 1660 Friends paid Robinson a nominal 10s to purchase the land as a burial ground "for friends of Sedbergh, Dent, Garsdale, Middleton, Killington and Ewbank". Fourteen years later, in 1674, they laid out another 10s for "three falls of land [about 30 square yards] in the corner of a close called Little Brigflatts, late belonging to Richard Robinson deceased". Here, the following year, they built the meetinghouse which stands to this day.

It was an astonishing act of defiance, for Quaker meetings were illegal and to attend such a place was to risk a punitive fine or a jail sentence. No architect designed it. Sympathetic farmers and craftsmen built it much as they would build a substantial barn, with no frills, no nonsense. They were sufficiently up-to-date to use the technique, relatively new in the area, of erecting load-bearing lime-mortared stone walls to carry a flagged roof, which distinguished it from the surrounding wood-framed, ling-thatched houses - though some of these, too, were beginning to be rebuilt in the new way. The stone and the stout oak timbers for the roof were supplied by Friends and carted to the site at their own expense. "The decision to use flags was bold," says David Butler, historian of the architecture of Quaker meetinghouses, "and it was in keeping with Friends' ideas on the rightness and permanence of their way of worship. At the same time it is possible to believe that some of the worshippers may have regretted the decision, when the wind drove flakes of snow between the stone slabs in spite of the moss packed into the cracks every winter".

When it opened in 1675, the meetinghouse was indeed barn-like, with a beaten-earth floor, no galleries (except perhaps at the west end), and no ceiling. But that the wooden galleries and wide staircase which are now the glory of the place were planned from the start is apparent from the disposition of the windows: none on the north, east or west, where the gallery was to run. It wasn't actually built till 1714, when the joiner, John Coupland, was paid £5 for his masterpiece! The following year a plastered ceiling hid the hitherto exposed undersides of the roof flags. The first wooden floor had been laid in 1681. In 1720 the narrow benches designed for discomfort-loving Quaker bottoms were improved for a softer generation by the addition of backs and, later, a strip along the front to extend their width and thus accommodate a little more thigh. John Holmes was entrusted to do the work and "see that it be well Done". The marks and lines he made when setting out each joint on the bench-backs, determined to see that the job was indeed "well Done", are still visible.

The result was and is a perfect monument to plain, no-nonsense Quaker simplicity. No-one thought to make it beautiful, but its simplicity and functionality are its beauty. A fragment of stained glass, the merest hint of a cross, would be a blasphemy here. But this was no cell-retreat, no hiding place from the wicked world outside. This was a powerhouse where men and women would plot to mend the world, and together seek inspiration for their revolutionary task. That is what Basil Bunting, poet and plotter, loved about the place. As the critic Peter Quartermain wrote in his essay "Basil Bunting: Poet of the North", he "shared with Quakers distrust of any authority save your own".

So it is Bunting as much as Fox who occupies our thoughts as we wake this Sunday morning. We have been accommodated in the little upstairs room which was partitioned off in 1749 "for convenience of Women Friends Meeting", and converted in 1905 into a bedroom for the caretaker who by then was living in the room below. Our bed is clearly a relic of the days when Quakers believed there was positive merit in extreme discomfort. When warden Melvyn appears and asks cheerfully if we had a comfortable night, we cannot tell a lie. "I've been meaning to throw that bed away for years", he tells us - and we understand he did so the following week. May future pilgrims be grateful for our plain speaking.

Just before 10.30am the first-comers arrive for meeting for worship.

We make our entrance direct from the bedroom to the gallery and descend the old stairs, through what is said to be an old dog pen, where Quaker-shepherd dogs sat quietly through meeting (which I doubt), and into the body of the meetinghouse. The old forms are arranged around a plain table in front of the platform built to raise weighty ministers above the common level. The table has upon it a plain vase of wild flowers, a bible and a copy of *Quaker Faith and Practice*. Some of the forms have cushions: experience has taught us to make sure we choose one of these.

By a little after 10.30 there are perhaps twenty Friends present and the silence deepens as the meeting "centres down" - a phrase I dislike for its New Age mystique, but one modern Friends have come to use to describe the process of settling into a state of focused meditation or concentration. Friends claim to have no ritual, but if this isn't a ritual the word has no meaning. What is happening? Twenty Friends would probably give twenty answers. Worship for some means opening the mind to a real, objective God out there: a dialogue of prayer. Others would speak of meditation and contemplation rather than worship. Others again seek to focus on "God" as a metaphor, Bunting's "symbol", of the values which, though we know them to be the products of human culture, we choose to treat as absolutes. Some invoke a "presence in the midst": but this is no seance, no conjuring of spirits. Our sense of a "presence" is real enough, but it is the sense rather than the presence which is real.

After perhaps twenty minutes, a woman stands to read an "advice" warning against "too much busyness". A man follows, linking the may blossom, Bunting, Fox and our journey, which he calls a pilgrimage. The rest is silence, broken only by the gastric symphonies generated by partly digested breakfasts. No hymns, spoken prayers, bible readings. A few minutes before the end, a dozen boisterous children burst in from the Sunday school or children's meeting, seek out their parents, whisper noisily and wait impatiently for the ritual hand-shakes which say it is all over bar the communion coffee or lemonade.

Hazel, the clerk, welcomes visitors and gives out the notices: an Amnesty meeting, a peace vigil, a project to support homeless "travellers" (Melvyn's special concern), and notice of some pending act of civil disobedience. It is often the notices as much as the unprogrammed structures of "worship" which mark out a Quaker meeting from most church services.

Meetings were rather different in the 1650s. There are few Quaker accounts to draw on, but Francis Higginson, vicar of Kirkby Stephen, gave this hostile description in 1653 in *A Brief Relation of the Irreligion of the Northern Quakers*:

"For the manner of their Speakings, their Speaker for the most part uses the posture of standing, or sitting, with his hat on, his Countenance severe, his Face downward, his Eyes fixed mostly towards the Earth, his Hands and Fingers expanded, continually striking gently on his Breast; his Beginning is without a Text, abrupt and sudden to his hearers, his Voice for the most part low, his sentences incoherent, hanging together like Ropes of Sand... sometimes full of sudden Pauses; his whole Speech is a mixt bundle of Words and Heaps of Nonsense, his Continuance in speaking is sometimes exceeding short, sometimes very tedious, according to the Paucity or Plenty of his Revelations. His admiring Auditors that are of his Way, stand the while like men astonished, listening to every Word, as though every Word was oraculous; and so they believe them to be the very words and dictates of Christ speaking in him."

Higginson appears not to have noticed the women speakers and "auditors". But it is still posible to hear (and deliver) ministry "hanging together like Ropes of Sand".

Over coffee we find ourselves discussing the personality of George Fox. Marjorie Henson thinks he enjoyed being a stirrer - "like you", she says to her husband George. "And you", says Anthea to me. George sees him as a "practical visionary" and envies him his certainty. He is a good subject for stories for the children, "to instil values into them - or rather", he hastily corrects himself, "to help them find their own". Someone else objects to the certainties George

Henson envies: "Fox saw everything in black and white, but I'm very suspicious of that. I don't think I'd have liked him much".

The *Journal* is silent about the two days, June 7th and 8th, following the Borret meeting with the Seekers. Perhaps Fox was resting, but more likely he was meeting more of the Seekers and excitedly comparing ideas and insights. But Wednesday the 9th, "Comonly Called Whitsonwedonsday", was the day of "a great fair at Sedbergh for hiring servants", and he was not one to resist a crowd. So

"I went to the fair and declared through the fair the day of the Lord, and after I had done I went into the steeplehouse yard [adjoining the market square where the fair was held] and got up by a tree, and most of the people of the fair came to me, and abundance of priests and professors. There I declared the everlasting Truth of the Lord and the word of life for several hours, and that the Lord Christ Jesus was come to teach his people himself and bring them off all the world's ways and teachers to Christ, their way to God; and I laid open all their teachers and set up the true teacher, Christ Jesus; and how they were judged by the prophets, Christ, and the apostles; and to bring them off the temples made with hands, that they themselves might know they were the temples of God. And never a priest had power to open his mouth. But at last a captain said, why would I not go into the church, for that was a fit place to preach in. I said unto him I denied their church for the church was in God as in 1 Thess[alonians] 1.1. There stood up a Separate preacher, one Francis Howgill, that had not seen me before, and he began to dispute with the captain, but he held his peace. Then said Francis Howgill, 'This man speaks with authority and not as the scribes'. So I opened to the people that the ground and house was no holier than another place, and that the house was not the church, but the people which Christ is the head of: and so, after a while that I had made a stand amongst the people, the priests came up to me and I warned them to repent. And when I was passing away a priest said to the people that I was distracted; his mouth being stopped by the power of God for opposing, that was his only cover to the people, and so they turned away, but many people were glad at the hearing of the Truth declared unto them that day, which they gladly received."

The speech was clearly, and no doubt deliberately, provocative. Fox's venue was the church yard and his hearers included an "abundance of priests and professors", which suggests word had got around that the fair was going to be hijacked by some visiting controversialist. But despite, or more likely because of, the many clerics who had come to hear him, Fox chose to home in on one of his favourite themes: the falseness of the official church, the emptiness of "steeplehouse" religion, and the evil of priestcraft and a "hireling" ministry.

The *Journal's* summary is couched in the relatively inoffensive language of post-Restoration Quaker polemics, but the verbally-violent anticlericalism of the pioneer period is better reflected in Fox's 1652 pamphlet *A Paper Sent Forth...Why we Deny the Teachers of the World*. Here Fox attacks "such Ministers as go to Oxford and Cambridge, and call them the Well-heads of Divinity... and there they study, and read books, and old Authors, and furnish themselves with Philosophy, and fine Words, and other men's matter, and when they come again, they sell it to the poor". Warming to the theme, the clergy "with feigned words, and through covetousnesse, make merchandise of us, and do upon the people, who by oppression maintain themselves and wives in pride and idlenesse, in hoods, vails, and changeable suits of apparell, who go in the way of Cain, to envy, murder and persecute". They

"take Tythes, the tenth of man's Labours, and estates, and those that will not give them, they sue at the Law, and hale before the Courts, and Sessions, yea, even those they call their own People, their own Parishioners, [and] besides their Tythes of corn, hay, beast, sheep, hens, pigs, giese, eggs, cheries, plumbs, take 10s for Preaching a Funerall Sermon, more or less, as they can get it, and 10s for the death of a man, and money out of Servants wages, and money for smoke passing up the Chimnies, and Easter Reckonings, and Midsummer dues, and money for Churching women, and thus by every device get Money, and burthen poor People that labour very hard, and can scarce get food and rayment, to main tain them in idleness and pride".

This is written, he adds,

"for the cleansing of the Land of all false Teachers, Seducers, and Deceivers, and Witches who beguile the People... All People that read these things, never come ye more at the Steeple-House, nor pay your Priests more Tythes till they have answered them; for if ye do, ye uphold them in their sins, and must partake of their plagues".

This 1652 pamphlet was reprinted in 1654, 1655, 1656, 1657 and

1659. In 1659 Fox directly addressed his enemy:

"Come, Priests, did not the Whore [the Roman Catholic Church] set up your Mass-Houses with the Cross atop of it, with their Pictures and Bells, and call it Holy Ground where it stands, and name them St Paul's, and St Peter's, and St Michael's etc. Come, Priests, have you not drunken the Whore's Cup here? Is not this the Whore's Cup? Guilty or not Guilty? If Guilty thou must drink the Cup of the indignation of the Wrath of the Almighty".

And the following year, as the clergy found fresh courage in the imminent restoration of monarchy and the Church of England, an anonymous Quaker pamphleteer warned them that their enjoyment of power would be short-lived, that they would "soon return to their holes", where "there is a Cup prepared for You, being mixed with Plagues, Woes, Miseries, Sorrows, Torments, and eternal Burnings... You are Antichrist, Deceivers, Sorcerers, and Ravening Wolves: FLAMES, FLAMES, FLAMES OF FIRE is prepared by the Lord to consume you as dry stubble...BURNINGS, BURNINGS, BURNINGS with unquenchable Fire, is your Portion from the Lord God of Heaven and Earth".

Such language explains why Fox and his friends aroused such violent antagonisms among the clergy and drew a following from among those who resented the financial and other burdens imposed on them by clerical authority. Our critical observer Francis Higginson described Quakers as "a Generation whose mouths are full of bitterness... The Billingsgate-Oister-Women are not comparable to them". More importantly, Cromwell himself - a markedly more tolerant man than his Quaker critics - was both alienated by such rhetoric and troubled by the frequent breaches of the peace which it provoked, and in 1655 announced his intention to enforce the law against disorders in religion. But in 1652 such restraints lay in the future, and we may suppose that the inflammatory language of the pamphlets, rather than the moderated phraseology of the *Journal*, was the language Fox was speaking in Sedbergh church yard on Whit Wednesday. Note too that it is the language of class war as well as spiritual warfare. Quakerism was the gospel, the promise (and the warning) of the Levellers revived.

The fair over, and Sedbergh no doubt seething, George Fox was taken to Draw-well, the home of Thomas Blaykling and his son John, two Seekers he had first met at Borret. It is to Draw-well we make our way after meeting, walking from Brigflatts through Ingmire Lane to cross the Sedbergh-Kendal highway and join the Roman road running above the east bank of the Lune. Ingmire Hall on our left was the home of the Otways, royalist cousins of the Roundhead Captain Alexander Hebblethwaite of Dent. It may well be that Richard Robinson and his Brigflatts neighbours were among the Otways' customary tenants, which would compound their social, political and spiritual rebellion.

Draw-well was and is a little farmhouse below the Howgills, looking across the river to Firbank Fell. Till after the second world war it retained its seventeenth century character and the open well at the door which gave it its name, but the well was subsequently paved over and the house converted into a holiday cottage before being renovated recently as the home of Janet and James Postlethwaite. They welcome us inside and show us the much-modernised interior. "We had to do it", they tell us. "The timbers were all rotten and the place was falling down". I remark on the adjoining barn, which dwarfs the house, and wonder aloud whether it has been rebuilt since it hosted many a Quaker meeting in the early years. James thinks not, and points out that the house has no gable wall of its own but is built against the barn. This certainly suggests that the barn is at least of an age with the house, but the present barn structure lacks the crucks which one would expect to find in an early seventeenth century farm building. We are shown the little room in which George Fox was said to have hidden from Government troops, but Fox was not the hiding sort, and at this stage the New Model Army troops were more likely to cheer him on than arrest him, so the legend has no basis in fact.

The Blayklings had become instant converts on meeting Fox at

Borret. The son, John, was a year younger than Fox, already a public-spirited worker - he was a trustee for orphans in Howgill and adjacent parishes and "a great supporter of such as were in low circumstances" - and destined to become a much travelled and much imprisoned ambassador for Quakerism. "His Testymony was but short, yet powerful and peirceing agst deceit, and was as a nail fastened in a secure place". His sister Ann was such a one as must have put the fear of God into her adversaries. She became one of the first women to take the new northern religion to the south, and was imprisoned once for heckling a minister in church and again for calling another a "greedy, dumb dog". This was not quite as Billingsgate-oyster-woman an insult as it sounds, as "dumb dog" was a contemporary epithet for priests who didn't bother to preach sermons.

In 1665, when the state, the church and the army were securely back in the hands of the royalists, a meeting at Draw-well was raided by the local militia, led by Ensign Lawrence Hodgson of Dent, "Curseing and swearing and Threatening that if Friends would not depart and disperse he and they could kill and slay and what not, he houlding out a pistoll Cocked, and also armed with a sword, and made himself very furious and terrible". Friends tried to ignore their visitors, which must have been difficult, but eventually "with harrying and thrusting and beating they [Friends, not their visitors] were forced out" and driven to Sedbergh market place to be "put before the leading men of the parish". Ann Blaykling was refused permission to turn back for her hat. If she was going to prison, she wanted to be properly dressed for the occasion. But the "leading men" were not sure what to do with Ensign Hodgson's captives and released them without charge, whereupon they walked back to Draw-well barn and resumed the meeting which had been so rudely interrupted.

Later, in 1675, Draw-well was the venue for an important conference between the leaders of two factions which had arisen within the Society, one the Fox group and the other, led by John Wilkinson and John Story, critical of Fox's authoritarian leadership style. Gervase Benson was at this time one of Fox's critics, and William Penn and Margaret Fox represented the dominant group, Fox strategically absenting himself (though he may have been ill at the time). John Blaykling worked to bring the factions together, but Quaker liberty and Quaker discipline were hard to reconcile. I fancy I hear the heated arguments still in the Postlethwaites' quiet living-room.

On his first visit George Fox spent four nights with the Blayklings, and it seems likely that some of the prominent Seekers and "professors" called to see and discourse with him. The only one he mentions in the *Journal* is Captain Henry Ward of Sunnybank, Grayrigg, who "said my very eyes pierced through him, and he was convinced of God's everlasting Truth." The 65-year-old captain (thought to be the captain Fox mentions as present at the Sedbergh churchyard meeting) had a radical record to be proud of. Thirty years earlier, he had been in serious trouble as one of the leading actors in the Kendal stage play which had attacked King James's personal and arbitrary decree attempting to abolish northern tenant-right. The play represented the king and his lords as "greedy eagles and devouring vultures". The same Henry Ward of Grayrigg was again representing tenants in a dispute in 1636, and in 1650 had given evidence on behalf of the tenants of Lady Anne Clifford who was attempting to raise their customary rents. As John Breay writes in *Light in the Dales*, "it can no longer be doubted that many families which had been deeply involved in tenant-right struggles embraced Quakerism after 1652". After the Restoration, the septuagenarian veteran was arrested on suspicion of involvement in the Kaber Rigg plot to restore the republic.

We cannot linger as Fox did, but must move on to his next triumph. Following the old track now signposted "Dales Way" down to and across the Lune (by footbridge), we are heading for Firbank Fell, on the Westmorland side of the old county boundary. The lane is brilliant with buttercups and bluebells, cow parsley and red campion, delicate white stitchwort and deep mauve wood-cranesbill. But the strong wind is back, and patches of sunlight race across the purple Howgills at our backs. Blackheaded gulls take a quicker route overhead. Reaching the Firbank road, we pause to chat to a lady who is tending her pretty cottage garden. She tells us the rough uphill track opposite was once the carriage-way up Firbank Fell, though why carriages should attempt the journey is a mystery. We take it, but after a quarter of a mile or so it becomes indistinct, and before long we are climbing barred gates to reach the summit.

It seems that "a great meeting of the sober people of the country" had already been arranged here for the Sunday after Fox's arrival in Sedbergh. On the fell summit, under one of several rocky outcrops, stood Firbank chapel, built here, it is said, because it was more or less equidistant from the thirty or forty families in the Firbank division of Killington-and-Firbank parish, who farmed both sides of the hill. The chapel was perhaps abandoned in the general collapse of church authority during the civil wars, and had been claimed by the separatists. The preachers billed for the Sunday morning were Francis Howgill and John Audland, the two Seeker lay-preachers who had filled the breach caused by Thomas Taylor's temporary defection to the "sprinkling" congregations of Swaledale. Howgill had been among Fox's audience in Sedbergh churchyard the previous Wednesday, promoting him as one who "speaks with authority and not as the scribes" - a provocative quotation of words originally spoken of Jesus himself. He was about five years older than Fox, a tailor by trade but also a farmer at Grayrigg. Brought up an episcopalian, and probably intended for the church, he had tried in turn the Independents and Baptists before joining the Seekers. One account calls him a Grindletonian. A prolific writer and unwearying traveller for Quakerism, he was eventually to die in Appleby jail in 1668, where he had been committed for refusing to swear the oath of allegiance.

John Audland was only 22 but already in much demand as a brilliant speaker and teacher. John Blaykling and other "moderate people", taking Fox to the meeting, were concerned lest their guest should let off one of his blasts against "parish teachers", directed at Howgill and Audland, who were paid stipends which laid them open to denunciation as "hireling priests". But Fox kept them in suspense. "Though I had little in me to declare publicly against them, I told them they must leave me to the Lord's movings". They found the little chapel full to bursting, with many people outside. Howgill later claimed that Fox peeped inside while he was preaching, an appearance which so shook him that Fox "might have killed [me] with a crab-apple".

The morning service done, some of the people "went to their dinners", but many more stayed or returned in the expectation of hearing more. Fox refreshed himself with water from a beck, then climbed to the top of one of the rocky outcrops, "even as Christ had done before", he says, inviting direct comparison with the sermon on the mount. A crowd gathered below - "above a thousand people", Fox claimed, and for three hours he delivered his own sermon on the fell, again "opening to the people" that "the steeplehouse and that ground on which it stood were no more holy than that mountain", that the days of priests and tithes were over, that Christ had come to teach his people himself. "All those several Separate teachers" in his audience were convinced, he wrote in his *Journal*, though "many old people that went into the Chapel and looked out of the windows... thought it a strange thing to see a man preach on a hill or mountain and not in their church (as they called it)". Howgill and Audland quietly abandoned their stipends.

There is no trace of the chapel today. It was taken down, stone by stone, to be rebuilt on a more convenient site. But a rough walled enclosure still stands, with one visible gravestone. Rearing up behind it is the outcrop, "Fox's Pulpit", marked by a metal plate commemorating Sunday June 13 1652 when Fox preached "here or near this rock". "Great power inspired his message and the meeting proved of first importance in gathering the Society of Friends known as Quakers". The plate is headed: "LET YOUR LIVES SPEAK".

Today there is not a living soul in sight - and, nearly two thousand feet above sea level, we can see the sea in one direction and, we fancy, Pendle Hill in the other. But as we walk down Shackla Bank and back towards Brigflatts, it isn't hard to imagine the excitement of those farmers and craftsmen and their wives and families whose emotions had been so stirred and hopes so renewed. The civil wars had changed nothing. Cromwell's republic, it seemed, had changed little. There was still grinding poverty and corruption, overlaid by the guilt and despair engendered by a religion of hellfire and damnation for all but the lucky elect. But George Fox preached hope. A day of deliverance was dawning, when the mighty would be put down and priestcraft abolished, when the burdens of tithes would be lifted, the oppressive power of the pulpit silenced and the tyranny of the Book dissolved away. A darkness had been dispersed. Fox's metaphor of Light, inward and outward, seemed to promise a new heaven and a new earth.

John Cooke

The Resurrection of Free-born John

DAY 10. Firbank-Preston Patrick

The great Firbank meeting over and the crowd dispersing down the fellside, George Fox accepted John Audland's invitation to stay the night at his home at Crosslands, nearly ten miles south, towards Preston Patrick. We have spent a second night at Brigflatts, which is in the right direction. We plan to take the Kirkby Lonsdale highway towards Four Lane Ends, cutting through Beckside woods to join the old Firbank-Killington road - undoubtedly Fox's route - at Killington New Bridge.

We are wakened in the early hours by the loud, distressed cries of a curlew, its nest under attack, perhaps, from a night predator. This time last year we had almost walked into a ground-nest only a yard or so from the path across the meadows to the meetinghouse, with four large speckled eggs neatly laid, the small ends pointing inwards. It is raining: the "soft, refreshing" sort, we persuade ourselves, which is one of the good gifts around us sent from heaven above. Once off the main road, the verges are again a heart-stopping kaleidoscope of colour, the mass of bluebells at Beckside beginning to fade, perhaps, but making way gracefully for golds, and whites, pinks, yellows and mauves. Crossing the bridge over the Lune and back into old Westmorland, we turn towards Killington through a deep and ancient holloway. Fox, Audland and excited hangers-on are striding ahead of us, praising the Lord and plotting the new Jerusalem. I am suddenly reminded of the Aldermaston marches when we too, with hope in our hearts and telling ourselves we would never walk alone, stepped out for good against evil and argued each other into the ground over which we tramped.

Killington is a sleepy village. Not far to the west the M6 cuts through the hills, and many a motorist has enjoyed a good fried breakfast in the most beautifully-sited service area in England, overlooking Killington lake. The village boasts a splendid mediaeval hall, originally built as a central tower with substantial cross-wings on each side. The south wing still stands as an eerie, roofless shell, the north has disappeared altogether. The front elevation has some strikingly beautiful 17th century windows of two, three, and four square-headed lights with stone mullions and labels. In the gable of the north dormer is a stone inscribed with the initials T.K and L.K. and the date 1640. T.K. is Thomas Kitson, gent., whose sister Elizabeth married into the Hebblethwaite family, kin to the Quaker Alexander Hebblethwaite of Dent. Across the road from Killington Hall is the church, which contains fragments from the 14th or 15th century. When Fox and Audland passed this way the Hall was accessible only by drawbridge over a natural ravine, but this has long been replaced by a stone-arched bridge.

Killington was also the home in 1652 of 19-year-old George Harrison, son of a minor-gentry family which bitterly opposed his decision to move from Seekers to Quakers. The young man threw himself into the travelling ministry, though he seems to have had a startlingly direct style of evangelism. *First Publishers of Truth* records him preaching in Dover in 1655, after which "Thomas Euerden, a very zealous Professor among ye Independants, Asking him some questions, George, Lookeing Wistly vpon him, said, 'Thou art a Dog', & so left him. Which words confounded him, & he meditateing long vpon them, Wrought such an Effect, That he could neuer get cleere of them, Till he receiued and liued in ye Truth, & became a Preacher himselfe".

Another blunt remark by Harrison was the means of converting the great Leveller leader John Lilburne. "Freeborn John" had done more than any other Englishman alive to push forward the cause of the people's liberty and commonwealth. He had fought against the king; been captured and released in an exchange of prisoners; had refused to take the Covenant because, like the future Quakers, he would not swear an oath of allegiance; had fallen out with Cromwell and accused him of high treason against the sovereign people, organised agitators in the army, founded Britain's first secular republican party and been jailed by Cromwell as an incorrigible subversive. His *Declaration to the Freeborn People of England* and a host of Leveller tracts which he wrote or had a hand in are the foundation literature of British democracy.

In 1655 he was a prisoner in Dover Castle jail, but was apparently allowed out by the jailor to attend a Quaker meeting. George Harrison was preaching, and Lilburne was heard to say something to the effect that he "liked well" what he heard. As he left, to return to jail, Harrison ran after him and they had a brief discussion in the street, at the conclusion of which Harrison told him, "Friend, thou art too high for Truth". These words, Lilburne said later, gave him "such a Box on ye Eare" that, as *First Publishers of Truth* puts it, he was "stund... Insomuch that he could neuer get from vnder them; but liued & died in ye profession of ye Truth". A few days later he wrote to his wife referring to "those preciousest (though most contemptible) people called quakers, the truly beloved objects of my soul", and the following year he announced his new allegiance in *The Resurrection of John Lilburne.*

With his immense reputation and fearsome energy, Lilburne might have emerged as a Quaker leader, perhaps a rival to Fox, had he not spent the few remaining years of his life under house arrest and exile. Friends' radical politics might have had more cohesion had he been free to fight yet another day. As it was, so many former Levellers joined Friends that contemporaries were not altogether unjustified in seeing the new movement as a reincarnation of the old. Lilburne's even-more radical comrade Gerrard Winstanley, leader of the communist "True Levellers", was also working with Friends by 1653 and was certainly assumed to be one by his conservative enemies. When the Quaker Edward Billing published 31 proposals for reform in 1659, his manifesto was rightly seen as a resurgence of Leveller demands. So too was George Fox's pamphlet the same year, *To the Parliament of the Commonwealth of England*, with 59 proposals, which advocated the conversion of Whitehall palace into an almshouse! The agitation against tithes was an integral part of the Leveller programme before it was taken up by Friends.

George Harrison (I can't help imagining him looking just like his Beatle namesake) had no opportunity to keep in contact with his illustrious convert. His restless ministry took him from Dover to London and thence to Essex, where, on a bitter December night, he and Stephen Hubbersty were refused shelter at the local inns. A sympathiser at Haverhill, Anthony Appleby, put them up, but a mob collected outside the house and eventually broke the door down, dragging out the two Friends "and most desperately did beat them to the ground, kicking them in a sad manner, driving them along the town, halloing them and stoning them all along to the end of the town, and this did not the townsmen seek to prevent but set others on". Harrison never recovered and died shortly after. He had been away from Killington for just eight months.

*

We climb out of the village and drop down to Three Mile House and Tarneybank. A wide stretch of bare moorland now separates us from John Audland's old home, Crosslands, but an ancient trackway is marked on the map, crossing in a more or less direct line. Fox and Audland either came this way or skirted the moor by cutting north to Old Hutton or far south to Old Town, which seems unlikely as they were at the end of a long, exhausting day. It is the rain which exhausts us, no longer soft and refreshing but the kind which stings your face, fills your boots and turns your skin to blotting paper.

To make matters worse, we miss the start of the track and have to retrace our steps, think we've found it but haven't, climb a wall or two, strike lucky, then crouch in a ditch to munch our soggy sandwiches. Anthea admires a patch of purple pansies but I am not in the mood for awe and wonder. The indistinct track acquires a metalled surface after a mile and a half and we pass three sinister bunker-like structures half-buried in earth ramparts, with high wire "keep-out" fencing around them, and a radio-communications mast. I am put in mind of the secret "Regional Seats of Government" which, as CND activists and "spies for peace", we hunted out and gleefully publicised in the 'sixties. Could this be another, so lonely and remote that even the Ministry of Defence has forgotten it?

We reach the Kendal-Kirkby Lonsdale road and there are Audland reminders all around us: Audlands Park and Low Audlands to our left, Far Audlands further south. Crosslands farm is straight ahead, a little house dwarfed by huge barns and outbuildings. It is said to contain a spice box bearing the initials of John and Ann Audland and the date 1656. A farmer's son, John was a linen-draper before becoming a Seeker minister and then a travelling Quaker, a man "of a sweet, ruddy and amiable countenance, and of a cheerful spirit... Immortality shined in his face and his voice was as thunder".

When, a few months later, Friends organised their first missionary forays to the benighted south, Audland's allotted task, with his friend John Camm, was to take Truth to Bristol and the west country. He seems to have done so with pentecostal fervour. "Full of dread and shining brightness on his countenance, he lifted up his voice as a trumpet and said, 'I proclaim spiritual war with the inhabitants of the earth, who are in the Fall and separation from God, and prophesy to the four winds of heaven'... But, ah! the seizings of souls, and prickings at heart which attended that season: some fell on the ground, others crying out under the sense of opening their states." The welcome Audland and Camm received from the Bristol Seekers was if anything even more enthusiastic than the one Fox received from their Westmorland gatherings. "We are with them from six in the morning", wrote Camm: "they will come to us before we get up: and unto eleven or sometimes one at night they will never be from us. Go into the fields, they will follow us, or go into any house, the house will be filled full, so that we cannot tell how we should get from them." It is a telling indication of the widespread thirst for pure waters from fresh fountains. But imprisonment was to follow for both missionary-agitators, and Audland too died early, before his 34th birthday.

Fox was at Crosslands for three nights, during which time he was visited by John Story who invited him to share a pipe of tobacco, saying "Come, all is ours". Tobacco was as fashionable among 1650s radicals as cannabis was among 1960s hippies. So-called "Ranters" saw God in all creation, "yea, in every stone", and certainly in tobacco. George Fox thought young Story "a forward, bold lad. Tobacco I did not take, but it came into my mind that the lad might think I had not unity with the creation, for I saw he had a flashy, empty notion of religion; so I took his pipe and put it to my mouth and gave it to him again to stop him lest his rude tongue should say I had not unity with the creation". It is an odd image: George Fox having a quick drag for religious reasons. Story's "flashy, empty" Ranterish notions soon gave way to Quakerism, but he was to lead an anti-Fox faction twenty years later. Indeed, Fox probably tells the smoking story years later to suggest that his rival, once a Ranter, was always a Ranter.

From Crosslands Fox moved on to Preston Patrick through the network of little lanes joining outlying farms and hamlets. We take a route which passes Warth, home of an early Friend, Richard Sill, and leads on to Camsgill, where lived John Camm, a prosperous farmer of whom it was said that "the world seemed to smile upon him, and riches... had exceedingly increased". Though of yeoman status, like his Seeker friend Gervase Benson he chose to style himself "husbandman" after joining Friends. He was in his late forties in 1652 and Camsgill had been his family's home for several generations. He rebuilt it when he married his wife Mabel, and together they carved a panel for the brideswain: JMC 1641. On his death in 1655, Mabel married Gervase Benson, whose first wife Dorothy had died in jail.

We approach the secluded farmhouse by dropping down through Hellgill, and meet its present occupant, Mr Gaitskell, who says his nickname is "the Chancellor", after Attlee's minister and successor as Labour leader. Yes, he tells us, the brideswain panel is still to be seen, though not in its original position, and yes, he does get the odd Quaker plodding down the lane to take a look. "I used to let parties inside, but my wife put a stop to that when we found a bus-load of children jumping around on the furniture". In her little "handbook for the 1652 country", *The Birthplace of Quakerism*, the late Elfrida Vipont Foulds writes that "to visit Camsgill is to stand at the roots of Pennsylvania, for John Camm, in the course of his travels, convinced Thomas Loe of Oxford, and Thomas Loe in his turn reached the heart of young William Penn". Not only did John and Mabel Camm and their son Thomas become travelling ministers for Friends, but so too did their serving maids Jane and Dorothy Waugh. Dorothy made a hazardous journey to America in 1657.

Hellgill, the deep and wooded ravine alongside the house, was said to have been used by Preston Patrick Friends for secret meetings after the second Conventicle Act prohibited public and open dissenting gatherings. Indeed, one of the charges laid against the Story faction by the Foxites during the split in the 'seventies was that through fear of informers they had forsaken open meetings and hidden themselves away in "gylls, woods and unaccustomed places".

Beyond Camsgill we take the access road, still unmetalled, towards

Preston Patrick. We might be back in the 17th century - till the 20th intrudes in the shape of the M6 motorway on a fly-over above us, and the angry roar of heavy lorries thundering past at seventy miles an hour. On past Preston Patrick Hall, a 14th century manor house where Thomas Camm, John's son, made regular appearances in the handsomely beamed courtroom at which his goods were ordered to be distrained no fewer than 33 times for non-payment of tithes and church taxes. Camm would perhaps have derived some satisfaction had he been able to foresee that the hall would become a Quaker family home.

Audland had two good reasons for bringing George Fox to Preston Patrick. First, the chapel there was the centre of the Westmorland Seekers, where Audland himself and Francis Howgill had assumed their joint ministry after Thomas Taylor's departure. Second, a general meeting of Seekers was held there every month (such monthly meetings would become an integral part of Quaker practice and organisation) and one was planned for the Wednesday of that week, June 16, so Fox would meet yet more of the separatist band. The Seekers met in the chapel itself, but on this occasion Fox waived his usual objection to preaching in steeplehouses, though he drew the line at entering the pulpit, choosing instead to take a seat on the back row with John Camm. Francis Howgill was conducting the service, but he was clearly overawed by Fox's presence. He "seemed uneasey, and pulled out his bible, & opened it, & stood up severall times, sitting downe againe and Closeing his Booke, A dread and feare being upon him yt he durst not begin to preach". After half an hour of silence, Fox got to his feet and put poor Howgill out of his misery. His message, to an audience of "sevrall hundreds", was the same as at Firbank and Sedbergh: "I... showed them that the end of my coming into that place was not to hold it up, no more than the apostles going into the Jewish synagogues and temple and Diana's was, but to bring them off all such things". The event was vividly recalled by John Camm's son half a century later: "A nottable day Indeede never to be forgotten by me, Thomas

Top: packhorse bridge near Downham.

Right: Yockenthwaite

Above: Semerwater.
Below: authentic 17th century road . . . and authentic 17th century door!

Right: *River Clough, Garsdale Foot, Sedbergh (the 'Sedgwick Trail').*

Below: *Camsgill . . . and glimpses of Lakeland hills from the south.*

Top: Draw-well (left)   Bouth Old Hall (right)
Middle: Dandra Garth, Garsdale (left)   Scale House, Grisedale (right)
Bottom: Burial ground, Firbank Fell

Camm... I being then present at that meeting, A schoole boy but aboute 12 years of age".

Preston was an ancient sacred place with a pre-Christian holy well claimed for the church and dedicated to St Gregory. It was a priest-town before the Norman conquest. A Premonstratensian abbey was sited here in the 12th century, but the canons perhaps found the place too busy and removed to remoter Shap. After the dissolution of the abbeys and monasteries, the property was one of many in the north-west acquired by the Wharton family. Philip Lord Wharton was one of the few powerful landowners who zealously supported the parliamentary and Independent cause: "new men" like Gervase Benson owed much to his protection and promotion, and his own steward, Philip Swale, would become a Friend. It seems likely that it was under Wharton's patronage that the old Church of England chapel here was taken over by the Seekers. In any case, Preston Patrick was one of those chapelries (Dent was another) which had somehow acquired the right over the centuries to have its minister nominated by its parishioners, so that a concentration of Seeker-Separatists here would account for the leadership of a Taylor, an Audland or a Howgill.

The present church is a rebuild. So too is the Quaker meetinghouse, which mostly dates from 1869, with the adjacent cottage added six or seven years later. Fox's own *Journal* account of his June 16th sermon "bringing off" the people from church worship adds that "after, they met in houses". For many years a custom-built meetinghouse wasn't necessary: the meeting simply did the rounds of farmhouse kitchens and barns. A meetinghouse was eventually built in 1691 on a rood of land bought by Thomas Camm for £6. It was modelled on Brigflatts, but without the double-storey porch.

Barbara Humphrey, resident in the cottage, has offered to put us up for the night, but she is not at home when, wet, cold, and dreaming of steak and chips, we knock on her door. Half an hour later a lady drives up, tells us she is a friend of Barbara's, that Barbara's car has broken down, and she has been sent to recover the key from a secret hiding place so that we can let ourselves in. Unhappily, the hiding place proves so secret that, despite Barbara's instructions to her friend, we cannot locate it, so our Good Samaritan drives us to her own home to revive us with the oil and wine of a nice cup of tea. Barbara eventually picks us up, and after a meal at the local we are joined by Eva Hopwood, a Quaker magistrate who sits on the Kendal bench with Anthea, and Barbara's daughter Laura, who is involved with the Franciscan order, the Poor Clares. Laura tells us how similar she finds Quaker and Franciscan spirituality. She probably thinks I am being flippant when I say I know St Clare primarily as the patron saint of television, but it is true. Pope Pius XII rather imaginatively bestowed the title after recalling that during her last illness she was said to have miraculously seen the midnight Christmas mass in the basilica of San Francesco from her room on the far side of town: mediaeval television, no doubt about it.

Before retiring, we wring out our socks, stuff old newspapers into our soggy boots and promise to be good for ever and ever if only we are granted just one little glimpse of a proper flaming June on the morrow.

Sedition and Subversion

DAY 11. Preston Patrick-Kendal-Tullythwaite

Sunshine! Dawn promised a day which, if not exactly flaming, looked to be warm and dry - which was more than could be said for our boots. The paper we had stuffed into them was now as soggy as the leather. But we eased them on, and were soon on our way.

First we detoured to take a more considered look at Preston Patrick Hall. We were met there by Jennifer Pumphrey who is not only owner of the Hall but hereditory lord of the manor: very much a working lord, too, in green wellies and get-on-with-it clothes. She kindly gave us the run of the place, especially the second-storey courtroom, reached from the courtyard by a flight of outside steps. For centuries this was the "big house" around which a whole little local world revolved. Today it is a beautiful, dignified relic of the past, but the modern world has caught up with it in the shape of the motorway. Though a few hundred yards distant over flat farmland, the hum and drone of traffic never quite disappears.

Fox stayed the night at the Camms' before striding on, apparently alone again, to Kendal. His route no doubt took him, as it takes us, through Goose Green, a cluster of houses in one of which lived pipe-smoking John Story, and through Gatebeck to Low Park farm, where the great anti-slavery Quaker campaigner John Woolman would stay in 1772. At Birkrigg Park we take the old bridleway over the hill to Storth End, passing a tiny walled enclosure used by Preston Patrick Friends as a burial ground. John Camm and John Audland were buried here, but only two broken stones are visible today, neither of them theirs since Friends were not given to raising stones, even the simplest, plainest kind, before the 18th century. The bridleway itself is well wooded, overgrown, and carpeted with masses of pink-mauve cranesbill.

At Storth End we turn north along the main A65 road, stopping for a soup and roll at the Punchbowl, Barrows Green, then passing first the Iron Age Castlesteads fort high on the Helm to our right, then the site of a Roman fort on our left. The dales are behind us, the Lakes ahead, and Kendal's traffic is all around us.

Mid-seventeenth century Kendal had a population of around 2000, making it the largest town in Westmorland, more populous than the county-town, Appleby. Sir Daniel Flemming of Rydal described it in 1671 as "the chief town for largeness, neatness, buildings and trade in this county... a place of excellent manufactury and for civility ingenuity and industry so surpassing that... it deservedly carries a great name". The town was "seated in very good air, and its healthfulness is improved partly by the cleanliness of the people, and partly by its situation on a hillside, the river carrying away whatever filthiness the descending rain washes out of it". Even Celia Fiennes, who was generally appalled by the hovels she saw on her 1682 journey through the area, thought Kendal "a good trading town... rich and populous". While both these accounts refer to the post-war Restoration period, there is no reason to suppose Kendal was substantially different in 1652, though its recovery from the civil wars would be only just begun.

Already Kendal was an industrial centre, the industry being wool. Wool was collected from farms in the outlying villages, washed by one set of workers, carded or combed by another, then put out again for spinning into yarn, then dyed, then put out to weavers or knitters before being collected in again by the wholesale merchants or chapmen. As local poet Richard Branthwaite, who called himself Dapper Dick, wrote in 1615,

"Each plies his work, one carves, another spins,
One to the studdle goes, the next begins
To ravell for new wefte, thus more delay
But make their webb up 'gainst each market day."

Local "worsted", though derived from the worst grade of wool, was common throughout the kingdom. A statute of Richard II in 1390 referred to "Kendal Cloth" being made by "common custom... in diverse Counties of England". A "Kendall cote" was the summer wear of a serving man in Elizabeth's day, but better-quality gowns were also made from Kendal cloths. Treasury accounts of 1497 refer to the purchase of "grene Kentdalee", and in 1505 the royal tailors bought "ten ells of Kentdale to be one cote to the King". When Katherine Parr of Kendal castle married Henry VIII she gave him a lover's gift of a coat of Kendal cloth which so pleased him, John Satchell tells us in *Kendal on Tenterhooks*, that he ordered another for himself and one for his fool. William Camden noted in 1600 that the inhabitants of Kendal "carry forward an extensive trade for woollen goods known in all parts of England", and later in the century Thomas Machell recorded that Kendal "cottons" (which, confusingly, were woollens), in cloth or knitted stockings, were sent to London every week by four carriers who set out every Monday in turn. There was a lively export trade, with goods being taken by packhorse for shipping from Southampton even in the sixteenth century, and perhaps earlier. Over a 15th century wool merchant's window was inscribed the couplet,

"I thank God and ever schal
It is the shepe hath payd for all".

One and a half centuries after Fox's visit it was largely Quakers who were thanking God for the sheep which paid for all, since Friends came to dominate the town's trade and government, much to the disgust of the old landed gentry.

Because so much of the work was cottage-based in the 17th century and earlier, each family unit had a certain independence, and this is one important factor which helps account for the marked tendency towards political radicalism found in most textile centres. Although the surrounding countryside was dominated by royalist gentry (with the important exception of Lord Wharton), Kendal was puritan and parliamentarian at the onset of civil war in 1642. Gervase Benson was mayor in 1643 and Henry Masey, a presbyterian protégé of Wharton, was vicar.

This changed when the weight of the Scots army was thrown into the struggle. The Scots too were presbyterian - but first and foremost they were Scots, the traditional border enemies of the dalesfolk, hated as raiders and reivers all. Kendalians bitterly resented having Scots troops billeted on them, or being taxed to feed these unwanted allies. Benson and his friends warned the army high command that they were finding it almost impossible to hold the town for the Parliamentary party, and the situation only eased when the Scots changed sides to make common cause with the king. By 1652, with Charles Stuart defeated and beheaded, the Scots back in their own land and Cromwell firmly in control in England, Kendal was war-weary and politically cynical. It was also hungry. A succession of three appalling harvests had reduced the poorer population to near starvation level. The religious confusion which marked the nation as a whole was by no means lacking here. Masey, the vicar, a stern advocate of presbyterian discipline and conformity during the war, had swallowed Cromwell's Covenant in order to hold his living, Thomas Taylor had attacked clerical "sprinkling" in street meetings, and from 1647 the Seekers had been holding their Quaker-like silent meetings. And of course there was growing popular agitation for the restoration of such popular pastimes as dancing, feasting, drinking and play-going which the more zealous puritan kill-joys had declared inimical to a godly community.

Crossing Nether Bridge to enter Kirkbie Kendal via Kirkland,

George Fox found himself in High Street, which at a rise in the ground becomes Stricklandgate, dropping down to river level again at the north end of town. The town is wedged in a narrow valley bottom, with steep fellside on the west and the river Kent to the east. Kirkland has the wide-naved parish church and a mediaeval Abbot Hall, rebuilt in the 18th century. High Street and Stricklandgate were lined in Fox's day with thatched, timber-framed houses and workshops, backed by long burgage plots, strips of garden and orchard destined in later centuries to become a warren of yards and back lanes. Finkle Street - the name supposedly derived from Old Scandinavian for elbow, and already encountered in Sedbergh - ran then as now down to Stramongate and over the river by Stramons Bridge towards the already deserted and ruined Norman castle, once home of the Parr family which provided Henry VIII with his final wife. Presiding over the market place in the centre of town was the Moot Hall - court, local government centre and public meeting place - which was to survive for another three centuries, till fire gutted it in the 1960s.

Fox must have noticed the swathes of cloth stretched on wooden tenterhooks on the open fields by the river and high on the western fellside. (Their positions are clearly marked by John Speed in his 1614 town map). Thirteen tenters were still there in 1883, and traces of tentering terrace still survive on Prickley Fell and Kendal Green. The frames were about four and a half feet high and up to a hundred yards long, set in parallel rows. Here the treated cloths, bleached in vats of urine and washed in the river, were set out to dry - though, as the town's most recent historian Roger Bingham acknowledges, "any attempt to dry anything outside in Kendal has always been an exercise of hope over experience". He even suggests that "the expression 'to be on tenterhooks', meaning jumpy and anxious, could derive from the need of the shearman to be up and down, coming and going all the time to check whether his cloth was either being soaked or frizzled". Bingham notes that no fewer than 44 mayors between 1575 and 1636 were chapmen, shearmen or otherwise engaged in the wool trade. Stricklandgate housed 26 shearmen in the 1690s, while Stramongate was the home of independent weavers. (Bingham's one reference to George Fox in Kendal gives rise to my favourite misprint: Fox is unaccountably indexed as the "Fox and George Inn").

Fox walked through a clean town if the by-laws were properly observed. One order stipulated that dung-heaps were to be kept only on the "backesydes" or rear gardens, and that "tymber, loggs, wood or stoones" were not to be stacked on High Street or Finkle Street. Every householder was responsible for paving the area in front of his own premises and for "cowling" or raking up garbage. Every house was required to have a chimney. George Fox would certainly have approved orders, which long predated the republic, regulating plays and other "delights and fantasyes" and forbidding "cardes, dyce, tables bowells" and other gambling games in the alehouses, of which, however, there were many.

The *Journal* tells us very little about Fox's short time in Kendal: only that "a meeting was appointed" for him in the Moot Hall, and that, in an echo of the Story story, "one Cocks met me in the street and would have given me a roll of tobacco, for people were much given to smoking tobacco, so I accepted of his love, but denied it". Tobacco is said to have been introduced to Westmorland by Thomas Tolson of nearby Staveley, who reputedly built his home, Tolson Hall, on the profits of his trans-Atlantic trade with Virginia. There are mentions in the Chamberlain's accounts of "Christo tobaco" and "Varinas" from the 1620s onwards, "Christo" being a cheap brand imported from St Kitts and "Varinas" an expensive one from Venezuela. Tolson's contemporary "Drunken Barnaby", another local poet, cursed the men of Kirkland as

"... vermin
Who'd rather smoke a pipe than hear a sermon".

He was particularly contemptuous of

"Great men's kitchens where I suppose
Less smoke comes from their kitchens than from their nose."

We do not know where George Fox stayed or who he met, though we can be fairly sure that he made himself known to the Independent party and the town's separatist groups. That he must have caused a stir which, uncharacteristically, he fails to record in the *Journal*, is suggested by the hint given later by Margaret Fell that she first heard of him when news reached her in distant Swarthmoor Hall of a powerful travelling preacher in a white hat who was setting the town alight.

*

Our destination in Kendal is the meetinghouse in Stramongate, where we are to meet Jill from Border Television who wants to interview us. Jill clearly doesn't know her Quakers from her Shakers, but that is probably an advantage since most of the viewers who catch a glimpse of us between the shredded wheat and lager commercials will know as little and care much less. She has us walk up and down a bit, in medium and long shot, with a close-up of our boots, then has us chatting outside the meetinghouse. We try to talk in sound-bites, but are not very good at it.

A meetinghouse was first built on a burgage plot here when the site was bought in 1687 by a tanner Friend, Thomas Wilson, next to his tan-pits. The smell must have been horrendous. The original building was extended several times over the next thirty years, and even a seating capacity of 600 was considered insufficient for the accommodation of a Northern Counties Yearly Meeting in 1716. In 1815 the place was pulled down and a large new elegant architect-designed building erected, advertising the changed wealth and social standing of the local Quaker community since Fox's day. One innovation was that there was "some plan for warming the building with hot air", but this seems not to have worked since ten years later a more conventional heating system was installed. The new meetinghouse held 850 people in comfort - but almost before the plaster was dry the fellowship was racked by schism and resignations which cut membership down to about 130. By the 1990s it was much smaller still, and the Society faced difficult decisions - not eased by the fact that, as a listed building, the structure was virtually unsaleable to any commercial interest since it could be neither demolished nor disfigured by radical alteration.

Rescue came in the shape of a bright idea. In 1981 Anne Wynn-Wilson was running a children's class in a gloomy room in the meetinghouse at Taunton, Somerset. The room needed cheering up and it was put to the children that they might paint some colourful pictures of Fox's journeys to hang on the walls. But one young lad, knowing of his teacher's interest in embroidery, suggested that instead of painting the pictures they should have a go at embroidering them. Anne had been studying the 11th century Bayeux Tapestry and was immediately fired by the vision of an embroidered tapestry telling the story of Quakerism.

She set about creating a craft project that would come to involve more than four thousand Friends in ten countries. Instead of a single long strip-cartoon tapestry, as at Bayeux, the Quaker story would be told in 77 separate panels, each 25 inches by 21. A common style of picturing and lettering was devised, 120 natural dye colours selected, a variety of stitches employed to suit different ages and abilities, and the whole unified by use of the ancient method of laying threads called Bayeux Point.

Work on the panels proceeded throughout the eighties and in 1989 those that were finished were exhibited in Aberdeen Art Gallery, the Royal Festival Hall in London, at Bayeux, and subsequently in Lincoln Cathedral and the House of Commons. The project caught the imagination of many beyond the Quaker sub-culture. But it needed a permanent home. Where better than Kendal? So the Stramongate meetinghouse was converted to house the Quaker Tapestry as a permanent exhibition: a celebration of Quaker work, a novel addition to Lakeland's tourist industry, an imaginative exercise in "outreach" - and a remarkable work of art.

So we call to see the Tapestry and meet Chris Nash, the energetic administrator who has the tough task of both making it work artistically and making it pay for itself. Someone has told us he is a descendant of the Camms of Camsgill. Thomas and John and Mabel would be proud of him. We mingle with a Women's Institute coach party which has scheduled a one-hour stop. Some are fascinated by the stitches, some by the Quakerism, but all are fascinated. When the coach driver calls "Come on, ladies, time's up", one old lady complains "Hey, I've only got to panel ten, I'm not going yet!" And the coach eventually leaves half an hour late.

There are panels on Quaker history, on "publishing Truth", on meetings and meetinghouses, on trades and industries and science and arts, on Quakers in criminal justice and prison reform, on peace and conscientious objection, relief work, abolition of slavery, and Friends around the world. There is a ruminative Fox in leather breeches at Fenny Drayton, a Hobbit-like Fox with his back to us on Firbank Fell, and a brave Fox facing a devilish mob of lewd fellows of the baser sort at Ulverston. A panel on Margaret Fell and her household, embroidered by children, depicts a happy family with the conspicuous exception of Margaret's son George, who rejected Quakerism. He is seen alone in the corner, the picture of sulky discontent. Even Karl Marx has a walk-on part in one panel, describing Fox's friend John Bellers as "a very phenomenon in the history of political economy". Bellers proposed a united Europe, a world council of churches, employment exchanges - "the poor without imployment are as rough diamonds: their worth is unknown" - universal education, democratic elections, a national health service and the abolition of the death penalty for theft. He was ignored, but wrote before his death in 1725: "...if a man shall not be heard in the age and country he lives in... he may be more minded in other countries or succeeding generations".

A few weeks earlier I had been asked to write up the official opening of the exhibition for *The Friend*. I had approached the task without much relish, unconvinced that the huge diversity of Quakerism could be adequately represented in 77 cartoons, and inwardly kicking against the reduction of a great revolutionary heritage to mere embroidery. But I was won over. There are sometimes too many words on too-crowded panels, the necessity of imposing a common style has probably inhibited individual creativity, and because each panel must be self-contained the vital flow and movement of the Bayeux continuous strip is missing. But the Quaker Tapestry is nevertheless a triumph, giving a new lease of life to the meetinghouse built by the descendants of those who heard George Fox preach in the Moot Hall in June 1652.

*

When Fox left Kendal, striking out westwards towards Underbarrow, he was not alone. "Several people came along with me, and great disputing I had with them, especially Edward Burrough", who was soon to play a critical leadership role in the new movement. Burrough had just turned 19 when he met Fox, undoubtedly at one of the Seeker meetings, describing himself as "a Puritan and a Roundhead". At 17 he had joined a separatist congregation, believing himself one of God's elect: "Whom God loves once, he loves for ever". Perhaps this Calvinism lay at the heart of his disputing with Fox as they took the high road over Scout Scar. But not only was the young man convinced: he threw himself into his new life's work so wholeheartedly that, according to Howgill, during the ten years from convincement to his death in Newgate jail in 1662 he never had one week to himself. "He was bold and manly, dexterous and fervent, and what he took in hand he did it with his might". His disgusted parents disowned him.

Burrough is seen by some historians as the early movement's chief political spokesman, even its political leader. He made contact with the defeated "True Leveller" leader Gerrard Winstanley in London in 1654, reporting that "Wilstandley sayes he beleeves we are sent to perfect that worke which fell in their handes. He hath bene with us". The two men shared the view that Quakerism was a movement of protest against the suppression of the Good Old Cause - or, more precisely, was itself the Good Old Cause revived - though Burrough's cause was a spiritualised radical democracy, Winstanley's a spiritualised communism.

It has been suggested that the subject over which Fox and Burrough disputed was the use of force. This betrays a common misunderstanding of early Quakerism. Burrough was certainly no pacifist, either before or immediately after his Quaker conversion. But Fox was no pacifist either, not for another ten years, and not only is there very little trace of political pacifism (as distinct from an impressive refusal to return violence for violence in private life) in 1650s Quakerism but, on the contrary, there is abundant evidence that the movement supported Cromwell's military conquest and backed the army as the instrument of revolutionary change. "We look for a New Earth, as well as a New Heaven", wrote Burrough, and it clearly never occurred to him, or to most Friends, that there was any way of creating a New Earth other than by revolutionary politics, in a day when politics and force were inseparable. With Samuel Fisher, Burrough addressed meetings of "some hundreds of officers and souilders" in 1659, reporting fears in enemy quarters that "ye hole armie should be seduced to follow us". At the same time he assured the Army Council that, if they carried through their programme of radical reform, "Oh then we should rejoice, and our lives would not be Deare to lay downe". He was proud the Quaker preacher-reformer like himself was considered "a sower of sedition, or a subverter of the laws, a turner of the world upside down, a pestilent fellow".

There were Quakers in Cromwell's army and navy, but no-one - including Fox - suggested that their position was anomalous. Indeed, by 1659, with the threat of the restoration of monarchy, Quakers were clamouring to join the army, and General Monck was trying to keep them out, not because he doubted their willingness to fight but because he feared their militancy. Colonel Benson's close friend and colleague on the bench, Anthony Pearson, tried to raise a military force of northern Quakers to resist the Restoration. Fox himself seems to have been side-lined at this critical period. He claimed later that he "forbad" Quaker participation in the military resistance to the Restoration, but that was after the event. No doubt the failure of Quakers and their allies to create a "New Earth" by political and military means was a crucial factor in swinging Fox and the whole movement over to the clear pacifist stance of the historic 1660s "Peace Testimonies". But in 1652 that was all a decade and a counter-revolution away.

*

The land to the west of Kendal rises steeply to the long rocky escarpment of Scout Scar. We reach it by way of the narrow, often stepped lanes of Fellside, open pasture and tentering grounds above the burgage plots in Fox's day, later so densely built over that the area became a notorious slum, rife with cholera and typhoid till cleared in the late 19th and renovated in the 20th century. Today this is the prettiest part of the town, virtually unknown to the tens of thousands of visitors who do not think to explore beyond the traffic-bound high street. The road over the Scar is the ancient route north of the Sands to Furness, followed as a packhorse track by Fox, turnpiked in 1763, much altered and improved since, and still down for further re-engineering in the county's roads programme.

The roads of Westmorland were notoriously bad in the seventeenth century. Kendal was not an easy town to get to or get away from. Three soldiers in 1614 battled through "such wayes as we hope we shall never see againe, being no other than climing and stony and nothing but boggs and myres and the tops of those high hills, so as wee were enforced to keep to these narrow loose stony base ways though never so troublesome and dangerous". And that was the Great North Road, now the main A6! Nor did they think much of the locals, whose directions they could not understand. "If a man markes his way not very well, and so chance to be out a wea bit, the rude, rustical and ill-bred people... have not will enough to put us in. We could not understand them nor neyther would they understand us". Note the We *could* not and the They *would* not!

An overpass takes us across the modern western bypass and on to the great limestone scar, towering above surrounding slate. Scout Scar is said to have been a natural boundary between the English farming the better soils of the Kent valley and the Norsemen rearing stock on the poorer acid land below the Scar to the west. Perhaps scouts from both communities used the tops to spy on their neighbours. Once we are free of the birch, oak, sycamore and spruce cover, the views across to the blue-grey Lakeland hills literally take the breath away. Below us is the dip and roll, the humps and bumps of green farmland dotted with friendly farmhouses. The Scar shelters wild rock-roses, pignut, meadow rue and dropwort - "good", say the old herbalists, "for the stone, gravel, and the stoppage of urine".

We follow the road down to the scattered village of Underbarrow, looking for Tullythwaite Hall, the home of one of the leading landowners of the parish, Miles Bateman, with whom Fox lodged the night. Bateman had invited the local "priest and a many professors" to meet his by now notorious guest, and inevitably there was "a great deal of disputing". Supper was laid on, but Fox decided he was not to eat with them, suggesting they organise a public meeting in the steeplehouse on the morrow. "A great deal of reasoning they had about it, and some were for it and some were against it". The argument was still raging the next day. Fox took an early morning stroll, followed by his still-disputing hosts, and there, he writes, "as I was walking upon the top of the bank there came several poor people, travellers, that I saw were in necessity". The argumentative church-folk "gave them nothing but said they were cheats. But when they were gone into their breakfast it grieved me to see such hard-hearted people amongst professors that I ran after the poor people a matter of a quarter of a mile and gave them some money".

Back in Tullythwaite Hall, the professors seem to have quickly agreed to call a meeting, but when they went out to tell Fox they were disturbed to see him a full quarter of a mile off. "They said I could not have gone so far in such an instant except I had wings; and then the meeting was like to have been stopped, they were so filled with strange thoughts, and that quite put the meeting out of their minds, and they were against it; for they could not believe I could have gone so far in such a short space". But one of their number, Stephen Hubbersty - who was to join Friends - insisted that the meeting go ahead. "Many of Crook and Underbarrow were convinced that day", though the priest "fled away". The chief constable debated the scriptures with Fox in the steeplehouse yard when the meeting was over. Bateman himself was convinced and later gave a piece of land at Crag, north of Underbarrow, as a burial ground - "yett afterwards he being but young in years went up to London, and letting his mind run after noveltyes, the soules enimy prevailed over him more and more till att Length he quite Revoulted from truth... and when he came home pulled downe one side of the burrying-place wall againe and layed it to his field to be plowed as formerly". (But it may have been Miles's son, who was also named Miles: or even another Miles Bateman, since Batemans abounded, and an uncommon number seem to have been called Miles).

George Fox's charity towards the poor travellers, apart from emphasising that he matched deeds to words, raises a fascinating question, the answer to which is something of a mystery. What did he do for money, given that he seems to have abandoned for ever both his trade as a cobbler and his former work as a shepherd? Several times he tells us in the *Journal* that he refused money from well-wishers, and several times he gives some away. Passing through Kendal again on his way back from Swarthmoor, he notes that he had silver in his pocket and "was moved to throw it out amongst the people as I was going up the street". He must also have paid for much of his food and lodgings on his journeys, especially when he stayed at inns rather than with friends. From time to time he hired a horse. Given that there were no banks in his day, did he always carry cash around with him? Was there in the depths of those leather breeches a pocket stuffed with coins? And where did it come from in the first place?

Fox's American biographer Larry Ingle has helped provide answers to the latter question. His parents appear to have been well-off: rich enough to leave significant sums of money to each of their children, and to pledge a £100 bond to the Derby authorities when George was jailed there in 1650. Fox admitted that he had "wherewith both to keep myself from being chargeable to others and to administer something to the necessity of others", and his family confirmed that he had left home with a "great" sum, perhaps a legacy from a relative. The vicar of his home parish charged that when he left his pockets were "full of gold and silver". Critics within the Quaker movement later accused him of salting away between £1200 and £1300 and hiding it from the tithe collector. He denied the charge of cheating the taxman, but not of possessing the money, which he called his "birthright". After his marriage to Margaret Fell he was scrupulous in refusing to share her considerable wealth. But from the start, as Ingle points out, "his inherited wealth placed him among that tiny and fortunate minority of English people whose lives were free from the need to earn a livelihood by the work of their hands and the sweat of their brow". Few of the "hireling priests" whom Fox castigated for selling the gospel belonged to that fortunate minority.

In the hamlet of Tullythwaite we think we have located Miles Bateman's home and are delighted to find that Mrs Mairie Parker there does evening meal and bed and breakfast. Only when we are inside do we learn that Tullythwaite Hall is down the road: this is

Tullythwaite House. But we have taken a fancy to Mrs Parker's elegant dwelling, as we do to her mushrooms in garlic, chicken breasts in stilton sauce and rhubarb crumble. Historical authenticity is all very well, but it has its limits. So we stay put, reassured that Fox's B & B is only a few minutes walk away.

An Earthly Paradise

DAY 12. Underbarrow-Newton

There can be no doubt that, by now, George Fox was deliberately making for Swarthmoor Hall, Ulverston. Had he been content merely to strengthen the relationship with the Westmorland Seekers he would have remained in their Kendal catchment area. Had he decided to follow up his Westmorland successes by taking Truth to the numerous Cumberland Seekers he would have struck out northwards. Instead, he turned south towards the sands of Morecambe Bay and the remote hamlets of Furness, where the Roundhead Judge Thomas Fell kept order for Cromwell and the republic.

But Swarthmoor was still two or three days distant, and Fox was clearly in no great hurry to get there as he was prepared to follow up other contacts which took him away from the most direct route. From Underbarrow he followed the road to Crosthwaite, probably in the company of "an old man, James Dickinson", who lived there and whose hospitality he accepted. Then he left the main road to follow the tracks through the Winster valley to High Newton, to meet one James Taylor whose home we have not been able to identify (though Taylors still live hereabouts). Here there were "many professors" gathered to hear him. Next day, Sunday June 20, he seems to have walked three miles north to Staveley-in-Cartmel, where he was brutally attacked in the church while attempting to cap the minister's sermon with his own, followed by a six-mile trek southwards again to preach at Lindale church that same afternoon, ending up, in all probability, back at James Taylor's at Newton Hall. We shall cover the same ground, half today and half tomorrow.

Before leaving Underbarrow we take a look at the real Tullythwaite Hall, home of Miles Bateman. Virtually nothing remains of the old house Fox stayed in: the present hall is a nineteenth century rebuild. It is said to contain a cast-iron fireback depicting Adam and Eve and the Tree of Knowledge, and even some of Bateman's furniture, but as we arrive the man we take to be the current owner is driving off on his tractor so we don't get to see the relics. The chapel where Fox preached has since been pulled down and replaced by the modern church, but Chapel Lane remains defiantly unmetalled.

Underbarrow itself is a delightful, sprawling township with several 17th century houses, including a former corn mill which is now the village pub. Miles Birkett, the miller, was an early convert and travelled widely before joining the Wilkinson-Story group in its criticism of Fox's later leadership. Another convert was Miles Halhead of Mountjoy, a farm at the northern end of the village. Halhead was also a compulsive traveller, recorded over the next three years as agitating in Berkshire, Dorset, Devon and Somerset in the south, and in Durham, Cumberland, Yorkshire and Scotland in the north. He was jailed in Newcastle in 1653, where he made himself such a "Burdensome stone" to the authorities that he was released, just to be rid of him. The following year he was twice locked up in Berwick, once for "speaking to ye Mayr in his own shop". ("Shop" here probably means place - i.e. the mayor's official rooms. Older Cumbrians still use shop for place, as in "fire-shop"). In 1655 he was jailed for 13 months in Exeter as a suspected Jesuit because his testimony against swearing led him to refuse the new Oath of Abjuration denying the Pope's authority and the doctrine of transubstantiation. Miles was so long absent from Mountjoy that his longsuffering wife complained "Would to God my husband had been a drunkard, then I should have known where to find him - in an alehouse!".

Yet another Miles, Miles Hubbersty and his brother Stephen, were also Underbarrow men, probably from Hubbersty Head about three miles west of the village. Miles was drowned when, "rideing ovr The Sands wth severall in Company, he fell of his horse into the water". Altogether, six of the 66 men and women who came to be known as the "Valiant Sixty" or "First Publishers of Truth" came from Underbarrow, and no fewer than 40 from the area covered by the Westmorland Seekers. We have a keen sense of walking a landscape and breathing an air deeply impregnated with Quaker inspiration and adventure.

Skirting Lords Lot, we reach Crosthwaite where, at the Punch Bowl inn, we have arranged to meet two friends, Wendy and John Cooke. John is an artist who has turned his tiny studio-gallery in Dent into a mecca for collectors seeking distinctive watercolours and oils of the dales and Lakes. This is a saturated market: there are any number of painters turning out chocolate-box views for the tourists. John has survived and prospered because his work has a quality few contemporary painters can match, particularly in his often magical use of sunlight and shadow and a striking play of light in his waterscapes. Working in an unashamedly representational style, true to every detail of topography, he nevertheless projects a profoundly personal view: no-one can mistake a John Cooke. His collectors not only make their regular pilgrimages to Dent but also follow him down to London for his annual February exhibition there. We have invited John and Wendy to join us for the morning, partly because we thoroughly enjoy their company but also because I hope to inveigle John into doing some line drawings to enliven these serried ranks of print.

George Fox could have taken either the eastern or western bank of the Winster on his way to High Newton. We leave the Punch Bowl by a bridleway and choose the east side under the massive limestone cliffs of Whitbarrow Scar. At this point, Anthea develops a sudden brilliant insight into the mind of George Fox. He couldn't pass a great hill without having to go atop of it, could he?. Surely he would have taken the ridge along the top of the scar rather than the valley road below, wouldn't he? It occurs to me that Anthea's enthusiasm for a climb may owe as much to her desire to visit the Cumbria Wildlife Trust's hill-top Whitbarrow Nature Reserve as to her deep understanding of Fox's psychology, but John and Wendy cast their votes for the heights, so we leave the road at Broad Oak to follow a path which turns abruptly at Fell Edge - an old farmhouse recently gutted by fire - to wind its steep way through hanging woods to the top of the escarpment. No sooner are we on the windswept summit when the rains come sweeping in. Within minutes we are soaked. Huddled together under a lone tree, we pluck drier clothing from our backpacks and press on. The rain turns to hail, playing darts on our faces. Then the gods change their minds and bathe us in sunshine. This is summer on the top storey of north-west England.

There are few defined paths here and we are off-course for the reserve proper, but the turf beneath our feet is spangled with tormentil and wild strawberry. Rockrose, dark red helleborine and birdsfoot trefoil are all abundant, and there is more than one bank where the wild thyme grows. We have just missed the flushes of cowslips and purple and white orchids which are the glory of the place in the late spring, and the rare northern brown argus butterflies known to breed here refuse to honour us with an appearance. But a pair of ravens cavort above, perhaps to compensate us for missing the main attractions, perhaps just for the sheer hell of it.

If Fox had come over the top he would have had to find a way down at the southern tip of the escarpment, so we set out to do the same. But more easily said than done: the ridge is six miles long and the drop becomes more precipitous the further south you go. So after an hour of fruitless exploration we give up and retrace our steps to Fell

Edge and the valley road. Wendy and John leave us here to return to Crosthwaite, John's mind a gallery of potential pictures. We have a good dozen miles to go, over more high ground.

The little road south takes us through an enchanting pastoral landscape which even Wordsworth couldn't easily find words for. The Winster burbles poetry on our right and fresh green birch and juniper woodland softens the scar above us on our left. The scattered farms here seem deserted, but the luxuriant meadows and well-cropped pastures assure us they are not. Across the river are the hills of Cartmel Fell, dotted with settlements boasting names like Swallow Mire, Burblethwaite, Strawberry Bank, Sow How and Thorphinsty. Some farmhouses are whitewashed and glitter like diamonds in emerald. Wordsworth detested whitewash:

"The objections to white, as a colour, in large spots or masses in landscape, especially in a mountainous country, are insurmountable. In Nature, pure white is scarcely ever found but in small objects, such as flowers; or in those which are transitory, as the clouds, foam of rivers, and snow... Five or six white houses, scattered over a valley, by their obtrusiveness, dot the surface and divide it into triangles, or other mathematical figures, haunting the eye, and disturbing that repose which might otherwise be perfect. I have seen a single white house materially impair the majesty of a mountain; cutting away, by a harsh separation, the whole of its base, below the point on which the house stood."

He would have preferred the colour and texture (if not the crude discomforts) of Lakeland buildings as Fox must have seen them, with natural surfaces of rough stone overgrown with lichens, mosses and ferns, organic structures which might "rather be said to have grown than to have been erected". If they had to be artificially coloured, Wordsworth preferred "something between a cream and a dust-colour, commonly called stone colour". His ideal homes were those which, "by their colour and their shape, affectingly direct the thoughts to that tranquil course of Nature and simplicity, along which the humble-minded inhabitants have, through so many generations, been led". Fox would perhaps have approved the veneration of simplicity, if not of Nature.

Wordsworth's *Guide to the Lakes* rhapsodises the dales communities as "a perfect Republic of Shepherds and Agriculturalists", a "pure Commonwealth, the members of which existed in the midst of a powerful empire, like an ideal society or an organized community, whose constitution had been imposed and regulated by the mountains which protected it. Neither high-born nobleman, knight, nor esquire, was here" in this "almost visionary mountain republic". It is not hard to understand how Quaker-republican independence, equality and simplicity caught the mood and tradition of such places. With uncharacteristic modesty, when it came to describing such earthly paradises in verse Wordsworth chose not his own but Spenser's lines:

"Into that forest farre they thence him led
Where was their dwelling in a pleasant glade
With mountains round about environed
And mighty woods which did the valley shade,
And like a stately theatre it made,
Spreading itself into a spacious plaine;
And in the midst a little river plaide,
Emongst the puny stones which seemed to 'plaine
With gentle murmure that his course they did restraine.

Beside the same a dainty place there lay,
Planted with mirtle trees and laurels green,
In which the birds sang many a lovely lay
Of God's high praise, and of their sweet loves teene,
As it an earthly paradise had beene..."

Approaching Witherslack, we turn westward to cross the river below Slate Hill. George Fox himself would probably have bypassed Witherslack: the diehard royalist Barwick family was a powerful influence here. Newton Fell towers ahead of us and we must cross it. We plod up the steep, hard road to the top - only 500 feet, but the start is not much above sea level. We are rewarded by views across the Sands and behind us to the Howgills and distant Ingleborough. We try to pick out the bump on the skyline that would be Pendle but mists have snatched it from us.

At the summit we join a road from the right, along which lies the appropriately named Height meetinghouse. Tired as we are, we decide to take a look, and plod the extra mile and a half to reach it. Strikingly similar to Brigflatts, which preceded it by two years, Height, or Cartmel Fell, was built in 1677 on land given by Lawrence Newton, probably of Newton Hall, who also met much of the cost. His initials are carved above the arch of the porch: L.N. ANNO DOMINI 1677. As David Butler comments in *Quaker Meeting Houses of the Lake Counties*, the building is "a rare survival from the period before the Act of Toleration of 1689, as for many years before this date dissenters were not allowed to own or to use a meeting house and few were therefore built". The local meeting's minute book itemises the main building costs:

"Wood 29. 0. 0
Limestones, leading and breaking them 2. 2. 0
Coals to burn them with 1. 6. 6
Stones, flags and sand, laths and spars 3. 19. 1
Freestone 5. 15. 2
The wrights' diet 4. 9. 7
Malt and drink at the Rearing 8. 8
Getting moss and plaster making etc 1. 2. 2
Three trees and drawing them
    and leading boards and joists 2. 16. 6
Meat and drink for slate and
    sand leaders at several times 16. 9
Glass and casements 3. 10. 6
Hair for plaster, and a barel 1. 7. 7
Slates and dressing of them 7. 0. 0
Nails, smiths work and iron 4. 6. 4
Mens wages . . . . 25. 14. 3"

It is interesting that the single most costly item was the wood for panelling and, perhaps, furniture. After that came labour costs, suggesting that Height meeting did not have the luxury enjoyed at Brigflatts of a voluntary labour force. Limestone was burnt for mortar and plaster, flags were laid on sand for flooring (unlike Brigflatts which made do with a beaten-earth floor for some years), freestone was used for windows and doorways, entire trees supplied the roof beams, and both hair and moss seem to have been used to bind the plaster. And even sober-minded Quakers, the minute-book reveals, enjoyed a ceremonial drink at "the Rearing". Stables were added in 1691, a cottage in 1712, and the front-elevation windows enlarged and converted to sashes in 1772. Today, the meetinghouse is an artist's studio, its features lovingly preserved.

Across the road is the old burial ground protected by a high stone wall and reached by what, if this were a church, would be called a lych-gate. Smothering the neat rows of rounded gravestones are masses of now headless daffodils.

But for us it is one more heave, taking a track descending the western slopes of the fell, past two reservoirs (where we are met and accompanied for some way by a garrulous stonechat) down to Ayside, just north of High Newton. We are booked in with Tina Luke at Browside Cottage, but Anthea can barely hobble down to dinner on ankles which are hot and swollen. We calculate that we have walked 22 miles today, with some steep climbing to boot. Fox would have done as much, holding a couple of meetings on the way, perhaps taking a beating, and then being content to sleep under a wall with nothing more than a sip from the beck to refresh him. If his ankles hurt, he never mentions it in the *Journal*.

Headlong Over a Wall

DAY 13. Newton-Lindale

Wet and windy is the weather forecast, and wet and windy it looks outside Mrs Luke's window. She apologises, as if sunshine was something she absent-mindedly forgot to lay on for us. Anthea's right foot has recovered, but her left ankle needs bandaging. I encourage her with my amended version of the old evangelical hymn:

"Will your ankles hold in the storms of life
When the clouds unfold their wings of strife...?"

We find Newton Hall, the supposed home of Lawrence Newton, builder of Height meetinghouse, and idly wonder which of the neighbouring houses was the home of Fox's host, James Taylor. Little more is known of him, but he is presumably the same James Taylor who accompanied another Cartmel convert, Richard Roper, to Oldham, Lancashire, in 1653, where they were attacked by the minister, "Priest Harrison", and his churchwarden, John Tetlow. They were "struck & haled out of ye steeplehouse-yard... by John Tetlow, who thrust them over ye wall". Friends recorded the subsequent judgement of God on these two persecutors: Priest Harrison "afterwards had taken from him ye use of ye one side", while John Tetlow "soon after sold up that he had & went into Ireland, where he dyed suddenly". It could be risky to tangle with

God's faithful Quakers, who interpreted Jehovah's words, "Vengeance is mine, I will repay!" as a promise that their enemies would one day get their just deserts.

High Newton, with Low Newton half a mile south and Ayside half a mile north, straddle the busy A590 trunk road which carries today's traffic north of Morecambe Bay to the shipyards and factories of Barrow. The section running eastwards towards the M6 and Kendal is modern, crossing the foot of the Winster valley by a causeway over drained and reclaimed land at Meathrop Moss before finding the line of an older road running round the foot of Whitbarrow and across the Lyth valley via another causeway at Levens. Northwards from Newton the trunk road again borrows the line of an old track under Newton Fell towards Staveley-in-Cartmel and Newby Bridge at the southern tip of Lake Windermere. It is this track which Fox would have taken to Staveley on Sunday morning, June 20 1652, and which we take on Thursday morning, June 9 1994.

This must have been one of the quietest spots on earth in Fox's day, but not for us. The "track", now a trunk road, is a single narrow carriageway and heavy trucks are hurtling past in both directions. This is no place for pedestrians as there are stretches with no footpath where the backwash of a passing lorry only inches away presses us hard against the hedge. But after a couple of miles of hell we are able to fork right for Staveley, finding ourselves immediately in a quiet lane, winding through mature woodland bounded by ancient stone walls almost throttled by ivy, ferns and lichens. We are met by a party of bold bullfinches, fellow refugees from the traffic maelstrom, who merrily lead the way.

The church Fox was heading for appears on our right, almost lost in the woods and protected from the wild world outside by a high wall. Fox never forgot that wall.

"... and on the First-day I went to one priest Camelford's chapel at Staveley and after he had done I began to speak the word of life to them. Camelford was in such a rage, and such a fret and so peevish that he had not patience to hear. All was on a fire, and the rude multitude struck me, and punched me, and took me and threw me headlong over the stone wall of the graveyard, but, blessed be the Lord, his power preserved me. The kirk-warden was one John Knipe, whom the Lord after cut off, who threw me down headlong over the wall."

The Lord seemed to take a particularly dim view of those who threw his servants over walls. That aside, Knipe was and is a common name hereabouts and we are intrigued to find in the graveyard a memorial stone to the Knipe family, recording their dedication to the work and worship of the little chapel. If only churchwarden John Knipe had kept a journal which we could read alongside Fox's! No doubt it would record the sudden unwelcome appearance of a stranger who, without any by-your-leave, took over the pulpit one Sunday morning and refused to stand down or be silent. He had stirred up the congregation against their minister and set Christian against Christian, arousing their just indignation at his strange doctrines and horrid blasphemies. The good minister and people had looked to their churchwarden to do something about it, so he, John Knipe, had cleansed this holy place as Christ had cleansed the Temple, removing the heretic by force since he refused to budge. And when the insolent fellow had started his rantings and ravings in the churchyard, there was nothing for it but to tip him over the wall...

"Priest" Gabriel Camelford also appears in a different light when viewed through non-Quaker eyes. He was no King and Church man but a convinced puritan who would have the courage to refuse to conform to Restoration church discipline as prescribed by the 1662 Act of Uniformity, and in consequence would be ejected from his Staveley living. Seven years later, in 1669, we find him installed as the first pastor of a Baptist meetinghouse at Tottlebank, five miles from Ulverston. (The Five-Mile Act barred nonconformist "conventicles" from meeting within five miles of a corporate town). Associated with Camelford at Tottlebank were two men who would become fierce opponents of Fox and Friends: William Rawlinson and Robert Sawrey of Broughton Towers, both parliamentarians during the civil wars, and Sawrey an officer in the New Model

Army. It is clear from these later events, if not from the *Journal*, that Fox's fiercest quarrels were not necessarily with a rump of die-hard royalist episcopalians but often with fellow-dissenters, fellow-republicans, fellow-members of the "godly party". One of the reasons George Fox stirred up so much bitter resentment and violence was that he split the Independent party in the church, just as he split the political Left.

To Fox and the early Quakers, priests of the old Prayer Book Church of England were, like papists, beyond the pale. They were also a vanquished enemy, their structures dismantled, their power wrested from them by law, apparently for good. Fox wasted little time on them. His primary targets were the Independent ministers, and the developing struggle between the new Quakerism and the prevailing Independency (which included the Baptists) was a fight for the soul of a true, new, reformed Christianity. Fox's ambition was nothing less than the construction of a reformed "church in England" which would subsume all rivals. Understandably, the rivals fought back, and the intense bitterness of this civil war within the civil war (Friends called it "the Lamb's war") led to violent reactions.

The issues dividing the two parties, which would produce a torrent of pamphlets, broadsheets, books, charges and counter-charges over the next few years, were real enough. The Independent church - in effect the established church under Cromwell - was overwhelmingly Calvinist in its theology, as had been the greater part of the English church since the Reformation. An elect few were predestined to salvation, the rest no less irrevocably to perdition. It was for the elect to rule and for the rest to be ruled. Moreover, since wealth and success were seen as the marks of God's approbation, and poverty and failure the clear evidence of his disapproval, the elect had come to be identified with "the better sort" and the damned with the mob. Fox, who like many other sensitive young men and women of his time had himself been afflicted with tormenting doubts about his own eternal destination, had come to see that the Calvinists' God was a monster. Salvation was free and available to all - and this had profound social as well as theological implications.

Then, as we have already noted, there was the matter of the bible. Puritans of all persuasions had venerated the biblical scriptures as the inspired and infallible word of God ever since the infallibility of the Church itself had been discarded at the Reformation. Old and New Testaments alike were assumed to be historically accurate and spiritually unassailable. Above all, in an age, as it seemed, of unprecedented confusion and diversity, the bible was cried up as the one reliable anchor of the soul, the ultimate authority, the source of unchanging, unchangeable, absolute Truth. Fox and his fellow-radicals dared to assault even this holy of holies. While Fox's language is probably more thoroughly permeated with biblical metaphor and allusion than that of any contemporary, and while he never scrupled to quote scripture to buttress his own point, he insisted that the true word of God, the ultimate authority, was "the inward light of Christ in your conscience". The first generation of Quakers and their fellow-radicals - Fox, Winstanley and Samuel Fisher in particular - began the long, slow process of biblical criticism which would feed into the Enlightenment and open the way to a liberal, rational theology. Their Puritan contemporaries knew that the very foundation of their faith was under attack, and, clinging to it as the proverbial drowning man clutches at straws, they fought back.

While downgrading the bible's authority, Fox paradoxically relied on scripture for two of his most controversial teachings. One was his insistence that Christ's injunction "Be ye perfect" was to be taken literally. As we saw from the account of his meeting at Stonehouse, Dent, this doctrine of perfectionism challenged the orthodox view that we are all "miserable sinners" and can be no other, which, Fox argued, led to a crippling moral complacency. What was the point of reaching for righteousness if the stain of original sin made it unattainable? Indeed, was there any point if salvation was by God's grace alone, and allocated to some but not to others even before the foundation of the world?

The other biblical injunction which Fox (following a long-standing radical tradition) insisted be taken literally was "Swear not at all, but let your Yea be Yea and your Nay be Nay". He scorned the churches for approving oaths by which the godly swore allegiance to a supposedly godly government, and scores of early Friends spent months and years in jail for refusing to swear to anything, whether or not they actually approved the proposition in question.

Fox also aroused hostility by what seemed to many a highly unorthodox view of Christ. Compared with orthodox puritanism, he seemed to heavily downplay the historical Jesus. More important than what Christ is reported to have said is what we ourselves can say out of our own experience. Fox did not go so far as some contemporary radicals, some of them Quakers, in denying the existence of an historical Jesus, but his emphasis was on a present rather than a past Christ, a Christ-principle identified as the inward light of conscience. Moreover, he had no doubt that this Christ-principle was conspicuously present in him, George Fox: on more than one occasion he scandalised his hearers by calling himself the son of God. While this could be defended by recourse to John's Gospel, which promises that all who believe have the power to become sons of God, his audiences didn't always grasp the point - and one rather suspects that he didn't always intend them to. Then there was the question of Christ's second coming, eagerly awaited as a miraculous event by the orthodox faithful, who saw the "wars and rumours of wars" as a sign of the imminence of this event, and the execution of King Charles as the prelude to the reign of King Jesus and his saints. But Fox said the second coming was happening all around them, in human hearts. "Christ has come to teach his people himself".

But if Fox's *doctrine* aroused antagonism, even more so, as we have seen several times, did his direct, uncompromising attacks on "hireling priests" and the unholy tithing system by which they were maintained. Fox took to its logical conclusion the Protestant doctrine of the priesthood of all believers - which meant there was no place for a special, set-apart priesthood. And since the gospel was free, there was no place for paid ministers and pastors in the true church. Independent and Presbyterian ministers were no less false priests than their vanquished episcopalian rivals who had claimed their authority from St Peter. The Quakers would have no professional ministry, no distinction between clergy and laity. Fox would abolish church ministry and the tax system which supported it. Ministers like Gabriel Camelford would be out of a job: they would have to work for their living like everyone else (unless, like Fox, they could live on legacies!). In attacking church doctrines Fox challenged traditional beliefs: but in attacking the institution of the clergy he threatened one of the most powerful vested interests in the state. "No bishop, no king" James I had said half a century earlier, and "no clergy, no order, no morality, no stability, no civil society" said the Puritan ministers. Small wonder, then, that Fox was perceived and denounced as the subverter and destroyer not only of the church as the people of England knew it, but of English civilisation itself. (Quite what he would have thought of a much later generation of Quakers deciding to join the Council of Churches in Britain and Ireland is best not contemplated).

Then there was class. Seventeenth century England had a class system as deeply entrenched as any in the world. The civil wars themselves were class wars in which old wealth, represented by a landed gentry which owed its power and privileges to the crown, was challenged by new wealth in the shape of commerce, trade and a rising managerial class which had come to dominate the House of Commons. These two classes made up the political nation. Below them were the poor, landless and propertyless, the commons excluded from the Commons. The civil wars had given these commoners a new sense of their own combined power, and if royalist gentry and parliamentarian commerce each hated and feared the other, they both hated and feared the latent power of the underclass even more.

One reason Fox and his fellow Quakers were so detested by their betters is that they championed the poor and lowly in language all too reminiscent of that used by the revolutionary Levellers and Diggers in the latter stages of the civil wars. Fox urged the liquidation of the aristocracy (not, of course, in the sense of killing them off, but by the abolition of their status and the sequestration of their wealth). He never developed as coherent (if utopian) a political philosophy as Winstanley's, nor was he a power-politician like Lilburne, but time and again his language is theirs - and lords and magistrates did not fail to recognise the fact. Just as Cromwell's men had simultaneously beheaded the king on their right and crushed the incipient Leveller and Digger rebellions on their left, the cause of what they perceived as the mob was revived by these Quakers who persisted in turning the world upside down anew.

As if all this was not enough to provoke violent reaction, Fox's *manner* was not exactly conciliatory. Quaker tolerance, like Quaker pacifism, belonged to the future. In any case, tolerance and toleration were different things. Fox preached freedom for the "tender conscience", or the legal toleration of dissenting views (such as his own), but his least critical admirers could hardly call him a tolerant man. In preaching Truth, he conveyed the impression that Quakers in general and he in particular had a monopoly of it. Those who did not agree with him were not "in the light", and ideas not in accord with his were mere "notions". In these passionate early days, his was not a fellowship of reconciliation and he did not know the language of compromise.

Whatever violence Fox provoked he suffered without retaliation. This sometimes infuriated his attackers all the more, but it also won him grudging admiration and sometimes dramatic conversions. In Gabriel Camelford's Staveley chapel that Sunday was a young scholar named John Braithwaite who was taking down the minister's sermon in a seventeenth century version of shorthand. He transferred his allegiance to Friends, and, says Fox, "became a fine minister of the Gospel". He is recorded as working on Friends' behalf in Somerset and the south in 1656, and "finished his Testimony by Death" at Chippenham, Wiltshire.

Apparently not much the worse for his brush with John Knipe and the wall, Fox "went up to an alehouse where many people resorted betwixt the times of their morning and afternoon preaching, and had a great deal of reasoning with them", which resulted in more of Camelford's flock splitting away to become the nucleus of the Quaker meeting centred on Newton. We fail to find a nearby alehouse but eat our packed lunches in Mr Camelford's church hall which has been converted into a polling booth for elections for the European parliament. Apart from ourselves and the two election officers, the place is deserted: five voters only have exercised their democratic rights that morning. I ask, and am told that none of them are Knipes or Camelfords. But we read a day or two later that the sitting Tory was ousted from the seat.

That afternoon Fox walked to Lindale, attracted by the prospect of another church service and another opportunity. He puts the distance at "about two or three miles" but it is a good five as the crow flies and longer by road. Rather than walk back along the busy A590 we take the lane a little to the west, via Fiddlers Hall (once the home of the Knipes) and Field Broughton, entering Lindale via Hampsfield. The little Lakeland church is set into steep hillside, and here, "when the priest had done", Fox "spoke to him and the people". He adds that "there were great opposers but they after came to be convinced".

Lindale was then, and for at least another century, one of the most remote settlements in Lancashire North-of-the-Sands. To the south lay the treacherous tidal flats of Morecambe Bay, to the north the rocky barrier of Newton Fell and to the east undrained marshland. Further west in Furness there was a primitive iron industry, but this did not reach Lindale till the 18th century when John Wilkinson, "the father of iron", constructed a forge and furnace at Wilson House, a mile or so north-east of the village. Wilkinson dug a canal into the peat mosses along the river Winster and built the world's first iron boat to bring in peat for furnace fuel and clay for bricks.

In Fox's day, Lindale and the Cartmel penisula seem to have been notoriously under-evangelised by the established church. In 1644 a Puritan minister, John Shaw from Manchester, was invited by a local deputation to spend seven or eight weeks preaching there. In Cartmel itself he found "a very large spacious Church" - presumably the priory - with "scarce any seats in it", and "a people very ignorant, yet willing to learn". Such was the latent interest in religion that Shaw soon found himself, according to his own account, preaching to "some thousands of hearers... & finding also 4 chapels in the parish, I preached and catechised often, seven or 8 times in one week... and usually ye Churches were so throng by 9 a clock in ye morning, yt I had muchadoe to get to the pulpit".

One day he met "an old man about 60, sensible enough in other things" and "a good Churchman" who "constantly went to Common-prayer" at Cartmel Fell chapel, but was entirely ignorant of Christian doctrine. "I asked him, How many Gods there were? he said he knew not". Shaw mentioned Jesus Christ, "who as he was man shed his blood for us on the crosse etc. Oh, sir (said he) I think I heard of that man you speak of, once in a play at Kendall, called Corpus-Christie play, where there was a man on a tree, & blood ran downe etc". The Kendal Corpus Christi miracle play had been suppressed some forty years earlier in 1605, but it was the only memory this "good Churchman" had of hearing the name of Jesus Christ. The implication, of course, was that Cartmel Priory and its chapelries offered liturgy and ritual but no preaching or teaching.

Shaw's evangelism was abruptly cut short when Prince Rupert's royalist troops swept through the area on their way to raise the siege of York (and thence to the defeat at Marston Moor which proved to be the beginning of the end for the king's cause). Shaw got his wife away by sea and himself fled to Yorkshire. Eight years later it was George Fox's turn to offer religious enlightenment in this forgotten corner of England, where even Jesus Christ was known to some only as a character in a half-forgotten stage play.

But the rains have set in again, and after looking over Lindale steeplehouse we head back to Ayside, where we find Anne Hopper of BBC Radio Cumbria waiting to interview us. So, huddled together under a large umbrella in Mrs Luke's garden (because the BBC wants an authentic outdoor atmosphere, and what more authentic out-door sound is there than raindrops bouncing off a stretched umbrella), we talk of Fox and the passions he aroused, and the relevance it has three and a half centuries later. Then we tuck into our supper, and Mrs Luke's bread and butter pudding. Walking is wonderful; but, as every walker will testify, the best part of a day's trek is when it is over, and the boots are drying by the fire, there's food on the table, and between today and tomorrow there is tonight.

John Cooke

The Captain who was not Convinced

DAY 14. Ayside-Swarthmoor

George Fox will have resumed his journey to Swarthmoor by first heading north again, using either the road below Newton Fell via Newton and Ayside or the parallel road further west via Field Broughton and Seatle. His starting point was Lindale (unless he spent another night with James Taylor at Newton Hall), but ours is Ayside. The rain is gone, the grass is sweet and we decide to avoid the roads and take a path across the fields to High Cark Hall. Here a woman driving a cow bids us good morning and asks where we are headed.

"Swarthmoor".

"Have you come far?"

"We started a couple of weeks ago, at Pendle Hill".

"Oh, you're the two who's doing that Quaker walk... George Fox, wasn't it? Heard all about you on the radio this morning, I did."

So Radio Cumbria had broadcast our interview already! We were hot news!

A minor road from High Cark would have taken us directly north again to join the traffic-congested trunk road at Newby Bridge. But our delight in this quiet, secret corner of the Lake District is such that we decide to keep striking west, over a forgotten network of tracks and bridleways finding their own tortuous routes through rocky outcrops and grassy hillocks. After all, Fox himself didn't always choose the shortest route between two points. Cuckoo calls accompany us and there is a profusion of hawthorn in blossom. In Seatle plantation, a forest of young hardwood, we hear a woodpecker tapping, and as we leave the trees behind and pick our way through golden gorse a yellowhammer offers its little-bit-of-bread-and-no-cheese. Over the shoulder of Bigland hill we get another panoramic view of the hills of Lakeland proper to the north, before dropping down through more woodland to cross the River Levens at Low Wood bridge.

George Fox almost certainly crossed the Levens by the bridge at Newby. This was actually in the process of being rebuilt in June 1652, and a month later, in July, the builders petitioned Lancashire Quarter Sessions for an order "that none should traile any draughts of Timber over the said bridge", as "trayleing of timber hath beene the great decaying of the same now of late yeares, and now the said bridge being verrie lately Finished and new builded, to the great Charge of the Countrie, and knowing that the lyme and sand and the other materialls is now all greene and unknitt and therfore will be great danger to the bridge yf any should trayle any timber over the same..." But Fox was not trailing timber and he could use the bridge without unknitting its lime and sand.

Another bridge may have crossed the river a couple of miles west at Backbarrow, but the bridge we use at Low Wood probably dates from the establishment of gunpowder mills here late in the 18th century. This was a perfect site for manufacturing gunpowder. The Levens, flowing out of Lake Windermere, provided ample and reliable water power and the easiest means of transporting the saltpetre and sulphur needed for the process. These had to be imported, but the third vital ingredient, charcoal, was available locally in virtually unlimited quantities. The charcoal burner's trade was an ancient one as charcoal had long been used to fire the iron furnaces. Willow and alder were considered the best wood for the process, but juniper or "savin" was also used as it was plentiful. The first gunpowder mill was licensed here in 1798. Although it was part-owned by a Quaker family, much of the powder produced was for use in the Africa slave trade, but when this was abolished in 1807 there was a continuing and more respectable demand for the mill's old-fashioned "black powder" for slate quarrying, as it was less likely to shatter the rock than modern explosives. In 1926 the mill was taken over by ICI, to be modernised in 1928 and closed in 1935. A fine 19th-century clocktower building which housed the offices and saltpetre and charcoal refineries is now home to several modern businesses, and the stable-block has become a handsome terrace of cottages.

Over Low Wood bridge is the western end of the old Lakeside and Haverthwaite Railway, built in the 1860s when the industrial revolution had transformed the Furness backwater into a busy and prosperous source of iron ore and coal. Those heavy timbers which had crushed the old Newby bridge and threatened its successor in 1652 had by then been replaced by new export products. But by the 1960s these too belonged to history, and the line was closed by British Railways, only to be purchased by a group of enthusiasts and re-opened for the benefit of Lakeland's one surviving non-agricultural industry: tourism. So Anthea and I spend a couple of hours forgetting George Fox, borne by a steam engine called *Repulse* down the line to Windermere Lakeside, where we bask in the sun, use a bottle of cheap Chablis to wash down cheese sandwiches, and then puff back to Haverthwaite, passing the site at Backbarrow where the Quaker Reckitts family contributed mightily to the cleanliness of pre-detergent generations by manufacturing their "dolly blue".

On foot again, we cross the inescapable A590 to reach the Kendal to Ireleth turnpike, the old main road north of the sands which Fox would have rejoined at Newby Bridge after his detour to Lindale. We are back in his footsteps after our short apostasy. As he did, we cross the "causey" over Ireland Moss and Rusland Pool to enter the little village of Bouth. A few well-kept cottages and one or two grander houses surround a village green overlooked by the White Hart Inn, and a plaque tells visitors that Bouth has won the South Lakeland Best-Kept Village trophy.

Bouth was not always the restful backwater it seems today. Even before the road was turnpiked in 1763 it was a busy highway where packhorses, carts and travellers broke their journey between Kendal and Ulverston. Known as the "capital" of the Colton district, a chapelry of the ancient and vast parish of Hawkshead, it boasted two fairs, at Whitsuntide and in October. There were once six inns and coachhouses, of which the White Hart was said to be the liveliest and, for a time, the most notorious, as the resort of off-duty seamen from Greenodd and the west coast ports in search of whisky and wild, wild women. Bouth was also an important centre for woodland industries: coppicing for the charcoal burners and for bobbins, barrel hoops and staves. In 1662 Thomas Massicks "sold fourteen wainloads of charrecoales unto Thomas Rawlinson of Graythwaite for xixs a loade". Rawlinson managed Force Forge works for the Fell family at Swarthmoor (and many years later fell out with Margaret Fox, who caused huge ructions in the local Quaker community when she wrongly accused him of dishonesty).

Fox had arranged to call on "one Captain Sandys" of Bouth Old Hall, a Cromwellian soldier from whom he seems to have expected much. In this he was disappointed. Sandys and his wife were not won over and Fox decided they were "hypocrites and he a very chaffy light man". Fox "admonished him of his lightness and of his jesting, how it was not seemly for a great professor as he was", whereupon Sandys, with infuriating insouciance, "said he had a son on his death-bed who did also reprove and warn him of it". Later, when Sandys tried to turn his friend Thomas Fell against Fox, Fox described him as "a wicked man... full of envy against me, and yet he could use the apostle's words and say 'Behold I make all things new'. I told him then he must have a new God for his god was his belly".

In a letter to the captain (omitted from modern editions of the *Journal*, presumably because it shows its author rather than the recipient in a distinctly unflattering light), Fox wrote:

"A.S. - To the light of conscience I appeal, thou child of the Devil, thou enemy of righteousness. The Lord will strike thee down, though now for a while in thy wickedness thou mayest reign. The plagues of God are due to thee, which thou has resisted and persecuted, thou art to be thrashed down, which is eternal, and doth comprehend thee, and with the light which thou despiseth, thou art seen, and it is thy condemnation. Thou as one brutish, and thy wife as an hypocrite, and you both as murderers of the just, in that which is eternal, are seen and comprehended and your hearts searched, and tried, and condemned by the light. The light in thy conscience will witness the truth of what I write to thee, and will let thee see thou art not born of God, but art from the truth, in the beastly nature. If ever thy eye see repentance, thou wilt witness me a friend of thy soul, and a seeker of thy eternal good. G.F."

But again, a little independent research throws up a picture rather different from Fox's. The Sandys clan of Bouth Old Hall, Graythwaite and Kendal were one of the leading families of Westmorland, having done well out of the dissolution of the monasteries in the previous century, when William Sandys was the king's Receiver-General of the Liberties of Furness. (He was "very riotously and wilfully murdered" at the house he built on the ruins of the old Conishead Priory in 1548). William's son Edwin was an Archbishop of York. The clan had Puritan and Parliamentarian sympathies during the civil wars, when Thomas Sandys of Kendal accumulated a fortune as one of Cromwell's sequestrators of royalist estates. In 1659 he left his town house in Kendal's Highgate as a hospital or almshouse which still stands today, with his coat of arms - two wool-combing bats with a swag of Kendal cloth draped over a shield - above the entrance.

Adam Sandys, 31 years old in 1652, had been appointed Chief

Constable of Ulverston by Thomas Fell of Swarthmoor. He was an associate of William Lampitt, the Puritan minister of Ulverston (probably another Fell appointment), and supported a Puritan ministry at Colton chapel, which served both Colton and Bouth. He gave one of his Bouth estates, Cowridding (perhaps the present Ridding Side farm where there are two fields called Cow Ridding) to the church "for the benefit of a preaching schoolmaster who is to officiate at the chapel". Thus Fox's "chaffy light" man, whose "god was his belly", is commemorated today as a benefactor of the little church and founder of the community's first school. Nor, it seems, did Adam Sandys wholly break his connection with the Fells of Swarthmoor. His daughter Hester married Thomas Rawlinson, the Quaker manager of the Fells' iron works at Force Forge, and in the Swarthmoor household accounts we find "Adam Sandges" in 1660 lending the Fell daughters £40 at a time when their mother was away in London on Quaker business and ready cash was short.

In Bouth we are told that a descendant of Captain Sandys is living at nearby Graythwaite, and a few weeks after the completion of our walk we drove over to Graythwaite Hall to see Major Mervyn Miles Sandys, former High Sheriff of Lancashire and a member of Montgomery's staff in North Africa and Italy in the second world war. He and his wife Helen made us most welcome, fascinated by our project and delighted to show us their scrapbooks of family history. It seems that at least two of Adam's kinsmen, in addition to his daughter Hester, became Quakers. Samuel Sandys of Roger Ground died a prisoner in Lancaster jail in 1663, and Elinor Hadwin of Fellyeat in Frostrow, Sedbergh, named her Quaker brother Stephen Sandys in Pennsylvania as one of her executors in 1697.

"Ah," chuckled the major when I brought up Fox's first meeting with Adam, "the chaffy light man whose god was his belly!" He bore Fox no ill will for this intemperate attack on his ancestor. "That's how they talked to each other then. I imagine our Adam gave as good as he got. Wouldn't do today. Took their religion too seriously". Sadly, Major Sandys died at the wheel of his car while returning home from a friend's funeral a few months after our meeting. His son runs the estates, stretching from Hawkshead to Bouth and Newby Bridge, which have been in the family's possession since before Adam's day, ensuring that Sandys remains a leading name in Cumbria life, today as in the sixteenth and sevententh centuries.

We meet a group of seven Morris dancers outside the White Hart and get chatting to the "father of the side", Bruce Wilson from Ulverston. When we say where we are walking from and to, Bruce tells us he used to attend Swarthmoor Friends meeting, and once played George Fox in a pageant celebrating the tercentenary of Swarthmoor meetinghouse. He never joined the Society. "Quakers see things in black and white. I see all the colours." He was one of the founders of Furness Morris, but apologised for the fact that they now did Cotswold rather than true Northern Morris. "Can't get the clogs, you know". We mentioned the Morrismen and women we had seen in Malham. "Women? Not proper Morris dancing, that. You don't get mixed sides in proper Morris."

We are interrupted by the landlord who says there's a phone call for us. Who on earth knows we are here? It turns out to be an embarrassed Anne Hopper from Radio Cumbria who tells us the tape on which she recorded our interview has been accidentally over-recorded. Does this matter, we ask, as it has already been broadcast once? Much confusion. It eventually transpires that what the lady at High Cark heard that morning was not our interview but a trailer for it. We have been promoted on air, only to be obliterated by the racing results. So we promise to say it all again at Swarthmoor.

After we have taken a look at Bouth Old Hall, a fine working farmhouse which shows its age, David Trotter, landlord of the White Hart, walks his dogs with us to a track through Moss and Height Spring wood, where trees are being coppiced in the traditional way. Trees and shrubs in a selected area are cut down to ground level, then allowed to grow again as "stools". Twigs and branches are laid over the stools to protect them from the deer which would otherwise make a meal of the new growth. In a good summer several new shoots will grow from the stool, and the long, thin rods can be cut for hurdle or charcoal making, swills or chair legs. Oak bark is also collected for tanning. The system lasted unchanged from mediaeval times to the 1950s, when it was abandoned. But now the Woodland Trust and Cumbria Broadleaves have revived the craft, and the result is that we pass stacks of wood and new-cut stools, just as Fox must have done when he came by.

On the far side of the woods we reach Colton, a tiny picture-book village looking down on the Crake river as it leaves Coniston, and across to the majestic peaks of Old Man, Dow Crag and Wetherlam. In Colton church, Wendy Smith is arranging the flowers for tomorrow's services and offers a friendly welcome. The church has one of the loveliest settings in Lakeland, and is built in plain roughcast with a square, embattled tower which houses a 14th century bell liberated from Conishead Priory at its dissolution. There was a "mean unconsecrated chapel" here before the church, in the charge of Furness Abbey, and before that a holy well dedicated to St Cuthbert. The church was consecrated by Archbishop Edwin Sandys, and a board inside names Adam Sandys as a benefactor.

Colton also proudly displays its copy of the "Treacle Bible", a translation commissioned by Archbishops Sandys of York and Parker of Canterbury in 1561. Based on the earlier English translations of William Tyndale and Miles Coverdale, and laying the basis for the later King James or Authorised Version, the 1561 bible gets its nickname from its rendering of *Jeremiah* 8.22 as "Is there no *tryacle* in Giliad?" rather than the more usual *balsam*. George Fox used a "Treacle Bible" and his copy is similarly displayed at Swarthmoor Hall.

We approach Spark Bridge down a tiny lane, noting some fine elms on the way: Dutch Elm disease hasn't found its way here yet. A family of robins are disturbed by our passing, and mother hops about distractedly as her fledgelings, which have only just left the nest, freeze on the road, trying to remain unnoticed. It's a good ruse: their speckled brown feathers make excellent camouflage.

There was once a bloomsmithy at Spark Bridge, which perhaps gave the village its name, but we are told that the furnaces and bobbin mill have gone and there remains one lone woodman crafting products from local coppicing.

George Fox may have crossed the Crake a mile further south at Penny Bridge, but we still want to avoid the dreaded A590 and strike uphill to High Scathwaite. Here the tranquillity of an ancient landscape is rudely shattered by a wind farm: rows of giant turbines dominating the skyline and emitting a ceaseless mechanical moan. They are championed by some as a cleaner, safer means of generating power than the nuclear alternative which was foisted on Cumbria by a combination of ignorance and deception. But the prospect of Lakeland's hills being blighted by the sight and sound of them is intolerable. No doubt there were windmills here in Fox's day, but they were in scale with the landscape and built from natural materials. These are aliens, but evidently destined to be the first of many.

We drop down to the Broughton Beck road and walk on to Ulverston. In Fox's time it was a market centre, more often reached by a hazardous and shifting "road" from Lancaster across Morecambe sands (which Fox is often wrongly supposed to have used on this, his first visit to Swarthmoor). The principal town of Furness, Ulverston was already full of domestic smithies, bloomeries and smelting works. Lord of the manor was Thomas Fell of Swarthmoor. Chief Constable was Adam Sandys of Bouth. Minister of the parish church of St Mary was William Lampitt. Built in 1111 by the monks of Conishead Priory, the church was given a thorough Victorian going-over which left a 12th century south door and a 16th century tower among the rare survivors. Monuments and effigies include one to William Sandys. The town had a school, endowed by Thomas Fell, and an open sewer called the Weint where, on a later visit, Fox was ducked by one of Sandys' constables. He was not fond of Ulverston. Its inhabitants, he recalled, were "liars, drunkards, whoremongers and thieves, and follow filthy pleasures".

The town we enter still radiates from its wide market square, though the old cross was replaced by a lamp standard in 1922, and then by a war memorial in the form of a mock-mediaeval market cross. The old bloomeries and smithies were replaced by elegant Georgian buildings in Daltongate, Soutergate and Hodge Puddle, and the Weint was long ago paved over. Our attention is caught by signs to a museum celebrating Ulverston's most famous son, but the object of devotion turns out to be neither Thomas Fell nor George Fox, but Stan Laurel.

Heading directly south from the centre, we strike a footpath from Springfield Road, pass some school playing fields, down into the little valley of Levy Beck, over a packhorse-style bridge, through a kissing gate, round an old orchard, through another kissing gate... And there is Swarthmoor Hall.

Our adventure is beginning to come to an end. George Fox's was coming to a new beginning.

Rocking the Nations

15. Swarthmoor

The *Journal* puts it in a simple sentence which (in modern editions) stands as a paragraph of its own:

"And from thence [Captain Sandys' home at Bouth] I came up to Swarthmoor to Judge Fell's."

Swarthmoor is a windswept low ridge a mile south-west of Ulverston. Troops supporting Lambert Simnel's insurrection had landed nearby and camped on the moor in 1487, and as they were led by a Captain Martin Schwartz it has been supposed by some that he bestowed his own name on the place of his encampment. But the "black moor" was so called long before Captain Schwartz pitched his tents, reflecting the desolate and barren topography which dominated here before cultivators took it in hand from the sixteenth century on. Late in Elizabeth's reign a gentleman's residence was built on the edge of the moor, with views from the upper storeys over the sands of Morecambe Bay to the east and towards the Coniston hills to the north. Swarthmoor Hall was bought by George Fell of Hawkswell, near Ulverston, whose family, like the Sandys, had done well out of land speculation in the wake of the Henrician dissolution of the monasteries and chantries. By 1632 it was owned by his son Thomas who that year brought his 18-year-old bride Margaret to live there.

Thomas Fell has always been held in high esteem by Friends because, although he never became a Friend himself, he gave his wife freedom to devote her energies to the movement, allowed the use of the Hall for its meetings, and more than once used his considerable political and legal clout to help get Quakers out of trouble. He famously listened in on meetings for worship from his study, without ever joining: he was the Society's first "attender". But recent research (summarised by Bonnelyn Young Kunze in *Margaret Fell and the Rise of Quakerism* and by H Larry Ingle in *First Among Friends*) has produced a more complex picture.

At the time of his marriage to young Margaret Askew of nearby Marsh Grange, Fell was a 33-year-old barrister of Gray's Inn, London. After marriage he seems to have spent more time in Swarthmoor than London, becoming a justice of the peace on his own home ground. It is clear that by the outbreak of civil war in 1642, if not earlier, his sympathies were decidedly parliamentarian. In 1643 he was appointed to the Lancashire County Committee for Compounding (responsible for confiscating royalist estates) and in 1645 became an MP for Lancaster (when the sitting royalist was thrown out). In 1648 he was ranked first in social status among the laymen of the ninth "classical presbytery" in the Furness district of Lancashire, but with the ascendancy of Cromwell his presbyterianism evidently gave way to republican Independency. As Justice of the Assize for the North Wales and Cheshire circuit he was a close associate and friend of John Bradshaw, Chief Justice of Cheshire and President of the court which condemned Charles Stuart to death. By 1651 he was Vice-chancellor of the Duchy of Lancaster, and by 1653 Chancellor.

At the outbreak of war in 1642 Thomas Fell's whole estate was valued at a modest £150 per annum. By this time he and Margaret had four daughters and a son to maintain. (Four more daughters followed). It seems clear that his appointment to the Committee for Compounding in 1643 gave him early knowledge of lands scheduled to be seized from vanquished royalists, and the opportunity to purchase them himself on favourable terms, or arrange for them to be made over to him as a reward for his labours: a not unusual practice at the time, and less unsavoury to the godly then than it seems to us now. By the end of the war Fell's property was worth not £150 but nearly £5000 - in addition to fees of several hundred pounds a year from his legal work. Ingle says bluntly that Fell was "considered a war profiteer by the king's adherents", and it seems that even Fell's own sister, Alice, accused him of cheating her out of her share of the family inheritance. Fell's accumulation of property seems to have continued unabated during the 1650s, provoking the uneasy thought that Swarthmoor was simultaneously the Quaker headquarters and a centre of war profiteering. By the time of his death in 1658 Thomas Fell was one of the largest landowners in Lancashire North-of-the-Sands, with an estate stretching some seven miles from Morecambe Bay to the Duddon estuary. Thomas Fell was one of those puritan gentry who firmly believed that God helped those who helped themselves.

It was, then, a rich and powerful grandee who combined political, legal and military power whom George Fox came to see in the last week of June 1652. But Fell was away on circuit. Margaret was also out. Instead Fox met another visitor, William Lampitt, curate of Ulverston. They took an instant and permanent dislike to each other.

Their problem was that they had much in common. Both were radical puritans, parliamentarians, republicans - and both were convinced of their own good standing with almighty God. Lampitt moved in Baptist circles (at a time when it was still possible to be Baptist within the loose structure of the national, parish-based church) and had served in the New Model Army. As we have noted, he was probably a Thomas Fell appointment at Ulverston. Lampitt and Fox each clearly perceived the other as a rival for spiritual supremacy in the Fell household, and therefore in the whole region. It seems very likely that Lampitt had heard of Fox from friends within the local puritan network like Gabriel Camelford and Adam Sandys, and he may well have been calling at Swarthmoor Hall to warn the family against the unwelcome intruder who was stirring up so much discord and dissension wherever he went. Fox decided Lampitt was "full of filth", an opinion he evidently communicated to the Fell children since little Mary, at the age of eight, wrote her parson the following letter:

"Lampitt, The plaiges of god shall fall upon thee and the seven viols shall bee poweered upon thee and the milstone shall fall upon and crush thee as dust under the Lords feete how can thou escape the damnation of hell. This did the Lord give mee as I lay in bed. - Mary Fell".

George Fox proudly included this in his *Journal*. Editors more sensitive to his and the Fell family's reputation dropped it.

When Margaret Fell arrived home, Lampitt had left but Fox was waiting. Fox records that "the children told her that priest Lampitt and I disagreed; and it struck something at her because she was in profession with him, though he hid his dirty actions from them". But it seems she had heard of Fox and the stir he had created in Westmorland. She had even had "a vision of a man in a white hat that should come and confound the priests". So she invited him to hang up his white hat and stay, and, says Fox, "at night we had a great deal of reasoning and I declared the Truth to her and her family".

Next day Lampitt came round again, and more argument ensued between the two men, with Margaret Fell listening in. Fox was apparently invited to stay a few more days, perhaps in the expectation that Judge Fell would soon be home, but when Margaret asked him the following Sunday to accompany her to church - Lampitt's church, St Mary's at Ulverston - he at first declined. But after thinking it over during a walk in the fields, he decided the Lord wanted him in the steeplehouse after all. He arrived late, in the middle of a hymn. "The priest Lampitt was singing with his people. His spirit and his stuff was so foul that I was moved of the Lord to speak to him and the people after they had done singing". Fox told the startled congregation that "he was not a Jew that is one outward, but he was a Jew that is one inward": appearances were deceptive: their minister was not the godly man he seemed.

"Then I showed them that God was come to teach his people by his spirit and to bring them off all their old ways, religions, churches and worship, for all their religions, churches and worship and ways were but talking of other men's words, for they were out of the life and spirit that they were in that gave them forth".

The church erupted. Justice John Sawrey, a friend of Thomas Fell and cousin of Adam Sandys, called on the local constabulary to throw Fox out, but Margaret Fell intervened: "Let him alone, why may not he speak as well as any other?". Lampitt took his cue from the lady of the manor and said "Let him speak", which Fox proceeded to do for "a pretty while". As he gave voice to his conviction that "the inward light of Christ in our conscience" took precedence over the authority of church and state, bible and pulpit, Margaret Fell was moved to tears. Fox went on to utter the single sentence which best expresses the essence of his message: "You will say, Christ saith this, and the apostles say this, but *what canst thou say?*" "This opened me so," Margaret Fell wrote later, "that it cut me to the heart; and then I saw clearly, we were all wrong. So I sat down in my pew again, and cried bitterly". In the confusion, Sawrey succeeded in having the trouble-maker removed. After calmly resuming his preaching in the steeplehouse yard, Fox returned to Swarthmoor Hall with Margaret, where she was "struck into such a sadness, I knew not what to do, my husband being from home". (As Bonnelyn Young Kunze drily remarks, this was almost the last time she felt any wavering on religious issues in deference to her husband, the last time she would play the "weaker vessel" role).

Over the next few days, using Swarthmoor as his base, Fox visited all the local churches in turn, spreading spiritual mayhem wherever he went. At Aldingham he took over the pulpit when the minister had finished his sermon, but the minister himself "got away". At

Rampside he preached in the chapel where Thomas Lawson was rector, and instantly won him over. Lawson broke with the Lampitt-Camelford group, "threw off his preaching for hire" and became a renowned botanist and Quaker schoolmaster. At Dalton "the people grew brutish and fell of ringing the bells" to drown his voice. On Walney Island, the priest "went to hide himself in the haymow" to avoid a confrontation.

Back at Swarthmoor, Margaret Fell openly declared for Fox, and "most of all the family" followed. (It would have been unusual for children and servants not to follow the temporary head of the household in her religious allegiance). But Fox now heard that William Lampitt had organised a meeting of local clergy at Kendal, "and mightily had incensed them against me and told them I held many strange things". So he headed straight for the lions' den "and answered all their objections". Lampitt, he boasts, "clearly lost the best of his hearers and followers and they came to see his deceit and to forsake him". From Kendal he revisited his Seeker converts at Sedbergh, where he seems to have met up with his comrades James Nayler and Richard Farnsworth, who had been making their own (sadly unrecorded) missionary journeys through the dales. We may imagine that, perhaps for the first time, there was now serious talk of giving the emergent movement some form and structure. Since Swarthmoor was as yet unsecured, the likeliest base of operations was Sedbergh itself, under the protection of Captain Gervase Benson. Within a few weeks the former Seeker leader Thomas Taylor would return from Swaledale, join Friends and take up residence in Sedbergh.

Meanwhile, George Fox received word from Margaret Fell that Thomas had returned home. As she recorded later, her husband was "much troubled... and surprized" at the change that had come over his household. Fell had been met as he crossed Morecambe Bay by Captain Sandys and Justice Sawrey who told him "that a great disaster was befallen amongst his family" and that his wife and children were bewitched. They had abandoned the church and embraced a new "Principle and Perswasion". Fell was "greatly offended; and any may think what a condition I was like to be in, that either I must displease my husband or offend God; for he was very much troubled with us all in the house and family, they had so prepossessed him against us". But she persuaded him to meet Fox and form his own judgement. Accompanied by Nayler and Farnsworth, Fox hurried westward again, where Fell civilly entertained them to dinner, and no doubt appraised them, before interrogating his principal guest.

It is clear from the *Journal* account of the meeting that Fell's first object was to establish Fox's political rather than his religious credentials. Perhaps Sandys and Sawrey had questioned his loyalty to the regime Fell served. "Art thou that George Fox that Justice Luke Robinson spoke so much in commendation of amongst many of the Parliament men?" he asked. Robinson was an MP, like Fell, and Fox had met him in Yorkshire the previous year and had clearly created a favourable impression which had been communicated to Robinson's fellow MPs, Fell included. Seizing his opportunity, Fox perhaps dropped a few more names of republican sympathisers who would be known to his host, because "Judge Fell was satisfied that I was the man". As the conversation continued, the tension eased. Fell said he wished Fox had met his friend John Bradshaw, the republican judge who would later be vilified as the chief of regicides.

So Fox came through his first test. Thomas Fell concluded that his wife's new friends were politically reliable supporters of the godly party, if given to more enthusiasm than his own taste allowed. But the following day Lampitt, Sandys and Sawrey called at the Hall to renew their attack. This was the occasion when Fox told Sandys that "his god was his belly", and Sawrey that "his heart was rotten". Caught between the vehement pressures of his local gentry and church associates and the wishes of his wife and family, Fell decided on the historic compromise which would hold till his death six years later: he would not publicly align himself with Fox and his Quakers, but he would allow his wife the freedom to do so, including the crucial freedom to meet in Swarthmoor Hall and use it as their base of operations.

It is unmistakably apparent that George Fox and Margaret Fell recognised each other instantly as soulmates. There was a kind of love at first sight, and it was soon expressed in endearments we are more used to find confined to private love letters. But the passion of Margaret's early letters to George is not the familiar passion of a woman for a man (though psychologists might diagnose it in terms of repressed sexuality: they usually do). What startles us is that the endearments offered to George are those addressed in the bible to Jesus: "My own dear heart, thou knows that we have received thee into our hearts, and shall live with thee eternally... My soul thirsts to have thee come over, if it be but for two or three days... Dear heart, do not leave us nor forsake us... O thou bread of life... We hope thou wilt not leave us comfortless but will come again... O our life, we hope to see thee again that our joy may be full; for in thy presence is fulness of joy... O thou fountain of eternal life... O thou father of eternal felicity..." But before we jump to the conclusion that this was the verbal love-making which anticipated their eventual marriage after Thomas's death, we must remember that extravagent language, borrowed from a bible which saturated the culture of the day, was the norm amongst deeply religious men and women. Other Quaker women wrote to Fox in equally impassioned terms, and other Quaker men addressed Margaret in like vein. James Nayler attracted similar adulation. Some of these letters were gleefully circulated half a century later in an anti-Quaker pamphlet *The Snake in the Grass*, but all they prove is that George Fox and Margaret Fell created a family of love as well as a religious and political powerhouse at Swarthmoor. (We are reminded that the Family of Love which preceded Friends was often accused of disregarding sexual norms, probably on account of its similarly highly-charged language).

That Swarthmoor Hall was a political powerhouse is often forgotten. But as Quakerism spread over the next decade - into Cumberland in the remaining months of 1652, down to Bristol and London over the next two years, throughout the nation before Cromwell's death in 1658, and to the American colonies and Europe before the movement's tenth birthday - it was the Quakers' political as well as their religious doctrine which threatened to turn the world upside down. Thomas Fell had first reassured himself that Fox was a good Roundhead, but was probably unaware of just how radical his republicanism was. The rise of Quakerism has been interpreted - I believe rightly - as the re-emergence in a new form of the Leveller agitation of the late 1640s. Many Quakers had been Levellers. Quakerism repeated the Levellers' hostility to all forms of priesthood, to tithes, to gentry rule. As we have noted, the Leveller leader John Lilburne became a Quaker, and the "True Leveller" Gerrard Winstanley told Edward Burrough in 1654 that Quakers "are sent to perfect that work which fell in [our] hands".

Fox and his friends aimed high. They intended to make a New Earth as well as a New Heaven. Quakerism was to be not a sect but "the church in England". The Lord would rule through his saints, said Fox, adding "of whom I am one". At first, Friends' political pronouncements lacked the coherence of those of their Leveller predecessors, but by 1659 Fox and Edward Billing had formulated them in a series of detailed propositions. Billing's were clearly Leveller-inspired: annual parliaments, constituency boundary reform, land reform, a bill of rights, annual election of magistrates, progressive taxation, prison reform, a new poor law, religious toleration and the abolition of "all servile tenures or copyholds, being the badge or yoke of the Conqueror". There "would never be a good world as long as there was a Lord in England", including "the whole rabble of Duke, Marquesse, Lord, Knight, Gentleman".

Fox's propositions were not as well focused but in some ways even more radical. He too wanted to abolish aristocracy and gentry, those who "cumbred the ground... and such gets the earth under their hands, commons wastes and forrests, and fells and mores and mountains, and lets it lie waste, and calls themselves Lords of it, and keeps it from the people, when so many are ready to starve and beg". His remedy was wholesale confiscation of land. All former monastic properties, glebe lands, great estates, churches and - a nice touch - Whitehall itself should be taken into common ownership and turned over to the poor. Lords of manors should have their fines confiscated, "for they have enough". Tithes, of course, should be abolished along with the clergy. And the gentry should be disarmed. Not since the hedge-priest John Ball preached Christian communism in the fourteenth century and the continental Anabaptists sought to dismantle temporal and spiritual power in the sixteenth had religion spoken in such plainly revolutionary terms. It was as well for Fox that this programme was not yet fully formulated when he met Thomas Fell in 1652, as it clearly threatened the annihilation of the Fell estate and titles. But the bones of the programme would have been discernible to an experienced politician, and it may have been political as well as religious doubts which kept the well-propertied Chancellor, Judge, MP and Lord of the Manor at arm's length from such zealotry.

Revolutionary politics do not sit easily with pacifism, but this was no problem to Fox and the Commonwealth generation of Quakers. As I have emphasised earlier, they were not pacifists, and the historic Peace Testimonies which many have seen as the distinctive mark of Quakerism belong to the post-Commonwealth Restoration period. As we have noted, Fox himself had refused a commission in the New Model Army in 1651, famously telling the recruiting officers that he "lived in the virtue of that life and power that took away the occasion of all wars". But his account of this episode was written many years later, and he may unconsciously have read back into his earlier life the pacifism of his middle age. He undoubtedly refused the commission, but it cannot have been on pacifist grounds, as his contemporary actions and writings clearly indicate.

It is noticeable, on his 1651-2 journey through Yorkshire and the North-West, culminating in his progress from Pendle to Swarthmoor, how often he sought out army officers as likely converts. More than half the men he names in his *Journal* between his release from Derby jail and his arrival at Swarthmoor were, with the exception of "priests" and JPs, men of military rank or men known to have served in the New Model Army or Parliamentary militias. The army was of course recruited by Cromwell, whenever possible from the ranks of the "godly": Independents, Baptists and Separatists with revolutionary views on politics and religion. They tended to be soldiers from conviction rather than conscription (though some were pressed), men who in Cromwell's words "had the fear of God before them and made some conscience of what they did". They prayed together, studied the bible together, and worshipped together without sanction of priest or church. They agitated for a levelling democracy, for the rule of the small over the great. There was never an army like it before, and as Noel Brailsford has commented in *The Levellers and the English Revolution*, "nor was there anything like it thereafter till the Workers' and Soldiers' Councils met in 1917 in Russia" - though, so far as we know, the workers and soldiers of Petrograd didn't hold prayer meetings.

Many early Quakers served their apprenticeship in this army. James Nayler was nine years a soldier, serving as Major-General Lambert's quartermaster. Preaching to his troops after the Battle of Dunbar in September 1650, Nayler so impressed one of Cromwell's officers that he was "afraid to stay, for I was made a Quaker". The very first Quakers, it seems, were made in the army - and before George Fox arrived on the scene. William Dewsbury joined the army in 1645 in obedience to the "light of conscience", and was a Quaker by 1651. Edward Billing resigned from the army to become a Quaker brewer, though he made it clear that he still "owned the sword in its place".

Some were demobilised after the decisive battle of Worcester in 1651, but many stayed in. Officers like Captain Gervase Benson, Captain Alexander Hebblethwaite and Major Bousfield still used their military titles when Fox met and convinced them. Not once does Fox rebuke these men for their calling or urge them to put away their sword. He objects to Captain Sandys' sense of humour and rotundity, but not to his military profession.

Not only are Fox's early writings non-pacifist, they are positively pro-army. He identifies himself openly and unambiguously with Cromwell's military rule, endorsing the Protector's conviction that it was the power of God which had given him victory. When he does criticise Cromwell it is for his military half-heartedness. Why stop at an English revolution? he asks, why not march on and make European republics? Why not topple the Pope from his throne?

"O Oliver, hadst thou been faithful and thundered down the deceit, the Hollander had been thy subject and tributary, Germany had given up to have done thy will, and the Spaniard had quivered like a dry leaf wanting the virtue of God, the King of France should have bowed his neck under thee, the Pope should have withered as in winter, the Turk in all his fatness should have smoked, thou shouldst not have stood trifling about small things but minded the work of the Lord as He began with thee at first".

In another pamphlet addressed directly to the troops, he urged them to "see that you know a soldier's place... and that ye be soldiers qualified". One Quaker soldier, he boasted, was worth seven non-Quakers. If the army grandees would not see the revolution through, "the inferior officers and soldiers" should take on the task themselves. Their job was to "rock nations as a cradle", and he urged them "never set up your standard till you come to Rome". In the parliamentary elections of 1656 and 1659 Quakers organised support for military candidates, especially the regicide John Bradshaw and Cromwell's own deputy, General John Lambert.

In the decisive year of 1659, when anarchy threatened and men of property began to look to the return of a king, hundreds of Quakers joined the army to resume the fight for God's own republic.

Historian Barry Reay, in *The Quakers and the English Revolution*, unearths evidence of Quaker recruitment in the army garrisons in York, Bristol, Holy Island and Berwick-upon-Tweed, Lancaster, Carlisle, Chester, Kent, Northamptonshire, Norfolk, Shrewsbury and London. Quaker JP Anthony Pearson set about recruiting a Quaker militia in the Kendal area. (When called to account for his actions after the Restoration, he saved his neck by denouncing Quakerism and spying on his former comrades). Twentyfive Quakers in England and Wales accepted appointments as military commissioners. Edward Burrough declared that the army had "some great work to do... with their outward sword, and that time is not long till a good thing may be accomplished by our English army". Even Margaret Fell described the army as "a battleaxe in the hand of the Lord".

It is no exaggeration to say that, throughout much of the republican 1650s, Friends and the junior ranks of the New Model Army together constituted a Quaker-Military alliance, Cromwell's militant tendency. As such, they were often a thorn in the Protector's flesh, ruthless critics of the balancing act by which he strove to hold together those who thought the revolution had gone quite far enough and those who urged its speedy completion. Cromwell was as ambivalent towards them as they were towards him, admiring their courage and integrity but offended by their extravagance and intolerance, particularly towards the puritan ministers of his own Independent churches. The confusing result is that we find Quakers in Cromwell's jails and simultaneously in his administration and armed forces. Restoration Quakerism is a less complex phenomenon, discarding its political garb, wrapping itself in the Peace Testimonies and magnificently turning its other cheek to its totalitarian persecutors.

So the English revolution was enacted in microcosm at Swarthmoor Hall. Thomas Fell and George Fox shared a common allegiance to the republic, to Cromwell as Protector, and to the New Model Army as guarantor of the new dispensation. They shared too the conviction that God was working his purpose out in the England of the 1650s and was offering them a place as co-workers in the building of a new republic of heaven. But Fox was a militant and Fell a moderate. Just as the survival of the republic itself depended on moderates and militants hanging together, so the survival of the family of love at Swarthmoor depended on an accommodation between the judge and the agitator-preacher. Margaret Fell brilliantly facilitated that accommodation, thereby preserving both a loving marriage and the partnership which nurtured a movement capable of not only surviving the catastrophic counter-revolution of 1660 but also of pursuing the Good Old Causes of toleration and pluralism to some kind of fruition.

*

It is late afternoon when we pass through the grand stone arch (which wasn't there in the Fells' day) at the entrance to Swarthmoor Hall. The warden, Steve Deeming, welcomes us with mugs of tea and shows us again around a house that has become familiar to us over the years. It is the house Fox made his headquarters in 1652, and it is not: the Elizabethan structure survives largely intact, but it has been added to and subtracted from, its walls rendered, its rooms repanelled. It has lost the great barn which for centuries graced the courtyard, but the lawn Thomas Fell paced up and down with William Lampitt the morning after his meeting with Fox is green and pleasant as ever.

Steve tells us of Friends' ambitious plans to turn Swarthmoor into a powerhouse again. Where the barn stood, new buildings will rise to accommodate visitors and administrators. Swarthmoor certainly needs a transformation. For too long it has been both museum and centre of pilgrimage, but inadequate in both functions. Its collection of Quaker bonnets, curios, and what is alleged to be George Fox's travelling bed, along with other furniture of dubious authenticity, is not enough to meet modern museum standards, and as a centre of pilgrimage it lacks even the most basic facilities. Swarthmoor Hall has the air of a much-loved relic which no-one quite knows what to do with.

So the new powerhouse plans have come in the nick of time. But what kind of power will it generate? Friends and their fellow-travellers do not need another study centre imitating the good work of Woodbrooke College in Birmingham and Charney Manor in Oxfordshire. No-one needs another retreat venue for circle dancing and Quakerly versions of New Age spirituality. So what can Swarthmoor do that isn't being done by others?

It could, perhaps, take its cue from the 1650s, when the hall became a centre for "rocking nations as a cradle", making a New Earth as well as a New Heaven. It could revive the original radical Quaker concern for a political transformation in the name of social justice and equality, and it could perhaps do worse than start by looking again at George Fox's demands for the abolition of peerages and titles, measures to secure greater economic equality, and measures to end the continuing scandal of an established and therefore privileged Church of England. These were ends which Fox and his friends pursued religiously from Swarthmoor. Swarthmoor could pursue them religiously again. And if that means courses in obstructing motorway construction rather than bible studies, courses on sabotaging war plants rather than aromatherapy, so much the better.

We sleep tonight, the last night of our Foxtrot, in Swarthmoor meetinghouse, built at the expense of George Fox himself. At the end of his life he left to local Friends "the house and houses, barn, kiln, stable and all the land, with the garden and orchard, being about three acres of land, more or less... called Pettis at Swarthmoor", giving advice on how the buildings should be converted, a porch added, trees planted, and paths paved to keep Quaker feet walking cheerfully and free from Swarthmoor mud. "Let it be done substantially", he wrote. Friends were "not to be at a Farthing charge, but iff Friends off ye meetinge or thereaways will come with there carts and help to fetch stone lyme wood sand or slate, I shall take yt kindely". The gift was confirmed by deed in 1687 and the meetinghouse was built the following year - the year of Toleration. Over the porch was written EX DONO: GF 1688 - a curious reversion to Latin by a group which had once denounced the language as the mark of clerical obscurantism. The surrounding three acres of garden and orchard are now claimed by Ulverston's suburbia.

Before settling in, we do another take of our fated BBC Radio Cumbria interview for Anne Hopper. Then she drives us into Ulverston for a Chinese take-away. It is dark when we arrive back at the meetinghouse and spread our bed-rolls for the last time, our Foxtrot at an end.

Twentieth Century Fox

16: From the 1650s to the 1990s

Following in Fox's footsteps from Pendle Hill to Swarthmoor, we have walked not only through the dales of Yorkshire and Cumbria, but through history. Every day we have been brought face to face with continuity and change. The hills and valleys are those Fox saw, the names of hamlets and farms the names he too became familiar with. The homes he visited still stand, and the descendants of many of the men and women he convinced or antagonised are still to be met with in the same localities. The tracks he trod are still walked by ramblers. Meetinghouses built by his friends are still Friends' meetinghouses. This remains 1652 country.

But of course it is something else again. The hills are more intensively grazed, the valleys have lost their cornfields, roads have been covered with tarmac and lined with wire, and virtually every building has been renovated more than once, if not entirely rebuilt. Fox walked through a seventeenth century landscape on the margins of civilised England, a dark corner "of little note or praise" and avoided by sensible travellers. We have walked through a twentieth century landscape which, every summer weekend, threatens to sink under the weight of admiring visitors. Our world is not Fox's, and his cannot be ours.

If that is true of the physical world, how much more so is it of his and our mental worlds? It is not just the topography which has changed: a hayfield supplanting a field of flax, a pylon where a pinfold once stood, a phone box on the site of a mounting-block, a housing estate over rows of tenterhooks. The words we speak, the thoughts we think, the conceptual models which frame our understanding of the world and ourselves have undergone so profound a series of revolutions that we seem to inhabit not a changed world but a different world altogether.

And that raises the question: what, if anything, of Fox's message to Cromwell's world has any relevance to ours?

His was a pre-scientific world, a world infused with miracle, magic and holy spirit. It was a young world which had seen only a few score human generations since it was made by a personal God who continued to intervene in the everyday affairs of his creation. Fox's world was the large centre of a small universe. Truth was a matter of faith and inspiration, virtue a matter of conformity to God's will and purpose, and beauty a worldly distraction. God ruled as an inward light through his saints, "of whom", said Fox, "I am one".

This is not our world. The kind of search for truths which we call science, conducted by rational process involving experiment and verification, has opened up to us an immense universe of almost unimaginable age, in which all living creatures including humankind have evolved from the simplest organisms, not by supernatural agency but by natural selection and adaptation. Our world is but a speck in infinite space, and a speck with a limited life span. If there is a place for God in this world it is not the same place he occupied in Fox's day, and not quite the same God. God too has been revolutionised.

A scientific understanding of the world and of humanity's place in it has not abolished miracle, magic and the holy. Indeed, the more we know (or think we know, or know provisionally) of the wonderful complexities of the natural world (whether perceived directly through our own investigation or indirectly through television and books), the greater is our awe and wonder. But miracle is no longer divine or supernatural intervention. Miracle, magic and the holy are woven into the structure of every atomic particle, every spiral of DNA, every replicating gene, every exploding super-nova, and every spark of human consciousness. What price water into wine when the whole wide world is revealed as miracle?

The great transformations in our understanding produced by physical, biological and cosmological enquiry are themselves only part of the story. Our understanding of history, culture and language itself has been similarly transformed. And although we are only just beginning to fathom the mysteries of mind, consciousness and self-consciousness (*the* project for the twenty-first century, if we can sustain our planet long enough), the work of nineteenth and twentieth century psychologists has already opened yet another gulf between ourselves and Fox's contemporaries.

So what links can we sensibly make between Fox's world and ours? We could begin by acknowledging Fox's place as one of the makers of the modern world: he is himself a link. We have followed his footsteps, not out of a detached antiquarian interest, nor just for fresh air and fun, but because it seems to us that Fox can speak from his own condition to ours, and he can do that because his intense and profound dissatisfaction with his own world bred the spirit of enquiry which produced the humanist Enlightenment and our culture of diversity and pluralism. If ours is a different world from Fox's, Fox and early Friends bear historic responsibility for at least some of the differences.

If that seems a large claim, let us remind ourselves of what these early Friends achieved. The world they inherited, the world into which they were born, was one where the state and the church claimed to exercise an absolute authority as temporal and spiritual regents of God. That authority was written in the bible, spoken from the pulpit and enforced by the magistrate. There was dissent, but dissent was subversion. There was free thought, but it dared not show its face or speak its name. The world of the Stuart kings was what we would now call a totalitarian world, a systematic dictatorship in which the dictator was the Lord's anointed.

That world was shattered by the civil wars of the 1640s, when the writ of king and bishop ceased to run. The 1650s saw the historic attempt to settle the nation on new authorities: Protector in place of monarch, puritan minister in place of episcopal priest, and both under the primacy of scripture. But the first generation of Friends saw that the new authority was little better than the old. For them, the Protector's power was legitimate only in so far as it expressed the power of a sovereign people (or at least the godly party among the sovereign people). For them, the puritan ministry was merely the old priesthood in drabber clothing. But, most radical of all, the bible too was deprived by them of its status as ultimate and infallible word of God. Infallible crown, infallible church and infallible scripture were all denied and deposed by Fox and early Friends.

In their place Fox put two alternative sources of authority. One was what he sometimes called "the light of Christ in your conscience" and sometimes just "the light in your conscience". The other was experience: "this I knew experimentally", or experientially. These words, and the ideas they embody, are now so familiar to us that it takes a considerable effort of the imagination to appreciate their revolutionary effect at the time. If ultimate authority was internal not external, subjective not objective, all political and ecclesiastical power was fatally undermined and subverted.

Of course, he was neither the first nor the only child of his time to think in this subversive way. A similar revolution was beginning in philosophy. It is highly unlikely that Fox ever heard of Rene Descartes, who died in 1650, but "the father of modern philosophy" had spent the last two decades scandalising his academic contemporaries in France and Holland by his profound rejection of ancient and established authority and of everything handed down from the past. Descartes, like Fox, thought our experience of truth must begin with ourselves and not with second-hand learning.

There was a more direct connection between the Quakers and Descartes' follower Baruch Spinoza in Holland. After his expulsion from the Amsterdam Jewish synagogue, Spinoza flirted with the new Quaker community established there in 1657, William Ames reporting back to Margaret Fell that the philosopher whose name would become a byword for rationalist "atheism" "owneth no other teacher but the light" and was "pretty tender and doth owne all that is spoken". Spinoza appears to have translated one of Margaret Fell's pamphlets. Commonly credited as the first of the new-moderns to apply critical analysis to the bible, Spinoza was perhaps prompted towards this approach by the Quaker Samuel Fisher, whose own writings expressly criticised the text of the bible, and who visited Spinoza in Amsterdam while acting as Margaret Fell's go-between.

Fox himself did qualify the status of conscience and experience. Their authority, he said, depended on the indwelling of divine power. He made a distinction between the "natural conscience", uneducated and liable to error, and the conscience enlightened by God or "the spirit". Similarly, what was known "experimentally" was valued according to whether it was in or out of "the life". This blunted the revolutionary edge of his message. It led him, before long, to urge that individual conscience and experience be tested by comparison with the collective conscience and experience of the godly, which seemed to some to point to a back-door reinstatement of church and scripture as ultimate arbiters.

But by then the genie was out of the bottle. Even when the collapse of the experimental republic brought the Stuarts and their episcopal church back to power, individual conscience and experience proved irrepressible. "For conscience' sake", Friends and radical dissenters defied the Clarendon code of oppression which sought to bring them to the heel of the restored autocracy. Church, monarchy and scriptures never recovered their former glory. The church lost its moral authority, the crown its divine legitimacy as enshrined in the doctrine of the "divine right of kings", and the bible its unique and unchallenged place at the creative centre of English culture. A freedom of expression and diversity of belief and action unthinkable before the "failed" revolution began to be the mark of English liberty.

Fox's world began to become our world with the Quaker campaign for toleration. No state or church power, said Friends, had the authority to compel men and women to obey its dictates against those of their own conscience. By the end of the seventeenth century, after filling its jails with conscientious objectors, the state and its church were forced to concede the point. In opening the door to religious diversity, they also opened the flood-gates to political dissent. A new pluralism was born.

Fox's emphasis on "light" and the primacy of "experiment" or experience can be linked with similar contemporary preoccupations which we now see as laying the foundations of our modern world. While Fox developed the metaphor of light in relation to conscience and integrity, Rembrandt and Vermeer were experimenting with techniques for representing light in paint on canvas. Rembrandt explored the contrasts of searching light and deep shadow, the capacity of light to penetrate mystery and heighten emotion. Vermeer, who used a *camera obscura* projector to organise his light, aimed at a new realism in recording the eye's experience of the soft play of daylight or moonlight on varied shapes and surfaces. Such explorations would prove crucial turning points marking off late mediaeval from modern art.

No less important, and contemporary with Fox, Vermeer and Rembrandt, Isaac Newton was laying the foundations of modern science with his investigations into the nature and properties of light (which had also preoccupied Descartes). His methods, moreover, were not speculative but experimental. Newton was a member, and later president, of the Royal Society of London for Improving Natural Knowledge, which grew out of informal gatherings of "natural philosophers" or scientists in 1645, at the height of the civil war. The aim was to develop "experimental philosophy" and promote "experimental learning". When Fox urged the primacy of experience, saying "This I knew experimentally", he was speaking the new language of a new science which would change his world into ours.

These, then, were Fox's pointers from his times to ours: his emphatic rejection of the binding authority of ecclesiastical and biblical authority, coupled with his emphasis on the inner light of conscience and experimental knowledge. But George Fox was no speculative philosopher, still less a liberal humanist born three centuries prematurely. Fox was God-possessed, and to understand Fox, and to interpret him for our generation, we have to try to understand what Fox understood by God. Superficially, it may seem that Fox's God was very much the familiar God of sixteen centuries of Christian tradition. He was the creator-God of Israel, a lord and heavenly father who called to repentance and obedience. He blessed his followers and smote his enemies. (Till well into the eighteenth century, Quaker meetings kept records of God's judgements on their persecutors and critics, citing their illnesses, deaths or family misfortunes as the just deserts of those who opposed God's faithful Quakers). Although Fox placed no emphasis on trinitarian doctrine, he did not expressly break with a tradition in which God was father, son and holy spirit. God ruled in the heavens, and the day was coming when he would rule in the world, through his saints.

But if that sounds orthodox enough to us, there was nevertheless something about his theology which the orthodox of his day found heretical and blasphemous. Nor was his supposed heresy related solely to his contempt for clerics, his demotion of scripture and his radical social and political message. What disturbed the wider Christian community, most puritan nonconformists as well as those who supported a state church, was Fox's emphasis on the inwardness of God. A "God within" seemed to hint that there may not be a God without - which is why Fox was accused of atheism. Moreover, to claim a "God within" seemed to come perilously close to proclaiming one's own divinity - which is why Fox was accused of blasphemy.

Now Fox clearly did believe in God transcendent as well as God imminent: a God "out there" as well as a God "in here". And equally clearly he believed in the divinity of Christ as well as the divine indwelling of those like himself who were called to be saints. But in these crucial matters Fox, throughout his long life, was never able to free himself of misunderstanding and misinterpretation. Exulting in new (or newly-refreshed) metaphors for God, Christ and the holy spirit, Fox could not help exhibiting God in a new light, and this had consequences he could neither foresee nor control.

Some of his contemporaries, men and women of the same generation liberated in the same unprecedented explosion of intellectual freedom, went much further than Fox. They were declaring by 1650 that God was Nature. A "Ranter Christmas carol" mocked traditional believers:

"They prate of God; believe it, fellow creatures,
There's no such bugbear; all was made by Nature."

The creator was the creation. Jacob Bauthumley (who, like Spinoza, flirted with Quakerism) taught that God is in everyone and every living thing: "man and beast, fish and fowl, and every green thing, from the highest cedar to the ivy on the wall". And again, "All the creatures in the world... are but one entire being". Bauthumley said Fox spoke "the eternal truth" when Fox told a Leicester audience in 1655, "The Father and the Son [are] all in me, and we are one". Other Ranters went further than Bauthumley, arguing that God was not only in living things but in every rock and stone. Ranter panentheism survived the absorption of ranterism into Quakerism and has had new leases of life ever since, in Spinoza's idea of God in nature and nature in God, in the Romantic age as Wordsworth's "spirit that... rolls through all things", and more recently in New Age spirituality, including some varieties of Quaker universalism. Ranterism also pointed in another direction: if God was everywhere in general he was nowhere in particular. As the Ranter carol put it, there was "no such bugbear". If God was "in this tobacco pipe, in dog, cat, chair, stool", if he was the universe itself, in what sense could he be said to have any independent existence at all? One Wiltshire Ranter concluded he would "sell all religions for a jug of beer".

Another radically heretical conception of God was that of Gerrard Winstanley, who saw Quakerism as a continuation of his own 1640s teaching. To Winstanley, as to the Ranters, God was suffused throughout creation, which was "the clothing of God". But his was a panentheism with a difference. The God in all things was Reason. "In the beginning of time the great creator, Reason, made the earth to be a common treasury". "Reason is that living power of light that is in all things... Reason lies at the bottom of love, justice, of wisdom... It doth govern and preserve all things, for Reason gives them in order... and hath a regard to the whole creation and knits every creature into a oneness". Winstanley preferred the word Reason to God "because I have been held under darkness by that word, as I see many people are". He saw all around him those who worshipped "the outward God" - landlords, priests, magistrates - and concluded that "the outward Christ or the outward God sometimes proves devils... He who supposes God is in the heavens above the skies, and so prays to that God which he imagines to be there... worships his own imagination, which is the devil". So "we will neither come to church nor serve their God", their imaginary, fanciful and essentially *unreasonable* God.

Reason, for Winstanley, *was* the light within: a term fondly imagined by many Quakers to be of Fox's own coining. This light (which, like Fox, he calls "the light of Christ") is "in every man and woman without exception", but particularly in "the despised, the unlearned, the poor, the nothings of this world" rather than the scholars and divines who have "all advantages and meanes outward". This light of Christ and Reason was not the God of the church:

"You do not look for a God now as formerly you did to be a place of glory beyond the Sun, Moon and Stars nor imagine a divine being you know not where but see him ruling within you; and not only in you but you see and know him to be the spirit that dwells in every creature... He that looks for a God without himself and worships God at a distance he worships he knows not what but is led away and deceived by the imagination of his own heart... but he that looks for a God within himselfe and submits himselfe to the spirit of righteousnesse that shines within, this man knows whom he worships for he is made subject to and hath community with that spirit that made all flesh in every creature within the globe".

This was written in 1648. And Winstanley also preceded Fox on the primacy of experience, of "experimental" knowledge, over scripture and book-learning. In his last work, *The Law of Freedom*, published in February 1652 while Fox was beginning his travels in the north, Winstanley urges that the rational man "speak nothing by imagination, but what he hath found out by his own industry and observation in tryal". No less vigorously than Fox, he insists that what we know "experimentally", experientially, is to be preferred over tradition as taught by clergy and scholars. Their "studying imagination" is "the devil... who puts out the eyes of mans Knowledge and tells him he must beleeve what others have writ or spoke, and must not trust to his own experience". It is hard to imagine that George Fox was not reading and drawing inspiration from Winstanley at this critical period in his own development. Winstanley often seems to be making the same points as Fox, but with greater clarity.

Winstanley's deification of the rational impulse pointed in several new directions. It became an increasingly secular drive for revolutionary social transformation. It inspired as well as drew inspiration from the new spirit of scientific enquiry. In less visionary vein, it may also have helped give birth to eighteenth century deism, the idea that something called God had set the machinery of the universe in motion but had subsequently taken early retirement, leaving his creation to manage as best it could without him. Thomas Paine was a deist, sharing Winstanley's passion for reason and social justice, which led him to become a key player in both the American and the French revolutions. Paine was the son of a Quaker father, and wished to be buried in a Quaker burial ground (which Friends, to their shame, refused).

George Fox's God, as we have seen, was more traditional than Bauthumley's or Winstanley's. He was neither suffused into his own creation nor abstracted into reason. He remained personal, and he remained the God of Christian tradition in that he was God-become-human. But where Fox imparted a radical spin to this traditional theology was in his interpretation of the incarnation. God became man not only in the person of Jesus the Christ but in the whole of humanity. The incarnation was democratised. Jesus was the son of God, but so too was George Fox, and so too, in some measure, are we all. There is "that of God in everyone".

This theology of radical immanentism, democratic divine-indwelling, would stimulate creative minds every bit as much as panentheism and rationalism. If Wordsworth was the bard of panentheism, his contemporary William Blake was the supreme poet of that of God in everyone, the marriage of the divine and the human, of heaven and hell. He knew that "all deities reside in the human breast", all visions in the human imagination. For Blake, himself a product and an inheritor of the radical antinomian tradition which had produced Quakerism, there were not two realms, human and divine, but one, the human-divine. And this is most clearly expressed in one of the most perfect poems in the English language, *The Divine Image* (to which I have added my own emphasis):

"To Mercy, Pity, Peace, and Love
All pray in their distress;
And to these virtues of delight
Return their thankfulness.

For Mercy, Pity, Peace, and Love
Is God, our Father dear,
And Mercy, Pity, Peace, and Love
Is man, His child and care.

For Mercy has a *human* heart,
Pity a *human* face,
And Love, the *human* form divine,
And Peace, the *human* dress.

Then every man, of every clime,
That prays in his distress,
Prays to *the human form divine,*
Love, Mercy, Pity, Peace.

And all must love the human form
In heathen, Turk or Jew;
Where Mercy, Love and Pity dwell
There God is dwelling too."

Blake was an artist and a visionary, not primarily a philosopher or theologian, but the philosophers and theologians were also at work on the human-divine. In Germany, Ludwig Feuerbach published in 1841 *The Essence of Christianity*, which pushed God-in-us theology to its logical conclusion: God was the outward projection of humanity's inner nature. All the traditional "moral predicates" of God - mercy, pity, peace, love - are simply the moral qualities of humanity self-deprecatingly projected onto an illusory abstraction, a super-human called God. In contemplating God, "man contemplates his own latent nature". Thus humanism was the true essence of religion. To those who labelled this atheism, Feuerbach responded that "he alone is the true atheist to whom the predicates of the Divine Being, for example love, wisdom, justice, are nothing - not he to whom merely the subject of these predicates is nothing". Like Fox and the early Friends, Feuerbach rejected any priestly control of religion, including sacraments, creeds and ritual. *The Essence of Christianity*, translated into English by George Eliot - no wonder her *Middlemarch* portrait of the cleric Casaubon was so scathing! - was substantially the most important theological work of the nineteenth century.

Blake's God-of-the-human-imagination and Feuerbach's God-in-human-nature had one great strength. This God was capable of surviving unscathed the onslaughts on religious realism which marked the following century: Darwin's evolution by natural selection, Einstein's revelation of the relativity of time and space, and Wittgenstein's later understanding that our ideas are given such reality as they have by our "language games". Religious humanism did not need to ask why a loving God created bubonic plague and the HIV virus, or allowed the holocaust. The kind of God of whom such questions might be asked had simply ceased to exist, just as the tribal "eye-for-an-eye" God of Moses had ceased to exist for Jesus, and the God who ruled through kings and bishops had ceased to exist for George Fox.

Humanist theology had a hard time of it within the churches, but it has survived the anathemas of fundamentalism. Dietrich Bonhoeffer saw that God wants mature men and women to stand on their own feet, "living without God before God" in "a world come of age". For Thomas Altizer "Christian atheism" was the logical outworking of the doctrine of the incarnation. Since the word had been made flesh once and for all, the sacred emptying itself into the profane, Christians must rejoice in the death of the once-separate God, the illusory objective God, in a world suffused with divine presence. Harvey Cox, building on Bonhoeffer, finds himself coming full circle with Gerrard Winstanley in suggesting that a "secular theology... requires our dispensing with the word 'God'". Modern radical theology is atheology.

Ironically, considering Fox's view of the Anglican priesthood, it took three Anglican clerics - a bishop, a dean and a parish priest - to popularise this developing understanding of a God who was no longer a Father in Heaven but an inward light of conscience. Bishop John Robinson, with *Honest to God* in the 1960s, replaced the God "out there" with a God conceived as "the ground of our being". Since the latter phrase is somewhat opaque, the message that got through to the popular press was that even bishops could no longer hide their loss of faith in a real God.

But *Honest to God*, though it dominated popular theological discussion in pew and pub for several months, failed to effect any permanent shift in church-goers' understanding of the God they worshipped. Robinson himself seemed to retreat to a more traditional position in his later years. Then in 1980 the Dean of Emmanuel College, Cambridge, Don Cupitt, published *Taking Leave of God* as "a resumption of the discussion about the nature of God begun by John Robinson... and shelved for far too long". Cupitt suggested that "internalization, the process by which all meaning, including religious meaning, has come to be seen not as built into external reality, but as generated from within ourselves", coupled with new demands for "spiritual autonomy", meant that "conservative religion of the sort that sets God authoritatively over the believer has become an anachronism; it is spiritually behind the times".

Quoting the mediaeval mystic Meister Eckhart - "Man's last and highest parting occurs when, for God's sake, he takes leave of God" - Cupitt argued that "a stage has come in mankind's spiritual and moral development when we need to abandon theological realism, for an objective metaphysical God is no longer either intellectually secure nor even morally satisfactory as a basis for the spiritual life. Instead faith in God must be understood as expressing an autonomous decision to pursue the religious ideal for its own sake" - a faith "free, agnostic and no longer motivated by external guarantees or sanctions".

A dean is not a bishop, and Cupitt's work, though intellectually more rigorous than Robinson's, did not have the same popular impact until the BBC commissioned him in 1984 to make a series of television documentaries. He called the series and the book of the films *The Sea of Faith*, taking as his starting point Matthew Arnold's familiar Victorian poem *Dover Beach*, with its image of the decline of religion as an outgoing tide - the "melancholy, long, withdrawing roar" of the Sea of Faith. But a new tide had begun to flow: "a profound mutation has been taking place as religion breaks free from the outworn supernatural beliefs that at present stifle it". No longer fighting against, but wholly accepting the twentieth-century view that religion is simply human, he proposed (in a phrase that Quakers through the ages would have endorsed) that "Christianity should now be practised without dogma, as a spiritual path, an ethic, and a way of giving meaning to life". He concluded:

"We see that religion is wholly of this world, wholly human, wholly our own responsibility, and that it has become ethically active and militant. It is religion that has raised us out of the dark, chaotic unconsciousness of Nature and has made us human; for religion just is our values, expressed in our social institutions and practices... The historic task of religion, of embodying our values, witnessing to them, conserving them, setting them forth in symbols and securing their realisation in human life, remains unchanged. It will be performed all the better after the veil of illusion that has hitherto hidden its workings has finally dropped away."

This profoundly religious humanism, which Cupitt calls "non-realism" (in opposition to traditional Platonism which insists on the objective reality of values, and traditional Christianity which insists on the objective reality of God), has found a continuing expression not only in his own extraordinarily high literary output but also in the Sea of Faith Network, which links men and women wishing to "explore and promote religious faith as a human creation". Non-realism is at the centre of liberal theological debate in those churches where liberal theological debate is still part of the culture, and has become a live and lively area of discussion among Friends, despite the fact that in the Quaker tradition speculative theology has always been suspect. But given the clear relationship between classic Quaker emphasis on "that of God in everyone" and the inwardness of spiritual experience, it would be surprising if the Sea of Faith's religious humanism had not attracted those Quakers who attach at least as much importance to thinking as to feeling. Cupitt himself has described his position as a kind of "left Quakerism".

Indeed, when the parish priest of Staplefield, Anthony Freeman, published a book called *God in Us* in 1994, some Friends were quick to recognise how much of their own emphasis on inward experience had been taken up in the old enemy camp of steeplehouses and hirelings. But *God in Us*, a popular restatement of religious humanism which matched *Honest to God* in press reaction and made the nature of the deity as hotly contested in today's pubs as it was in Fox's alehouses, fell foul of Freeman's bishop, who gave him the distinction of being the first Anglican priest to be sacked for unorthodoxy this century. Ironically, even as we walked in the footsteps of George Fox who had called on priests to abandon their evil calling, we found ourselves actively involved in supporting a priest who had been fired for giving Fox's essential message contemporary expression.

Walking "among the rocks and winding scars" of the northern dales, we cannot know how this changed but unchanging landscape will look to our children and our children's children. Will it be ranched, built over, industrialised, or abandoned to the wilderness? Similarly, we cannot yet know whether the twenty-first century and the third millenium will see a significant and saving growth in reasonable faith, a wholly human faith based on the authority of conscience and experience, or will witness a growing rift between those who are learning to live as spiritually autonomous men and women in the present and those who insist that we must all worship an objective ultimate authority, a God as conceived by past generations.

"What canst thou say?" asked George Fox, and whatever reply we choose to make, it will derive its authority from conscience and experience, nurtured by reason and imagination. And conscience and experience nurtured by reason and imagination may even lead us, as they led Fox, to seek a new Earth, a transfigured world. The poverty, injustice, pain, and powerlessness which drove early Friends into revolutionary politics and social action are still with us after an Enlightenment, an "Age of Reason", an industrial revolution and a century of socialism and social democracy in competition with rampant capitalism - our "little systems" which "have their day and cease to be". Must we then accept, with Jesus, that "the poor are always with us", or do we dare try to prove him wrong? "Our principles you can never extinguish", Fox's friend Edward Burrough told the Restoration parliament just before he died in jail, "but they will live for ever, and enter into other bodies to live and speak and act". Winstanley too had insisted that "action is the life of all, and if thou dost not act, thou dost nothing".

Fox said it his own way: "Spare no place, spare not tongue nor pen... Be valiant for the Truth upon earth; tread and trample all that is contrary under... Be patterns, be examples in all countries, places, islands, nations, wherever you come; that your carriage and life may preach among all sorts of people, and to them. Then you will come to walk cheerfully over the world, answering that of God in every one".

We have walked in Fox's footsteps from Pendle to Swarthmoor and from the 1650s to the 1990s. We have been glad of his company.

Suggestions for further reading

The basic source book for Fox is, of course, his *Journal*, of which the Nickalls edition is the most accessible. *The Beginnings of Quakerism* (Sessions, York) by W C Braithwaite, although first published as long ago as 1912 and revised by Henry J Cadbury in 1955, remains invaluable. *First Among Friends* (OUP, 1994) by H Larry Ingle is by far the best modern critical biography of Fox, and *Margaret Fell and the Rise of Quakerism* (Macmillan, 1994) by Bonnelyn Young Kunze is an equally brilliant study of Quakerism's mother-superior. *The Birthplace of Quakerism: a handbook for the 1652 country* (Quaker Home Service, London) by Elfrida Vipont Foulds remains a most useful little guide to the "Quaker Gallilee", though now somewhat dated. *Quaker Meeting Houses of the Lake Counties* (Friends Historical Society, 1978) by David Butler is a marvellous treasure-trove. *First Publishers of Truth*, a collection of early Quaker records edited for the Friends Historical Society in 1907, is another. *The Quakers and the English Revolution* (Temple Smith, London, 1985) by Barry Reay will tell you more about the political activities of early Friends than most latter-day Friends want to know.

Of the vast number of more general books about the English revolution, *The Levellers* by H N Brailsford (Spokesman Books edition, 1976) is a good starting point, and *The World Turned Upside Down* (1972) is only one of a dozen seminal books by Christopher Hill which have turned the history of seventeenth century England upside down.

Of the equally inexhaustible quantity of literature on the Dales, there is still nothing better than Arthur Raistrick's *Old Yorkshire Dales* (Pan Books, 1971) and *The Pennine Dales* (Eyre Methuen, 1978). For studies of specific areas there is *Richard Robinson of Countersett and the Quakers of Wensleydale* (Sessions, 1989) by David S Hall; *Kendal: a Social History* (Cicerone, Milnthorpe, 1995) by Roger Bingham, and my own series on the Dent area: *Early Friends in Dent, Discovering Dent* and *Discovering Upper Dentdale* (all Dales Historical Monographs, Dent), and *Adam Sedgwick's Dent* (Hollett and Boulton, Sedbergh).

Index of names and places

Cam Houses 80, 82-4
Camm, John 27, 143-6, 150, 157
Camm, Mabel 145, 157
Camm, Mary 36
Camm, Thomas 36, 145-7, 157
Cam Road 80, 82
Camsgill 144-5, 149
Capstacke, James 89
Carlisle 18, 207
Carperby 70
Cartmel 173, 182
Cartmel Fell 169, 171
Cautley 119-20
Chagall 73
Charles I, king 9, 15, 152, 178, 196
Charney Manor 209
Charnley, Barbara 58
Charnley, Richard 58-9
Chester 71, 207
Children of the Light 9, 69
Clifford, Anne 134
Clubmen 11
Cockcroft, Barry 101
Cockermouth 32
Colthouse 82
Colton 188-92
Constantine, Penny 109
Cooke, John 167-9
Cooke, Wendy 167-9
Cortley, Thomas 72
Countersett 69-75, 78-9, 81, 85
Coupland, John 125
Coverdale 64
Coverdale, Miles 192
Cowgill 89, 93, 96-8
Cox, Harvey 223
Cragdale 67
Cray 65-6
Cromwell, Oliver 39-41, 44, 57, 71, 93, 100, 112,
    116, 118, 120, 131, 137, 141, 152, 159, 165, 180,
    189, 196, 203, 205-7, 212
Crook 162
Crosslands 139, 142-4
Crossley, Barbara 78, 81
Crossley, Bernard 78-9, 81, 96
Crosthwaite 165, 167
Cupitt, Don 224-5

Dalton 200
Dandra Garth 96, 99, 107
Dapper Dick 151

Darlington 74
Darwin, Charles 110, 223
Dawson, Edmund 93
Dawson, Em 93
Deeming, Steve 208
Dent(dale) 12, 58, 65-6, 79-80, 85-99, 107,
    109-10, 114, 125, 132-3, 140, 147, 167, 177
Derby 9, 11, 163, 205
Descartes, Rene 214-6
Dewsbury, William 205
Dickinson, James 165
Diggers (see True Levellers)
Dover Castle 141
Downham 17-8, 23, 26
Draw-well 132-4
Drunken Barnaby 154
Duerdon, Norman 67
Duffy, Jim 12-3, 105, 107
Dunbar (battle of) 205

Eccles, Solomon 43, 71
Edmondson, William 100
Einstein, Albert 223
Eldroth 35
Eliot, George 222
Elizabeth, queen 151, 195
Ellwood, Thomas 56
Ely, Isle of 27
Euerdon, Thomas 140
Ewbank 125

Fairfax, Thomas 39
Family of Love (Familists) 26-8, 116, 118, 202
Farnsworth, Richard 14-5, 17, 20-1, 23, 26, 38,
    54, 200-1
Fell, Alice 197
Fell, George (jnr) 157
Fell, George (snr) 195
Fell, Margaret 36, 71, 104, 134, 155, 157, 163,
    188, 195-7, 207, 215
Fell, Mary 198
Fell, Sarah 36
Fell, Susannah 36
Fell, Thomas 165, 188, 190, 194-204
Fenny Drayton 157
Feuerbach, Ludwig 222-3
Fiennes, Celia 150
Fifth Monarchists 70
Firbank Fell 132, 134-7, 139, 146, 157
Fisher, Samuel 159, 177, 215
Flemming, Daniel 150